The Search for the Unholy Grail:
The Race to Prove
Behavior and Personality are Inherent

By Faye Snyder, PsyD

November 3, 2016 (date of original print publication)

© 2016 by S. Faye Snyder, PsyD.
v1.1.110316

ISBN 978-0-9854714-8-4 (paperback)

All rights reserved. No portion of this document may be reproduced – mechanically, electronically or by any other means – without the permission of the publisher.

Clifton Legacy Publishing
Los Angeles, California

Printed in the United States of America
First published electronically November 2016

To Nicole, my daughter-in-law, for choosing to raise
my grandson in The Causal Theory.

Other Works by Dr. Snyder

The Handbook: The Supplemental Guide to the Miracle Child Parenting Series and The Causal Theory, 2009

The Manual: The Definitive Book on Parenting and the Causal Theory, 2012

ADHD: A Diagnosis in Denial, 2012

Healing Your RAD Child, 2012

The Politics of Memory: When One Is Requested to Shut the Eyes, 2014

The Predictor Scale: Predicting and Understanding Behavior According to Critical Childhood Experiences, 2014

Acknowledgements

This book was inspired by a lecture by Dr. Robert Geffner, who presented at the California Coalition on Sex Offending in 2015, reminding members that sex offending is precipitated by trauma—especially attachment trauma—as well as genetics. Having presented such a magnificent lecture, I asked him later why he hedged his bets. He told me to look up the Caspi study. I have reviewed many such studies, so I promised him I would prove to him genes do not influence behavior. Synapses influence behavior. Mirror neurons influence behavior. Synapses form from experiences and learning. Each one of us possesses shared learning such as language, and individual learning that forms our unique personalities and points of view.

I began to write an analysis for Dr. Geffner that could be shared with others as well, and as I wrote I became clear that the Caspi study could be perceived as the exception to genetic research if I did not reveal the history of genetic studies preceding it. By then, I was obligated to write this book, which I now consider the most important of my books.

I have collaborated extensively with my son, Scott Clifton (pka Scott Clifton Snyder) because his guidance and involvement became essential to getting this book written as soon as possible. He is a consummate debater, lover of truth and facts, and dedicated to logic and reason, so I have enjoyed the fruits of my labor, receiving guidance from and collaborating with him during this controversial endeavor. He has declined to share authorship with me "because it doesn't feel right," but agreed to write the foreword.

Unfortunately, it took me years to learn how to analyze research studies. I have come to consider myself an interpreter or decoder for others who don't have the time to figure out why scientists say what they say, or whether they are honest. I have been frustrated there is no pocket version of the research claims that laypeople, judges, attorneys and even other scientists can reference when facing assumptions that genes influence behavior. I have even wanted my materials handy in such a discussion over the purported meaningfulness of genetic research. Sometimes I forget a name, a date or a term, and I want to be accurate when confronting mythology-thought-to-be-science.

This book stands on the shoulders of many brave and great clinicians, scientists and critics. In the process of researching the existing studies by both pro-parent scientists and pro-child scientists, I have enjoyed the work of many brave, ethical and thoughtful researchers. They too could not help but notice the results that genetic behaviorists were producing didn't make sense. Further, these results are used to do harm. They have spent precious time unearthing the unsound evidence at the center of incredible claims and flawed logic. To be the person who starts to leak doubt about the process and face the ire of dedicated colleagues requires bravery and integrity. The researchers who question research are the ones who look to see *what is*, not *what they need to see*, and ask, "Why is the emperor wearing no clothes?" If one contemplates the ramifications of believing behavior is learned in homes and communities rather than inborn, we may have a whole new lease on human behavior. We may finally enter the true Age of Enlightenment.

My References are in no particular order filled with the work of heroes, especially Bessel van der Kolk, Allan Schore, Colin Ross, Alvin Pam, John Reed, Don Jackson, Jay Joseph, R. C. Lewontin, Martin Teicher, Ty Colbert, Robert Whitaker, Peter Breggin, Richard Bentall, Richard DeGrandpre, John Bowlby, Bruce Perry, Jonathan Leo, Harry Harlow, Mary Ainsworth and Mary Main, Rene Spitz, Daniel Stern, Daniel Siegel, Jeffrey Maason, and Alice Miller, to name such a few. It must be acknowledged that these greats stand on the shoulders of unsung heroes before and beside them.

Still, these amazing researchers do not write to the general public. They write to one another, and although I never cared to learn much about science, I have accepted my lot as interpreter and guide to the laypublic. As such, I find I am a researcher of research, having by necessity discovered how to do an autopsy on the veracity of scientific studies.

Lastly, I have decided to blaze a trail and confront the same old research tricks that appear to be showing up in epigenetic claims and studies. Even the heroes above seem to show deference to epigenetics. This is my gift to them, because I believe they will appreciate it.

A Child Lives What Is Modeled, by Dorothy Law Nolte

If children live with criticism, they learn to condemn.
If children live with hostility, they learn to fight.
If children live with ridicule, they learn to be shy.
If children live with shame, they learn to feel guilty.
If children live with tolerance, they learn to be patient.
If children live with encouragement, they learn confidence.
If children live with praise, they learn appreciation.
If children live with fairness, they learn justice.
If children live with security, they learn to have faith.
If children live with approval, they learn to like themselves.
If children live with acceptance and friendship,
They learn to find love in the world.

It's ironic that laypeople can see what scientists can't. --FS

TABLE OF CONTENTS

1: INTRODUCTION 15
2: GENES & ENVIRONMENT 101 22
   LAYPERSON'S GUIDE TO THE BRAIN 22
   UNIVERSAL GENETIC INSTRUCTION 26
      Cell Membrane as Gatekeeper 26
      Inborn Reflexes & Genetic Instructions 29
   ENVIRONMENTAL FACTORS TO CONSIDER 31
      Attachment 31
      Modeling 33
      Imprinting & Mirror Neurons 34
      Systems Theory and Practice 36
      Family Ethics 37
      Resiliency 40
      Healing 41

3: EVOLUTION OF MEDICINE 42
   TIMELINE 43
      Economics and Religion Instruct Society 43
      The Insane and Poor are Exiled 45
      Moral Management Retreats are Offered 45
      Mental Illness Becomes Medicalized 46
   FREUD 48
      Freud's Betrayal of the Child: Daniel Paul Schreber 51
      Freud's Betrayal of the Child: Adolf Hitler 53
      Three Babies of Germany 54
   WATSON 54

4: EVOLUTION OF GENETIC RESEARCH 59
   PEDIGREE STUDIES 60
   MENDELIAN MODEL REFRESHER 63
   ADOPTION STUDIES 64
      Twin Studies "Separated at Birth" 64
      Tienari (1963) 68
      Heston (1966) 69
      Danish Studies (1968, 1971, 1974) 69
      Veteran Twin Studies: Pollin & Hoffer (1970) and Allen (1972) 76
      Gottesman & Shields (1972 & 1982) 77
      Meta-Analysis (aka Average Risk Studies) 77
      Kendler: Equal Environment Assumption (1983) 78
      Koskenvuo, Langinvainio, Kaprio, Lonnqvist & Tienari (1984) 79
      Sherrington (1988) 79
      MISTRA (1990) 80

Finland: Tienari & Wynne (2004) *81*
SUMMARY CHART 83
HISTORICAL TRENDS 84
RESEARCH FLAWS IN FAMILY STUDIES 86
 Lack of Rule-Outs *86*
 Failure to Replicate *87*
 Revisions of Language *88*
 Data Tampering *90*

5: THE HUMAN GENOME PROJECT 93
SUMMARY 94
PLOMIN IS THE FACE OF HOPE 96
NOT ONE GENE HAS BEEN ISOLATED FOR BEHAVIOR 98

6: THE 50/50 GENETIC ASSUMPTION 101
THE CASPI STUDY 104
 Habituation *106*
 Poor Resiliency *108*
 Stress *109*
RESEARCH FLAWS OF THE 50/50 GENETIC ASSUMPTION, WITH CASPI AS EXAMPLE 110
 Lack of Rule-Outs *110*
 Revisions of Language *113*
 Apparent Research Motives *113*

7: EPIGENETICS 115
A HISTORY OF EPIGENETICS 116
 Attachment Research Called Epigenetic Research *117*
 Excitement in the Air, Again *118*
 The Way It Works This Time *119*
 Criticisms of Epigenetic Theory and Research *120*
PREPARING TO STUDY A STUDY 122
THE YEHUDA STUDY 123
 Detour for Definitions and Background Info *125*
 Back to Analyzing the Yehuda Study *127*
RESEARCH FLAWS OF EPIGENETICS, WITH YEHUDA AS EXAMPLE 135
 Lack of Rule-Outs *135*
 Failure to Replicate *137*
 Revisions of Language *137*
 Incentives (Patents and Grants) *139*
 Fixed Research Designs *140*
INTERGENERATIONAL TRANSMISSION 140

8: ANALYSIS 142
PSYCHIATRY AND THE RAMIFICATIONS OF GENETIC THEORY 142
 A Review of The Tulip Theory *142*
 A Failed Opportunity to Clear It Up *143*

    Denial and Pro-Parent Motives *144*
    The Patrons of Research *147*
  WHAT'S THE HARM? 150
    Betrayal of Trust *150*
    Misdiagnoses *152*
    The Human Cost of Medication *152*
  GROUP THINK 154
    Group Denial is a Historical Phenomenon *154*
    People Ignore the Truth for Acceptance *155*
  ORIGINS OF SELF-AWARENESS 156
    Clinicians Need to See More Clearly *158*
    Psychoanalyzing Scientists *159*

9: APPENDIX 162
  I: TYPES OF RESEARCH FLAWS 162
  II: DON JACKSON'S 11 CRITICISMS OF TWIN STUDIES 166
  III: KEY QUESTIONS TO ASK WHEN READING GENETIC RESEARCH 167
  IV: REFERENCES 168
  IV: EPIGENETICS LANGUAGING CODES (TEAR-OUT) 177

Foreword by Scott Clifton

I met the Night Stalker when I was six years old.

My mother had been making trips up to San Francisco County Jail, where she conducted a series of interviews with Richard Ramirez about the childhood that would inevitably lead to his more than thirteen murders and rapes in Southern California. He was an avowed Satanist, and during his trial he neither showed remorse nor fear of the gas chamber that awaited him. "Big deal," he told reporters at his sentencing.

In prison, he was allowed materials to draw and color, which he enjoyed. His art was mostly pornographic in nature, but he once asked my mother if her young son at home would like to put in a request. Cautiously, she relayed the message, and I wanted a Ninja Turtle. He matched the wrong weapon to the bandana color—an egregious error no child of the 90's would fail to notice—but otherwise, it was exquisite, and I cherished it. But there was also the matter of my mom leaving for days at a time, which I didn't much like. I wanted to see what she was up to. After months of my begging, she finally (and I assume reluctantly) invited me to come with her to see San Francisco, and, maybe, Richard.

I knew, abstractly, who he was: he hurt and killed people, he would probably hurt and kill many more if he could, and he would spend the rest of his life locked away because of it. But the thing was, I loved to draw, too. This was an existential riddle: how could one piece of this man's mind be so intimately familiar to me, and the other so incomprehensibly ugly? I had questions.

On the plane, my mom explained that she believed he was born good, just like me, just like all babies are, but his mommy failed to protect him from things worse than I could imagine, and he wasn't ever allowed to be sad or angry about it. "But what goes in must come out," she said. The idea was that if the man was made to swallow his pain and anger to protect his mother, it would have to escape him in other ways, compounded by time and pressure. This was all perfectly digestible to me, the six-year-old, even though a dismissive, "He was born that way," could have been easier.

He'd reported to my mother during their last interview that there was once a woman, whom he decided to let live. He broke into her den through a window and found her sitting on her sofa alone. She seemed to know who he was, and what he was about to do to her. With total sincerity, she asked him, "Oh my God, who did this to you?" Her humanization of him was completely destabilizing. He sat down with her. They talked for while, and he left.

My meeting with Richard was also the last time she ever saw him. He was already seated, peering through from the other side of the bulletproof plexiglass window, grinning. His smile wasn't menacing; it was charming. He was fit, and handsome, and he greeted me warmly when I put the handset to my ear. I don't remember what I said to him or him to me, except that he wanted me to know he could tell how much my mother loved me. It's no mystery why that moment was salient enough to stay with me.

When the conversation had ended—the following occurred with such swiftness and disorienting simultaneity that it's difficult to explain how it was possible, let alone to narrate—Richard hung up the phone and rose from his chair and, while my head was turned toward my mom leaning over to ready her belongings for our departure, the fly of his jumpsuit had already been undone, his penis in his hand, and he stood, posed, awaiting my attention. I turned back to him and froze, struggling to process what I was seeing. My eyes darted upward to find his index finger landing perpendicularly on his lips. "Shhh," he mouthed, before my mom even knew what had happened. "Don't tell."

I would later learn that Richard was born with an abnormally large penis, and that he had siblings and relatives who wanted to see it from the time he was a baby. It became an immutable piece of his identity, a source of attention and, perhaps, a measure of his self-worth.

I told. Immediately and dutifully, the moment we left him; it was a protocol my mom had ensured was drilled into me. She hung the 'privacy' card outside the door of the hotel room that evening, and encouraged me to cry, to rage, to tell her I hated her for failing to protect me. "Mommy is so sorry," she chanted, arms around me, holding back tears of her own. "Mommy is so, so, sorry."

How cosmically unfair the world is, that Richard—the other little boy who loved to draw—had his mother instead of mine. How blindly cruel is our design, that a child so tormented will become an adult so hateful, and in turn, so hated. And yet for those whose childhoods are charmed, a charming adulthood awaits. "The double-damned and the twice-blessed," my mom would call it. It's why she persists in her work. She thinks our belief in genetics impairs our ability to see clearly the effects of childhood, while children are still malleable.

The book you are about to read is not her life's work; it is an opportunity cost. In some ways, my mother's life and career could be described a series of opportunity costs. She wasted years of her life in bad therapy before meeting a clinician who could finally draw a straight line from her environment as a child to her behavior as an adult, which then began the process of her own healing. She became interested in how parenting causes behavior—both healthy and pathological—and why so many therapists seemed unable to help her, so she went to school to learn what the professionals were being taught. For thirty years she ran a private practice that allowed her to develop her theory of behavior until it became clear that the credential of MFT wasn't prestigious enough to be taken seriously as a theoretician. So, although she is prouder to call herself a marriage and family therapist than a psychologist, she went back to school in her mid-forties for her doctorate and psychologist license. At another point, she decided that in order to map her theory onto the legal reality of child abuse in the United States, she would have to understand the erratic inner workings of the Department for Children and Family Services. So for a short time, she became a social worker. Throughout her career, she would continue to be sidetracked by mortal threats, libel, litigious parents of past clients, and even her aging body, which her vibrant mind has no time to coddle. But there was never an obstacle more prevalent than the subject of this book.

Disproving the premise that psychopathology is inborn is neither her passion nor her hobby; it is simply the doorway through which many of us must step in order to hear her message and learn from her theory. **Forget genes; childhood is everything.** After you read this book, you just might allow yourself a blank slate for considering the causes of behavior and personality. You might also enjoy the best part of her theory, where she demonstrates with vignettes of famous people how parenting creates all the behaviors ever known: *The Predictor Scale: Predicting and Understand Behavior According to Critical Childhood Experiences.*

I wonder how Richard's mother might have treated him differently if she believed she was creating a killer.

1: INTRODUCTION

Early in my marriage, my husband and I began to garden together. Neither of us were experts by any means, so we experimented together. Today it seems illogical to me to have done this, but nevertheless, we sent away for 100 tulip bulbs from Holland to plant in Southern California. The Scandinavian bulbs arrived with very brief instructions: Do not worry about caring for these bulbs. You cannot harm them. They don't need fertilizer. They don't need water. They don't need sunshine. You can leave them on a shelf in a dark cupboard and they will still grow. For a second I was reassured, and then it hit me: My mom raised me within The Tulip Theory! It was an epiphany I had to proclaim outloud to my husband. Like the tulips, my mother believed I was born a certain way and I'd turn out fine, no matter how well or badly she treated me. The majority of society shares this attitude, and it's just plain wrong.

When I became a therapist I discovered an inordinate number of my clients believed their issues were inborn or at least partly genetic. They couldn't say what part was genetic and what part was not, because they didn't know. How could they? Often, they assumed their worst and best traits to be inborn. They didn't know how their own childhood affected them, and it seemed too often like "going there" was off limits. I hit resistance to searching for causes behind their suffering. They did not believe it was right to question their parents, even when they were not present or had died. Childhood was behind them, they thought, and what's the point in going into painful memories and dredging up trouble. On the other hand, I had narcissistic clients who believed they were inherently superior and more deserving than others. What brought that on? Why would someone *need* to believe they were better than others, and how did that harm their relationships? I wanted to explore from where or from whom their troubling behaviors and beliefs came, and again I often hit a wall.

I was shocked to find a significant number of clinicians with whom I would confer, also agreed with my clients that much of their personality was inborn. I don't even know how anyone can actually do therapy if they think that way. Nevertheless, in order to pass the California psychologist's licensing exam, which is geared toward genetics, one needs to assume genes play an important role in assessing psychopathology, and be on-board with prescribing medications to alleviate symptoms.

In the case of the self-deprecating, it was like we hit a bottleneck in therapy, where clients would rather blame themselves or their body than discover what happened to them so they could change it. It often seemed to turn into a discussion about beliefs, leading to an underlying philosophy that everyone is entitled to their own beliefs, right or wrong. But I often wondered aloud: what if your belief is harming you? The discussion often became about evidence and the Scandinavian studies. They would sometimes bring in articles on the most recent studies. I looked at these articles with a sort of disbelief, like I was looking at a puzzle. In all my jaded lessons from the 60s I had not learned scientists could not be trusted. I too believed researchers had taken a sacred oath of impartiality favoring evidence. These clients believed the evidence was in and the fat lady had already sung.

It appeared I would have to understand how I had been so wrong. I had to face my estrangement with science and dig in. I didn't expect to find there was a whole brigade of scientists who believed behavior was inborn, and another brigade who believed behavior was created from environment, experiences and family systems. These separate entities were producing different and contrary research, evidence and information, which I deemed **The War of the Researchers**. It seemed at first like no one else saw it. I felt like Alice in Wonderland. If clinicians saw, they still didn't seem to see the problem of disparity between scientists. I noticed therapists would shrug and assume the liberal and correct response was to accept both sides equally, even though they fundamentally disagreed on facts and causality for behavior, and those reported causes informed diverse practices. Trying to treat both sides with equal respect seemed schizogenic to me. Could it really be *both*, and how does accepting *both* affect clinicians, parents and patients? It appeared to muddy insight. I became rather disillusioned with my profession and realized I had to find out how scientists could arrive at contrary results. I was going to have to study science.

The conflict among researchers and theoreticians over whether or not behaviors and traits are inborn has history. It is the underlying schism of psychology, in which professionals fought over who would determine the causes of behavior and how to treat symptoms. It became progressively clear there were motives behind each position. These motives were complex, but they seemed to distill down to two basic perspectives: One insisted on immunizing parents, and the other held a perspective that hurtful and helpful childhood experiences have a long-term impact on people.

I began to call the geneticists **"pro-parent"** because at the heart of their beliefs was a refusal to "blame parents" or accept that parenting is key, such that they were willing to ignore the suffering of children, in whole or in part. They held that behavior was inborn, at least in part. The **"pro-child"** researchers were a smaller group of theoreticians and scientists who thought as I did. They appeared to understand the importance of nurturing and guidance in the formation of personality. They had performed an abundance of convincing research not reported by the press. The more the well-publicized twin studies from Scandinavia took root in the minds of the public, the less interest the pro-child studies seemed to hold.

The theoretical research war orients around the medical model and a power struggle about who will have authority over the mentally ill, as well as who or what is responsible for mental illness. The medical model attempts to identify the specific origins of all types of pathology, ironically often independent of genetic explanations. Many doctors who treat physical maladies hold that accidents and environmental toxins cause these maladies. Even recently the World Health Organization (WHO) announced that beef and pork are a major cause of cancer (WHO Website, October, 2015). Relatively few medical conditions can be traced to genetic anomalies (Ewald, 1994). Still, in the field of psychology the medical model is used to identify pathology in terms of genetic inheritance. Since the birth of psychology, psychiatrists have needed to see patients in terms of medical issues to justify their dominance over the profession. Psychiatrists are medical doctors who, after receiving their M.D., continue their education to specialize in issues of mental health, predominantly according to biological psychiatry. Some of the powerful quotes in this book are from brilliant and heroic psychiatrists who have dared to speak up about the way they were trained, challenging the mythology of their own profession.

Most of today's greats have alluded to or expressly acknowledged that our field is torn. The ultimate question is whether or not psychopathology is the result of genes or parenting. Do we go after inborn traits to understand the causes of mental illness of psychological suffering, or do we examine parenting and childhood experiences? How do we treat inborn traits? Many people think the only solution to that explanation is pharmaceuticals. Should we spend more money on research to prove inborn traits, or on treating and educating parents? Some fence straddlers have blamed television, music, street drugs, pharmaceutical drugs, poverty, and guns. While all of these may be triggers, they are not the primary cause because none of these elements drive everyone, but the environmental elements I will be presenting are elements that would affect all of us for good or bad depending on content and context.

I have obviously decided not to hide my bias, which I consider no more of a bias than the importance of protecting Jews from Nazis, especially with all discussion based on credible evidence. I see myself protecting children from pharmaceutical solutions and people who parent by The Tulip Theory. I see myself answering differently the question of what is wrong with society today, while others point to the music, television and guns.

As biased as I may seem, should I find out I am wrong, I can change my opinion on a dime because I *love* the truth like a lifeline. Any replacement theory will have to make more sense of available evidence than my Causal Theory. However, as you shall soon see, it appears I am onto something. The perspective of the geneticists is highly vocal and largely unchallenged, except by a small elite group of scientists who write mostly to one another, not to the general public. So if I appear biased, please consider this similar to a trial and you are the jury. You need to hear both sides. I am the voice for the current young children and the children who had to grow up.

Before we wander down the road into the thicket of the nature/nurture debate which appears to be coming to a head with the advent of real science, the reader needs the tools to critically evaluate reported research results and weigh both arguments one against the other. We need to understand the feasible explanations differing scientists offer for the same phenomena. This would include the rule-outs researchers must ethically consider before drawing inferences and conclusions. With two opposing camps, one invested in genetic explanations and one invested in parenting and environmental explanations, I propose we do need the facts, and we do need to decide how to intelligently process opposing research results. It will be important to understand (past) motives leading to today's actions and ramifications (of their impact on the future) as well as their research designs, protocol and ethics. I consider it my job to walk you through it and interpret where necessary. I believe anyone can understand pro-child research, but an interpreter or code-reader is required, even for other scientists, to understand the results of genetic research.

We will be evaluating genetic research, but first we need to understand what has already been shown, proven and replicated. If we don't know of demonstrated ways to explain behavior other than genetic instructions, we cannot think critically or comparatively, and may be persuaded to believe the research results, based on faith alone. Below is an overview of all the research that supports my theory, The Causal Theory. My theory is born out of this nature/nurture debate with a tendency to distinguish itself as theory that explains *all* behavior and personality as the result of essential experiences. The Causal Theory is premised on **evidence-based**, **replicated research** that actually accounts for the causes of behaviors in a simple cause and effect formula, which includes identifying factors that carry more or less weight, as compared to or combined with other factors. For a thorough explanation of this, read my book, *The Predictor Scale: Predicting and Understanding Behaviors According to Critical Childhood Experience*.

Page intentionally blank.

War of the Researchers and Theoreticians Grid

NATURE-BASED, PRO-PARENT

Premise: Parents are not the cause of child's personality or behavior. No need to explore childhood. Causes are inborn and more final.

Motives: Protect parents, feminism, pharmaceutical industry, AMA and daycare.

Sponsors: Neo-Freudians Internal Drive (inborn fantasies); AMA medical model; pharmaceutical industry

Practice: Denial/repression ethic. No-guilt parenting.. Parents, take care of yourselves, for your child's sake.

Presumption: Genetics, bad/good seed, 'chip off the ol' block", "luck of the draw". Astrology. Baptism. God's will. Reincarnation.

Ramifications: Bad parenting goes unnoticed, causes blindness to origins of pathology, including effects of premature separation. Unhealthy citizens.

NATURE-BASED, PRO-CHILD

Premise: Behaviors are learned, but parents have nothing to do with it. No bad seed. Can't see into "the black box" of someone's history or unconscious. Can condition new behaviors.

Motives: Don't blame parents or genes, but propose discipline and conditioning techniques and cognitive behavioral treatments.

Sponsors: Behavioral Theory, Cognitive Theory and Zen Buddhism.

Practice: REPRESSION ETHIC. Work on the here and now. Avoid childhood. No point making parents feel bad. Practice positive thinking and affirmations.

Presumption: Behaviors were learned, but parents are not to blame.

Ramifications: Those who are healthy enough can self-correct, but those who ere highly damaged are ignored.

NURTURE-BASED, PRO-PARENT

Premise: Bad things can happen to children, but it won't create personality or behavioral change. Nevertheless we should protect them from unnecessary suffering.
Motives: Protect child, AMA, and the status quo with compassion.
Sponsors: Teachers, social workers, nurses, pediatricians
Practice: Rescue and protect child, but don't blame parents for resulting behaviors.
Presumption: "Poor thing."
Ramifications: Most causes of pathology are not identified. No boats rocked. Blame the adult victim or his genes. Assume inborn knowledge of right and wrong.

NURTURE-BASED, PRO-CHILD

Premise: Quality of attachment determines resilience. Quality of individuation determines personality. Most bad behaviors driven by trauma. Greatness often comes from great parenting.
Motives: Prevent unnecessary suffering Identify real causes. Teach parents how to raise amazing kids. Recognize how healing works & ways of deep healing. Protect society from criminals & mentally ill.
Sponsors: Freudian Seduction Theory, Reichian Breath Work, Attachment & Trauma Theories, Systems Theory, Object Relations Theory, Self-Psychology, CAUSAL THEORY.
Practice: EXPRESSION ETHIC. Revisit causes to heal destructive drives. Observe and express feelings. Release (with empathy) heals and creates insight. Learn new coping skills.
Presumption: "There, but for the Grace of God, go I."
Ramifications: Clearer seeing. Healthier society.

2: GENES & ENVIRONMENT 101

> Instead of studying brains and genes, societal and research attention should instead focus on the familial, social, political and physical circumstances that cause children and adolescents to act out, harm themselves and others, suffer low self-esteem, and experience sadness, loss, fear, heartache, loneliness, aggression, insecurity, and other negative emotions—behaviors and emotions that psychiatric genetics and mainstream psychiatry decontextualize and subsume under the medical designation "child and adolescent psychopathology." —Jay Joseph, 2015, p. 199

I'd like to describe for you my internal visual representation to help your right brain out. This mental construct was formed over years of studying science from a layperson's perspective, with the help of some rather enlightening ah-ha moments. Although I'm no longer a layperson myself, I write as if I am explaining to a layperson. My intention is to first describe a big picture in story form without specific facts, citations and jargon, in order to help you mentally map the basics to continue through the escalated concepts later. It is intended to enhance communication between us and to facilitate insight. You are encouraged to check out any and all facts that would support or discredit this story, or seek the information you need to verify its relevance for yourself. Following this, I'll briefly review the same topic in a more formal format, for those in the profession.

LAYPERSON'S GUIDE TO THE BRAIN

When we are conceived, we are a merger of two cells, one from our mother and one from our father. They form a zygote, which is a cell that is the combination of the sperm and egg cells. The zygote will multiply again and again. After enough replications, these cells become stem cells. They are all alike, but each could become a heart cell, a brain cell, or become employed anywhere in the body. They all have the same special instructions contained in their nuclei. Mostly these instructions are used to build a being—in this case, a human being.

Multiplying is not the only thing these cells need to do to create functionality in our developing structure. They will need to diversify to perform different tasks. Some cells will have to work together to create a heart, while other cells have to work together to create lungs, while others unite to create the nervous system, *etc*. These diversified cells are considered invaluable in the field of medicine, which is why placentas, embryos, and aborted babies are so priceless. If and when they become available to people with devastating maladies, it is thought they could help rejuvenate damaged tissue.

The job stem cells ultimately inherit is determined by their location in the body. Still, something seems to instruct them *how* to organize. Enter DNA, the instruction manual located within every cell. DNA combines into the segments of chromosomes, which are the genes that encode function. Together with DNA's instructions from within, the cells will know precisely how to build the human. There is no evidence the DNA will determine what will happen to the human, just that it will have a skeleton, blood, a heart, a nervous system, skin, *etc.*, and DNA will tell it to specifically design a short female with brown eyes and curly red hair, for example. DNA will determine features such as how tall this baby will grow if it's nurtured and protected.

However, the DNA *does not* determine how the baby will think or act. We are a bag of cells. Every cell is an organism in its own right. Our cells make lots of decisions on their own that ultimately take care of us. Once our body is built, our cells won't think and act from the nucleus. Our cells will think and act from their membranes to make decisions. They will determine how to respond to the environment. They are the gatekeepers. They decide what part of their environment of fluids, substances and air are toxic, and what parts of the environment are helpful. They will let in nutrients we ingest and process, and they will exclude toxins. Sometimes they get fooled, and some toxins are admitted while some nutrients are forbidden entry through the cell membrane. Sometimes the cells are simply overwhelmed by the environment and can no longer function, perhaps leading to death. Many a time the cell membrane has been fooled, but the cell membrane learns. It may recall a toxin was harmful and remember next time to keep the gate closed. Whatever the membrane admits, the body must metabolize. When it can't, we're in trouble.

As I have mentioned, some cells specialize. Neurons are nerve cells predominantly located in the brain and spine, but are represented throughout the body in branches of connections that spread out to every area of the body. They keep the brain informed about the entire experience of the body. They let us know when something we are experiencing could be harmful because it feels bad. They relay information like a bucket brigade. We burn our hand and the brain tells us to lift it quickly. They connect at synapses between neurons via electrical or chemical conductors, forming relays.

Mirror neurons have a further specialty. Not only do they record and share information, but they fire when they witness another person having an experience relevant to any experiences we have already had. Even though each experience is unique, if there are enough components in our own experience to relate, these mirror neurons will fire, and we will identify with the experience of the other. These experiences of identifying with others, especially parents, create empathy and understanding. However, if our father beats us, taunts us and seems to enjoy it, never offering empathy or remorse, and our mother looks the other way, doesn't care or even tells the father exaggerated stories to get us in even more trouble, there are no mirror neurons available to relate to the suffering of another. Instead we would be predisposed to want to injure another person the way we have been injured. We would identify with the perpetrator, not the victim. Our mirror neurons would not fire over another person's suffering. There would be no recorded mirror neurons in our brain that could relate. Experiences and learning create synaptic neuro-connections in the right brain and left brain. Is it the human design at fault for this? Is a person responsible for knowing something they never learned? Can we expect someone to intellectually override something foreign to their own experience and learned drives? Is it the gene's fault? No. Does epigenetics explain it? No. Although, as we shall ultimately see, epigeneticists try.

The human design is brilliant beyond our wildest ability to understand. The designs of the human body and brain are far more complex and intricate than the design of the entire universe. Probably the most extraordinary aspect of our design is we are adaptable and not restricted by instinct. We have evolved beyond instinct. We become what we experience and learn second-by-second, and the seconds in the infant and toddler and more formative than at any other time in life. During the first years of life, personality, worldview and self-worth are constantly forming.

In fact, instinct may even be overrated. I know birds have to be taught to fly by their mothers and daddies, learning mostly by watching the 100 times they flew away and back, a lesson handed down from generation to generation possibly a billion times. I have seen that someone might have to show a newborn puppy where to go to nurse. I have seen cows ordinarily hang with cows when there are no other options, but I know of a cow that rescued a traumatized pig, staying with it every night for a month until it was ready to join the others in the barn. We are flooded with videos these days of animals and babies doing amazing things together. On the Internet, I have seen a dog rescue another dog off a freeway. In another video I saw a parrot feed a dog that couldn't reach its dish. I have seen an elephant whose best friend was a dog. I've seen a turtle chase a cat after it got tired of being chased. I've seen a bird groom a cat. I have observed that a dog kept in the backyard will be quite different than a dog that gets to crawl under your covers at night. So many such videos have convinced me we are here for one another.

We have even seen wild animals make friends with their normal prey. So even instinct or inborn behavioral programming will subordinate to experiences in animals, especially in the very young. What I have seen is everything alive wants to connect. It prefers to connect with the familiar, or what they already know. No one wants to be alone, even if they learn it's the only safe way to be.

Humans have a developmental design that takes us from conception, to old age, to death. I used to assume we were universally programmed for some behaviors, since we all roll over first, sit up next, then learn to walk and finally to run. I don't think so anymore. I call these inevitable lessons. They are events any and all of us are eventually challenged by and we inevitably decide to make it happen after watching others long enough. Figuring it out also helps our brain organize to solve problems. We sit up because it's the next experiment we need to perform to get ourselves into a vertical position like everyone else. We see everyone walking, so we want to figure that one out too. We see someone run and we want to walk faster. None of our behaviors are inborn other than the reflexes with which we are born, and those die away in a few months after experience has had enough time to take over.

There are universal experiences we all seem to need to have, even if they are not universal behaviors. We need to survive, so we need to eat and sleep safely. We need to attach and to be touched to form a mental and physical sense of ourselves, especially where we begin and end. We need affection. We need to feel regarded. We learn what we are worth by how others treat us. We need limits so we don't become entitled. We need someone to model values for us and teach us values, or we won't know them. All these things we need if we are to socially integrate and to be considered a sensitive, smart and cultured person.

Otherwise, we don't need these experiences. In another culture it could have been more productive for us to have to scrap for everything and to compete with others, except we need to proliferate. That means we still probably need to be able to have sex without rape. Certainly, for violent cultures other ethics are learned such as loyalty and submission.

Intelligent human beings have the ability to sense, especially to see and hear, recalling via pictures in their right brain. The right brain forms pictures (think R for "round"), while the left-brain creates formulas and works with symbols such as language (think L for "logic" and "language") to communicate and describe the pictures. The right brain and left brain work together.

When we are preverbal, we are mentally mapping out the world and our place in it. Yet we are less likely to recall specific events than when we are verbal. Language offers us the ability to reference experiences. Events experienced but not referenced remain influential to the personality, but they operate at an unconscious level. This is one of the reasons dreams can be so useful.

Intelligence must include the ability to perceive reality clearly and then represent our experience to others with language. The most intelligent among us are those who can witness and experience events, then explain what they just witnessed in language others can understand. It's a good idea for parents to give their children words for their most essential experiences. Eventually this skill, to include a good vocabulary, leads to objectivity and formulating common denominators, problems and strategies. The least intelligent among us are those who have been deprived of acceptance, experiences and communication skills, or they are the ones who have been told what to see, think, feel and believe, despite their experiences. When experiences don't match up with what we are expected to believe, we enter the realm of insanity, sometimes for a moment and sometimes for a lifetime. Or we can simply enter a world in which we never develop the capacity for independent or critical thinking.

All biologically normal babies are born with more brain cells than they can ever use in their lifetime. With every experience, the synapses make connections to represent the experience in the form of memories. Pictures are formed as we experience things. The more experiences we have the more pictures we form. These experiences are retained more indelibly when they are associated with previous experiences—previously painted synaptic representations. We have a tendency to associate new experiences with old ones, comparing them, affirming them or uniting them. The more we connect new experiences to old memories, the denser and easier they are to retain and recall, especially if we are verbal. Our conscious thought stems from neural connections in the brain, and these neurons are alive and processing all the time. If they are being forced to process events with information that contradicts their experiences, they will be handicapped. These handicaps can manifest in the realm of mental health, intelligence and social skills.

When there are no experiences, there are no connections. When there are no experiences, the synapses wither in a process scientists call pruning. When you meet someone with borderline or below average intelligence, barring a brain injury or genetic anomaly, you might speculate they have been deprived of experiences and dialogues.

We are ultimately able to explain those four-dimensional video recordings with language or other symbols via the left brain. The left brain will organize experiences according to previous experiences and beliefs, creating mental constructs that can become self-fulfilling prophesies. Beliefs can sometimes misguide the storage of experiences, which diminishes intelligence. Intelligence requires a clear lens through which to perceive, which means the fewer beliefs and more experiences we have the more clearly we can perceive.

UNIVERSAL GENETIC INSTRUCTION

Now that you have the big picture, I will share with you the research supporting it. The following may in some ways seem repetitious, but it contains more technical information this time. It is based on science, as I have seen my job in life as a translator, diplomat and mediator between researchers. I commit to taking the most representative of the various studies and knitting together a complete picture of how humans develop.

Cell Membrane as Gatekeeper

Possibly the beginning of awareness took place billions of years ago after The Big Bang, when particles of matter began to form groups, some of which, made of carbon, came to enjoy an optimal environment for cell life to begin, to include clean air, water and sunshine. Some of the earliest forms of life originated with the amoeba and the organisms they formed when they clustered. One of the earliest manifestations of awareness took place when the amoeba turned toward the light. It also had a cell body, the membrane of which made decisions about what was friend or foe. Those who study evolution will recognize that the human being passes through all the stages of evolution to become aware, conscious, and ultimately, self-conscious.

Neurobiologist Bruce Lipton (2001c) says, "The primacy of DNA in influencing and regulating biological behavior and evolution is based on an unfounded assumption." Another biologist, H. F. Nijhout (1990), explains that concepts of genetic "controls" and "programs" were originally born as metaphors to help direct research. With widespread repetition of the metaphor, scientists and the public began to take the metaphor as fact, which sent researchers on a wild goose chase in search of substantiation, which they never found but apparently believed they would find if they tried hard enough or spent enough money. Lipton (1991) clarifies on his website:

> The notion that the nucleus and its genes are the 'brain' of the cell is an untenable and illogical hypothesis. If the brain is removed from an animal, disruption of physiologic integration would immediately lead to the organism's death. If the nucleus truly represented the brain of the cell, then removal of the nucleus would result in the cessation of cell functions and immediate cell death. However, experimentally nucleated cells may survive for two or more months without genes, and yet are capable of effecting complex responses to environmental and cytoplasmic stimuli. Logic reveals that the nucleus cannot be the brain of the cell!

Lipton is addressing the assumption of conventional biology that the nucleus of a cell (including DNA) is the cell's "brain." Recent biologists say the brain of a cell is its membrane. Lipton (2001b) explains:

> The membrane provides a (genetically designed) interface between the ever-changing environment (not-self) and the enclosed controlled environment of the cytoplasm (self). The embryonic 'skin' (ectoderm) provides for two organ systems in the human body: the integument (the natural covering of an organism or an organ, such as its skin, husk, shell, or rind) and the nervous system. In cells, these two functions are integrated with the simple layer that envelops the cytoplasm (which is the cell's internal substance and sub-structures).

This membrane is the gatekeeper within which our receptor-effector molecules decide whether the environmental stimulus is something to let in or keep out. Protein molecules in the cell membrane interface with the environment. These protein membranes are control-molecules comprised of couplets. "The expression of the cell is primarily molded by its perception of the environment and not by its genetic code, a fact that emphasizes the role of nurture in biological control," says Lipton (2001b). He continues:

> ...Stem cells do not control their own fate. The differentiation of stem cells is based upon the environment the cell finds itself in. For example, three different tissue culture environments can be created. If a stem cell is placed in culture number one, it may become a bone cell. If the same stem cell was put into culture two, it will become a nerve cell or if it is placed into culture dish number three, the cell matures as a liver cell. The cell's fate is 'controlled' by its interaction with the

environment and not by a self-contained genetic program (Lipton, 2001b).

The first cluster of cells in the development of a human being, the morula, is all stem cells, and they all share the potential to form a normal human embryo and a normal baby. Then when the morula arrives in the uterus, it begins to receive fluid from the uterus. As this interaction begins to take place, the inner cell mass of the morula begins to differentiate from the outer cell mass, and the stem cells begin to take on different jobs. They have different properties depending on what is around them (Lipton, 2001b).

In the purest form this is called epigenesis, distinct from epigenetics. It's an ongoing adaptation that stem cells—not genes—make to their environments. More recent discoveries have suggested these molecules can learn from experience and they actually formulate "beliefs," some of which are not true. According to Lipton (2001b):

> Every cell is innately intelligent in that it generally possesses genetic 'blueprints' to create all of the necessary perception complexes that enable it to survive and thrive in its normal environmental niche. The DNA coding for these perceptual protein complexes have been acquired and accumulated by cells during four billion years of evolution. Perception coding genes are stored in the cell's nucleus and are duplicated prior to cell division…Changes in the environments generate a need for 'new' perceptions on the part of organisms inhabiting those environments.

Thus the number of potential environments a cell may face is not anticipated in the genes or even by the cell membrane. The number of potential environments is astronomical if not infinite. Membranes determine whether an environment is toxic or supportive. The body doesn't need a gene for every permutation. It just needs decision-makers who can say yes or no. Apparently these decision-makers, like us, can also make wrong calls based on previous experiences. According to Lipton (2001b):

> The cell membrane boundary enveloping each biological cell comprises the structural basis of a biological processor system. As a processor, the cell's membranes scan the environment for signals. Obviously the environment is awash in signals. If all the signals were audible, the environment would sound like blaring noise. However, the specificity of reception characteristic for each receptor IMP [Integral Membrane Protein] enables it to distinguish its complementary signal out of all the jumbled ambient noise…While the environment is in a sense 'chaotic,' with hundreds and thousands of simultaneously-expressed 'signals,' the cell can selectively read only those signals that are relevant to its existence…

The cell works like a microcomputer system of bits, each of which can switch on or off, or rather receive or reject receptor-effector complexes. These choices for every event enable genes to design membranes that can respond to an almost infinite number of permutations from the environment. Facts in evidence indicate we are designed to adapt to our environment rather than follow some sort of pre-program for every permutation of potential experiences.

There are some universal genetically instructed behaviors—which we call reflexes—but genetics-for-the-human-race is entirely different from genetics-for-individual-humans. We need to be clear about that. Scientists and the lay public are prone to conflate the two. Cultural anthropologists are pioneers in the issue of nature vs. nurture, having demonstrated repeatedly that we are the most behaviorally adaptable of all species because we have shed innate "human nature" (Fuentes, 2012; Geetz, 1973; Kluckhohn, 1959). Our brains are designed to make the most of experience. Cultural anthropologists point to our flexibility between cultures, but lately it seems they make a perfunctory nod to genetics, as it is out of their wheelhouse—possibly because their work would be criticized if they didn't—while continuing to explore various adaptive human measures in differing cultures.

Inborn Reflexes & Genetic Instructions

All babies are born with specific reflexes that last only a few months, until their genetic instructions fade away. All babies will **throw their hands and legs out** when they think they are about to fall (perhaps so we can catch them, or so they can break their fall). They also have **reflexes to crawl** (and even walk) when they are first born. When touched on their cheek, they have **reflexes to turn toward the stimulus** (so they can nurse). They also have **reflexes to grasp**. These reflexes die away by six months of age (Boyd & Bee, 2006).

We are **designed to be self-representing**. We want to **avoid pain and seek pleasure**, which includes a positive sense of ourselves. We want to thrive, and we are inclined to certain responses when threatened, including **fight, flight or freeze**. Our nervous system is wired to self-inform and self-represent, which is our genetic design. Whether or not that includes specifics that could still be discovered is uncertain. It may not be that we have any inborn behavioral instructions, but rather we discover inevitable ways to represent ourselves compatible with our physical design, such that we gain nourishment, comfort and skin contact by nursing. I couldn't say with any conviction whether these are inevitable lessons or genetic instructions. It may be that our genetic instructions simply design our bodies with a few temporary inborn reflexes, and the rest is to be learned in a legacy of generational transmission.

There actually are some other apparently gene-based drives common to the entire species that are not reflexes. They may be propelled by inborn drives or may once again be the result of learning ways to achieve pleasure and avoid pain. As we shall soon consider in more depth, the **drive to attach** is essential to the survival of all humans, and it calls for parents to do whatever is necessary to provide a continuous and safe attachment, and prevent broken attachments.

A broken attachment or an insecure attachment creates a fragile core identity, which will fail to handle assaults on one's self worth with any sort of resilience. A baby needs a grown-up who they come to know as their grown-up. Any old grown-up won't do; it must be *their* grown-up. Without a dedicated grown-up, trust cannot be learned. Self-worth cannot be learned. We need others to give us our self-worth, and we need it to come from someone who is *our* someone. Once again, this may simply be the drive to avoid pain and seek pleasure, as no two attachment behaviors are exactly the same. But without attachment, we die. With minimal attachment, our behaviors become perverse.

I know of no genetic research where scientists acknowledge the role of attachment in the formation of mental health, and/or how this drive, if frustrated, would create the foundation for mental health issues or a fragile core that could not provide resilience in stressful times. I speak of original causes for a chronically anxious or depressed personality.

Another universal need for all children is to **individuate**, which means they must develop their own autonomous and authentic expression of themselves. When children are not raised in a healthy way, the need to attach and the need for authentic expression come into conflict (Maté, 2015).

We all share the same design that brings emotional healing, something that seems counter-intuitive and has to be discovered if not taught and learned. All human beings are **genetically programmed how to heal**. If we are emotionally injured, we need to release our feelings and confused thoughts, ideally to someone who gives us understanding in order to recover from our injury. Those of us denied permission (repressed) to get our feelings out when we have been truly injured will be prone to scapegoat others (Miller, 1981, 1983, 1984, 1998, 2001) and those who loiter in the injury—internalizing the message, seeking rescue by acting helpless and acting as if the hurtful messages were deserved—will create self-fulfilling prophesies in the future (Snyder, 2012).

While all humans may share the same temporary inborn reflexes, our genes prepare us to handle unique situations as well by providing us the necessary equipment. Genetic instructions give us the tools to adapt to environment. Genetic instructions give us the human brain as it evolved to record experiences, infer lessons and retrieve information learned for future reference and communication.

Our nervous system and brain are the origins of our ability to self-represent. The brainstem keeps our body working for us. The right brain is fully formed at birth and sees more clearly than we acknowledge, more clearly than even adults can see, recognizing primary information, facial expressions and tones of voice. The left brain awaits language and codification for storage, retrieval, patterns and generalizations in order to develop resolution, reason, predictions and foresight. The corpus callosum connects the information from the right brain to the left brain, while Wernicke's area and Broca's area stand by to facilitate the communication of our thoughts. Wernicke's area allows us to interpret communicated sounds and Broca's area allows us to express what we understand in words. A person who has suffered damage to Broca's area can completely understand what people are saying when watching a televised news broadcast, but be unable to recreate a single word to communicate a thought. The hippocampus helps us retrieve our memories according to histories and associations. The amygdala stands by to handle assaults and self-defense. If the amygdala is denied a chance to represent itself, it builds up a grudge and undergoes a change in chemistry affecting our neurotransmitters and their abilities to metabolize trauma in a clear-headed way.

Genes do enough to deliver a miraculously designed body—fashioned brilliantly by evolution—but they do not do everything. They instruct our stem cells how to set us up for survival and success. They regulate the physical structure of the body. The microorganism within the human body that makes decisions on behalf of the body appears to be the cell membrane, which determines which chemicals are toxic and which chemicals are beneficial, and as a gatekeeper makes decisions of inclusion or exclusion. The misunderstanding by geneticists of the role of genes is based on an assumption that behaviors are pre-programmed, not adaptable. The brilliance of the human organism is that we are adaptable to environmental demands. We are flexible. We are able to learn from experiences and history. These experiences inform our choices reflexively, unconsciously and consciously.

ENVIRONMENTAL FACTORS TO CONSIDER

Attachment

All babies are born needing to attach. Whether or not they are born knowing they have a need for their mother specifically, they learn soon enough. It may be genetic instruction or just clarity that attaching to that grown-up is the only apparent way to survive; it's hard to say whether insight is inborn or quickly learned. One thing is for sure: Babies know they are babies and need help. Is that learned, or inborn knowledge?

It may also be we find comfort in the familiar, as information is power. Attachment has two primary ingredients: attunement and continuity. Babies need at least one primary caregiver who cares deeply about their experiences enough that they endeavor to relate to their child, to communicate that understanding to the child, and to put the baby's needs above their own. More than two such primary caregivers for a single baby may lead to some difficulties in the formation of identity, including fragmentation; issues of loyalty, trust, and commitment; confusion about values; and even disorientation. Attaching to our special person or parents affirms our existence and our sense of belonging. Multiple caregivers affirm our sense of tenuousness. The need for attachment tells us we need connection.

We have known there are primary issues of nurturance that come with attachment since Rene Spitz, Harry Harlow, and John Bowlby and his protégés did their voluminous and replicated research. We have seen the devastating impact on personality from depriving baby monkeys of maternal affection, while offering milk from wire monkeys (Harlow, 1964). We have seen securely attached adolescent monkeys introduced to feral "children" to teach them social skills when adult monkeys couldn't. Behaviors of all magnitudes and permutations can be learned, and can also become unlearned.

Some pro-parent researchers have attempted to discredit attachment researchers, despite their excellent research designs and replicability. I have in mind a couple of books I once came across critiquing the groundbreaking series of major research on attachment (Spitz, Harlow, Bowlby, Robinson, Ainsworth and Main), in which the feminist authors attempted to discredit Attachment Theory. While such attempts were very weak, it was probably useful for other pro-parent researchers who wanted to avoid alternative explanations for their results. The same thing happened following research on repressed memories of sexual abuse. I expect it to happen again over mirror neurons because mirror neurons are the real scientific explanation for different types of behavior. Some researchers will always be trying to prove behavior isn't learned at home.

Another factor in our disposition toward The Tulip Theory is that mothers are now committed to the work force, and the supporting theory is feminism—an essential element in my own identity. Unfortunately, the evolution of the human species never prepared our babies for daycare, to be cared for by strangers or rotating caregivers. We were designed or rather evolved to be nurtured by our tender and constant mothers from birth until we can walk away. For humans that is no earlier than three years of age and ideally, five years of age. It appears securely attached children are resilient in the face of traumatic events.

Continuity is a related issue facing society today, as babies need a continuous attachment, not one broken up into multiple weekly abandonments or more acute, longer abandonments. The infant needs fidelity for comfort, if only because it's more efficient to depend on someone we know than to depend on someone we don't know. Our fulfillment or frustration when attempting to attach to our primary parent becomes a fundamental part of our core personality. The results of secure or insecure attachments constitute degrees of resilience and show up on a continuum of behaviors from killers to saints. The more secure an infant feels, the more resilient she becomes. The more insecure an infant or toddler feels, the more susceptible she is to future insults and assaults, and the more pathological will be her adult behavior.

When babies are passed around to multiple caregivers, they learn not to attach to anyone because everyone leaves. They withhold trust. They no longer mold to their parents' bodies when carried. They would rather push away. They don't like eye contact and will point to a corner of the ceiling in order to "change the subject." Parents often think they are trying to show them something and that they are so smart. They become little prematurely independent islands, unable to be vulnerable or surrender and learn from parents and authorities. They grow into adults who don't trust, who have limited education (because they were too defended or proud to learn) and then have to cover up their ignorance as they get older. They seek power and loyalty for security. They live "underground." They do not reveal their true selves, except perhaps when they are being left or abandoned by someone they have finally come to include in their lives. Then they explode.

Gabor Maté (2003, 2015) was brilliant to reduce the human struggle into two drives: 1) the drive to attach and 2) the drive to become authentic or true to ourselves. We need to experience the lessons of a secure attachment that include how and when to trust and be vulnerable. We gain an inner security and feeling of worthiness when we are securely attached. We gain an internalized awareness of what healthy intimacy looks like. When we feel safe, we can learn easily, develop clarity and a sense of feeling significant. When we have achieved that goal, so to speak, we begin to represent ourselves in a healthy and respectful way.

Yet many of us never enjoy a secure attachment, so many or most of us are never free to become authentic. That is to say, we spend most of our lives caring about how we look and what other people think, so we forget to see the world through our own eyes. The degree to which we still need to be validated by others is the degree to which we will not be free to become whole or fully evolved with our own values, creativity and insight. We will never get to be our authentic selves, and while we don't really know why we have an amorphous unhappy or discontented feeling inside, we suspect something is missing in us. Only when one achieves authenticity do we discover how important it is. It is the source of personal security, resilience, creativity, healthy relationships, empathy, clear seeing, and even enlightenment.

The long-term effects and behaviors of securely attached infants vs. insecurely attached infants are profoundly different, and each result is unique. Pro-parent modern scientists have previously interpreted these children as having different genetic instructions rather than differing first years of life, as most of the pro-parent researchers appear to know almost nothing about Attachment Theory.

Modeling

Humans have known throughout human history that behaviors are copied, and how we treat others will come back to us. "Do unto others as you would have them do unto you." Children copy their parents. Children feel for their parents and each other. They imitate and internalize at a deep level the values practiced on them and around them. "Monkey see, monkey do." "Do as I say, not as I do."

Psychologist Albert Bandura was one of the first if not the first in the field of behavioral sciences to write about imitative behavior. He called the phenomenon "modeling" and the theory "observational learning" or Social

Learning Theory. He also developed a concept called "reciprocal determinism," which held that behaviors are mutually constructed. He came to the forefront of the field of cognitive psychology with his experiments with the Bobo Doll, a bounce-back blow-up doll children were allowed to hit and knock down after witnessing their parents aggress the doll, demonstrating children will imitate their parents, especially if their parents were praised for their aggressive behavior with the doll.

Imprinting & Mirror Neurons

In 1979, halfway through my therapy, I concluded behaviors were "imprinted" from observing others. I saw behaviors imprinted by children from parents, and I hypothesized the imprinting took place by the younger and weaker from the older and stronger. When I attended graduate school I learned Conrad Lorenz had described something he called "imprinting." He had observed if goslings hatch in the presence of a human, they will follow the human as their parent.

Behaviors become transmitted and replicated sometimes within less than one minute, as well as from generation to generation. In other words I have seen instant imprinting and I have watched children store up their experiences until they become parents themselves. Babies who had mothers who suffered from postpartum depression may also suffer the same when they finally give birth to babies, who may some day grow up to have postpartum depression after they give birth. What goes in must come out.

I have videotape of a father who threw a plastic block at his son's face, and his son turned around and threw a plastic block at a doll's face, as the son knew he was forbidden to retaliate. When children are forbidden to give their injuries back to their perpetrator, that becomes the foundation for later scapegoating, whenever the child has any sort of power differential over another: a smaller child; a girlfriend or wife; one's own child; a teacher and student; a cop and his captive; a bully and a smaller child; a coach and his child; a priest and his alter boy; etc.

I have identified the phenomenon as second generation. For example, a girl may be the victim of incest in her home and become histrionic as a result of first generation trauma. She may later have a daughter who imprints her mother's histrionic behavior as a result of second generation internalizing of her mother's trauma. The second-generation child may have a different take on the behavior, or she could be traumatized too, especially if she attracts further sexual abuse (bringing first and second generation trauma into her life). She could also be inoculated to her mother's behavior, if she has had the freedom to speak openly about what she sees and how it affects her mother and her.

I concluded there were two different definitions for imprinting. Lorenz's definition came first, but I would not give up mine. Still it was obvious imprinting is mostly done in infancy and youth, leaving a library's worth of experience and options for the adult. I have seen the power of attachment and the need to relate, such that animal life will attach to whoever is available. Years later, now I see the two concepts of imprinting are related and are perhaps the same. Further, it appears Attachment Theory and imprinting cannot be studied or understood separately.

If goslings can imprint from humans, the concepts imprinted from one human to another is incalculable. I have seen babies and small children driven to act toward others as their adults have treated them. We need to have others in order to develop ourselves; we are co-creators of one another. British pediatrician and psycholanalyst D. W. Winnicott wrote, "There is no such thing as a baby...if you set out to describe a baby, you will find you are describing a baby and someone" (Winnicott, 1992, p. 88). Clearly without someone, the baby will perish. Without someone, no identity will form. The law of relativity holds we can only know something in relationship to something else, and in this case, some*one* else.

Sometimes, witnessing a sibling or their mother being abused traumatizes a child. Psychotic parents tend to raise unhealthy children and healthy or nurturing parents tend to raise leaders, as we can see in Malala, Mother Teresa, and Nelson Mandela, to name a few. Mirror neurons afford us the opportunity to see ourselves in others and to modify ourselves to adapt to others and to be understood. We all share a design that causes us to share points of view via mirror neurons and to imitate and replicate the way we have been treated.

"Neuroscientist Giacomo Rizzolatti, MD, who with his colleagues at the University of Parma first identified mirror neurons, says these neurons could help explain how and why we 'read' other people's minds and feel empathy for them. If watching an action and performing that action can activate the same parts of the brain in monkeys—down to a single neuron—then it stands to reason the same would be true for humans" (Winerman, 2005, p. 48). Rizzolatti and his associates have surmised that mirror neurons give us the ability to understand others.

They dubbed their discovery "mirror neurons." With the humility of a good scientist who has an eye for ramifications, Rizzollati stated, "We were lucky because there was no way to know such neurons existed," he said, "But we were in the right area to find them" (1996, p. 131). Renowned psychologist V.S. Ramachandran, PhD, reportedly has called the discovery of mirror neurons one of the "single most important unpublicized stories of the decade" (Winerman, 2005, p. 48). He has suggested the discovery of mirror neurons may account for culture, language, empathy, and maybe even autism.

Some say it was wrong to speculate on the importance of mirror neurons in all these areas when the research has yet to be done to prove their applications (Hickok, 2014). That may be true. I doubt autism is caused by imprinting an autistic parent, but may more likely be caused by not imprinting involvement from the parent during a critical learning period, just as a person may lack empathy because they have never experienced it.

Mirror neurons make us versatile, not bound to genetic instruction. They may have been key to evolution. I suspect mirror neurons can produce indelible programming in some ways and reversible programming in other ways. I also suspect what has not been provided to imprint may be sought out later in life. People who have been deprived of empathy cannot produce it. What doesn't go in can't come out.

Researchers will find when one receives empathy in early childhood, they have it to give. If they hear languages, they learn to speak them. They will internalize the ways of their culture with mirror neurons. Children copy. They copy so well, you can see the behaviors, beliefs and attitudes of their parents very early in their development. Play is an opportunity to re-enact what they have imprinted. A child who has been ignored will seem to shrink inward. A child who has been hit will eventually hit others. A child who is yelled at learns to yell at others. I have never believed these behaviors were genetic because one can witness them in real time.

Some people observe something they can't repeat and still understand it, like sports fans (who can't play) or people of the opposite sex who somehow are able to identify with their partner. We can imagine ourselves in the point of view of others and still not be able to physically act it out. However, when we are treated in certain ways, especially in infancy, we internalize what we learn to a greater and more profound degree, especially when it is chronic or acute.

Some say mirror neurons don't drive behavior because people can rebound and attempt to behave in opposite ways from how they were treated. The success of such an endeavor requires a great deal of self-awareness I call "conscious override." Mirror neurons record and drive us on an unconscious level, but experiences can be transcended or over-ridden on a conscious level. This is one of the reasons it is important not to program children, repress them or deny them expression, lest they not be able to self-reflect. People who have been raised to have a voice and represent themselves freely and cogently will be able to transcend imprints and make conscious new choices. Self-awareness is necessary to outsmart what we have imprinted.

Systems Theory and Practice

Unfortunately, behavioral geneticists do not know about attachment and imprinting. They don't know about family systems theory from the 1960s either.

Murray Bowen, the psychiatrist who developed family systems theory, focused on how the mental state of parents is transmitted to their children consciously and unconsciously, which he first coined the "intergenerational transmission process." It's especially clear to trained clinicians that people telegraph their attitudes to one another. Research studies have demonstrated babies become withdrawn if mothers or primary caregivers don't acknowledge them. It's what bonding is about.

Family systems theorists and clinicians have been telling researchers and clinicians for decades children learn their behaviors from their environment, like a micro-culture, especially the family. Grown children then transmit those experiences to their own families for generations to come. Systems theory has always been straight forward and easy to assess. It's a cause and effect theory. It was formulated more than a half century before the discovery of mirror neurons, and it sufficed. It represented natural cures, prevention and pro-active ways to raise healthy families and healthy children.

Intergenerational transmission is observable in an instant and it is observable over generations. We see it in language, culture, religious beliefs, attitudes, bias, and sophistication, or the lack thereof. It's an understatement to say we copy or mimic one another. We metabolize one another. We intuit one another according to our experiences.

Family Ethics

The first thing I look for when I meet people or work with them is how they seem, whether they seem authentic or underground. I notice those who are underground do not seem as creative, honest, self-aware, perceptive, intelligent and alive as the others. They seem to be rule followers or rule breakers. They need guidelines to live by or authorities to disregard. Both are confused about ethics, at best. Two major family systems transmitted with devastating effects or that empower are the **repression vs. expression ethic** and the **blaming vs. person responsibility ethic**. The inclination to live underground, as we have seen, is either the result of insufficient attachments or family ethics or both, as second-generation behavior can become a family ethic.

Repression Ethic vs. Expression Ethic

When families put pressure on children not to complain or express the truth, especially their feelings, then healing and resolutions cannot be had. On the other hand, families that allow for honest expression of feelings and observations will raise a child who can heal from the most difficult of experiences. The body knows how to heal injuries by expressing them. Repression keeps them inside and makes us symptomatic. When researchers use self-report to determine how much a person has been abused or neglected, they need to identify repression ethics as well, or these self-reports cannot be valid. Most serial killers will lie about their abuse and neglect to protect their parents. If they were able to tell the truth about their abuse, they would not become killers.

Repressed children learn to keep the truth a secret. Many of them have not been directly taught to withhold the truth of their thoughts and feelings. Many simply have just never been asked. Sometimes they see family members rally to protect someone in the family from the truth because they are too fragile. They learn not to tell the truth about what they see and think and feel to avoid getting in trouble or hurting their parents' feelings. Others are directly threatened not to talk. These children figure out how to live underground. Secrecy is important to them. Sometimes therapists confuse confidentiality with secrecy and don't recognize secrecy as a symptom. Unfortunately the emphasis on confidentiality can be mistaken as reinforcement for underground thinking. We should be careful to address this openly and inform our patients that authenticity is far more precious than living underground.

Repressed children will not learn how to live authentic lives. They will tend to act their way through life. They will be unconscious, thoughtless and lack the ability to perceive and understand others. They will begin to scapegoat others. They will become judgmental and form superficial explanations for other people's behaviors, such that it must have been inborn. The repression ethic provides us scapegoats, people we can righteously love to hate rather than seek to understand. Ironically, scapegoaters prey on scapegoaters. The most abused among us are the children who grow up to become serial killers or time bombs, and we love to hate them for how they turned out.

As I have already said, and it bears repeating, Gabor Maté makes the observation that children come into this world with two needs: one is to attach and the other is for authenticity—to have one's own voice and feel safe speaking according to our own observations, experiences, needs and our own lessons. He makes the observation that for many if not most, these two needs are in conflict. For many of us, we have to sell out our own authenticity in order to preserve our attachment with our parents.

A host of great thinkers in our field have addressed the problem of repression and denial. Some have said denial, repression or resistance is the illness, rather than the trauma itself. Unfortunately, some of the experts on the causes of trauma are not the experts on how to heal it. Recently, experts have been suggesting the key to healing trauma is to avoid re-injury or remembering. I believe the opposite is true; once the trauma is remembered, it can be expressed and healed.

Blame Ethic vs. Personal Responsibility Ethic

In an unhealthy home, children learn to blame lest they be blamed. When families exercise blame instead of personal responsibility, members of that family will have major difficulties in life and will have many victims. On the other hand, when a child grows up in a family that encourages self-reflection, the child will be able to learn from mistakes and grow. They will have far healthier relationships. These are critical elements explaining behavior and predicting outcomes that are ignored in genetic research and therefore not ruled out as causes for the phenomena they claim to observe over generations.

I find if you get into a conversation with a stranger, a judge, a cop, your parent, someone else's parent, a teacher, or a neighbor about personal responsibility, you will find about half will say their parents taught them character and supported their curiosity and modeled for them how to self-reflect. They believe if there is a disagreement with a parent they should talk it out. If they remember something from their childhood that still affects them, they are willing to go talk to their parents about it openly with compassion and respect until both parties experience resolution.

The other half experience these as fighting words, possibly becoming enflamed. If we look closely enough we will see hypocrisy. They may reference the "abuse excuse" but somehow hold their parents immune to criticism. Their logic might begin to escape you. They believe their parents had nothing to do with how they turned out, or if they did, their parents get credit for the good stuff and blame genes for the bad stuff. In any event, they will likely be quite vociferous about blaming others but protective of their parents. They may say we need to do something about the ways children are turning to violence and drugs, but, "Don't mess with Mom," as one of my professors once said.

All of this is to say most children learn to think in a pro-child way or a pro-parent way. The former will be curious and tell the truth respectfully. The latter will become so loyal to their parents that they grant them a sort of immunity; they will live in denial for them, and they will defend them to the end of their lives if anyone suggests their parents should have not hurt them. If they were whipped with a belt, they will say they deserved it or, "I was a difficult child." As a matter of fact, some of them will take up the banner for all parents against all children, such as biogeneticists.

Resiliency

The following chart represents all the environmental causes of resiliency and lack thereof, the most influential of which is attachment. These are two brothers, same parents.

Good Brother, Resilient	Bad Brother, Not Resilient
Good bonding and attunement	Poor or unattuned bonding
Continuous Attachment	Broken attachment(s) or major abandonments at young ages
Nurtured	Neglected
Rocked	Not rocked
Touched and cuddled	Barely touched
Protected	Unprotected, overprotected, or parentified
Appropriate and gradual separation	Multiple pre-mature separations
Parents "see" or perceive child	Parents don't see child or project onto child
Allowed to express negative feelings, even to parents (Parental Responsibility)	Required or expected to repress feelings for parent's sake (Parental Immunity)
No secrets	Secrets to keep to protect adults, especially hurtful ones or ones about harmful events
Not abused	Abused, with no avenue to vent
Child had enlightened witness	Child had no enlightened witness
Intimacy available from loving caregivers	Intimacy only available with negative influences or abusive caregivers
Good projections (Hero Child)	Negative projections (Scapegoat Child)
Hero has self-fulfilling prophecies or projection of being lovable; enjoys being good under good projection	Scapegoat has self-fulfilling prophecy or projection of being unlovable, feels angry and hurt; hard to be good when parents are not good to him; acts out negative imprinting
Parents enjoy rewarding child	Parents have a drive to punish and blame child
Good projection gets better (Twice Blessed)	Bad projection gets worse (Double Damned)
Good modeling	Parents make and model selfish choices
Parents discipline consistently with natural consequences	Parents discipline erratically if at all, or parents discipline brutally
Child has ethical and/or religious training	Child has no ethical training or has extreme religious training
Creativity encouraged	No creative outlet
No head injury	Head trauma

Healing

> Parents who freely acknowledge the harm they have done can experience enormous moral relief and rediscover their potential to positively influence the lives of their offspring. —Peter Breggin, MD, 1991, p. 40

The purpose of life is to become self-aware. Taking it one step further, I believe self-awareness is a holy state, when one is closest to divinity, however you conceptualize it. When we review our earliest years and the formation of our values and beliefs, we have an opportunity to redesign ourselves. When we consider how our choices have created the results of our life, we discover how we can redirect our life. When we become conscious of our own motives and beliefs, along with the ramifications of our actions, we enjoy a process some call enlightenment. The veil of assumption drops away, we see what we have been unable to see, and we have clarity. We see what has been before us all along that we learned not to see. Of course, vetting our therapist guide is essential, as this process needs to be done with someone who has done the work and has his or her own clarity as a result.

The work is hard but not hard. If you consider it difficult to explore your true feelings and acknowledge truths you buried long ago, then the work is hard. If you relish understanding why you do what you do and think the way you think, it's a wondrous adventure. The first thing I learned is feelings—even very "bad" feelings—are temporary, and they don't harm us. They are just feelings. They inform us, and when we deny them, they get stronger and start kicking us around, running the metaphorical show. I also learned seeing is change. When I discovered what had injured me and how I had taken it, I could then change my mind and recreate my own "program," so to speak. Now as an adult, I can see what was once adaptive as a child, didn't work as an adult in the greater world. I learned I could review my childhood and family philosophies, and update them with self-reflection and courage to reinvent myself. It changed my world from drudgery to inspiration. I learned the true meaning of legacy.

> We are healed from suffering only by experiencing it to the fullest. —Marcel Proust

3: EVOLUTION OF MEDICINE

There are often motives behind beliefs other than simple observation. Culturally, beliefs may support power, established authority or an established behavioral system. We learn much of these beliefs in childhood and they are usually taught to us.

Some people learn beliefs through observation and experience, which creates higher intelligence and more awareness. Others are taught exactly what to believe, and they learn to minimize what they see and experience. This is somewhat of a handicap in the real world. Further, there are often ramifications that come with any given belief, as beliefs inform practice, and they tell us what to see or not see, and what to do or not do. These beliefs can become flashlights or blinders. They can affect the politicians you follow, the career you choose, the religion you embrace, the partner with whom you make babies. They can come from a diminished, appropriate or excessive belief in oneself. They can come from a regard for others, or feelings of being threatened by others. They come from lessons learned, whether the information is useful or harmful. We often ingest harmful beliefs to be in accord with our society or our parents, so they will continue to love and protect us.

Judges, doctors, scientists, law enforcement officers, teachers and clergy have beliefs that direct them to see no evil, or to see evil where there is none. We live our lives according to which beliefs we embrace, which beliefs we are willing to examine and which beliefs we have indelibly affirmed. We sometimes confuse equality before the law and freedom of religion with equality of beliefs. Not all beliefs are equal, especially those that aren't true, are harmful to others and embraced to remain safe and accepted. These indelible beliefs can and do affect scientists, cops, judges and clinicians, along with the rest of us. Further, we can see how people who gather together in the name of their beliefs, reinforce one another to see what they are supposed to see. At some point, loyalty becomes the shield that prevents self-reflection.

Children are often taught what their parents believe and learn to see and think according to those beliefs. Perhaps the most impactful of any single belief is the one about how we are to look at our parents. In a healthy home, children learn to treat their parents and all people with respect. They learn to be humble, like a child, and they learn to apologize when they hurt someone. They learn grown-ups are kind and considerate leaders who know more, and they are in charge of us and they will protect us when we truly need it. They learn right and wrong and the ability to discern the difference. They learn to love the truth and tell the truth. These children will seem healthier, more intelligent and more honorable than most other children.

Others learn to be afraid to hurt their parents' feelings with the truth of what they have experienced or how they feel. They learn to act the way their parents want them to act, which is quite different from learning to be true to themselves with integrity. Unfortunately, most parents don't know the difference and assume forced compliance equals good ethics and good parenting. Most parents would do things differently if they thought what they were doing would harm their children.

In the pages to follow, the reader will learn the legacy of psychological theory and research. The issues will become clearer as you take a journey through the shadowy history of pro-parent theories of mental health. This history will cover ramifications of nature theory over nurture theory, to include wars of beliefs, including The War of the Researchers. By following history we can see the motives and ramifications of diverse behavioral theory.

TIMELINE

Economics and Religion Instruct Society

Self-awareness applies to societies *and* individuals. **In order to understand anyone or anything, we have to know its history.** When we look at its history we will see the causal and driving forces, to include beliefs and economic incentives, and we will see the ramifications of those beliefs, including who was harmed, if anyone, and who benefitted.

The history that led us to today's issues began thousands of years ago. The beliefs and motives driving historical events continue to drive current events in variations on the same theme. What is considered bad behavior and by whom? Who or what is responsible for bad behavior? How do you make people comply? The answers often lie somewhere between forced behavior and ethics.

In order to lay out the progression of economic forces behind the struggle for dominancy in the arena of medical and mental health, it would be helpful to explain the four economic stages of civilization to-date: communalism, slavery, feudalism, and capitalism. Each had a religious counterpart that established the philosophy of the economic powers-that-be.

In **communalism**, families were mostly matriarchal or of matrilineal dissent, and the leaders were shamans. The objects of worship tended to be from nature, like trees and animals. At some point communal economies were overthrown by competition, especially in a struggle for "energy" sources or ideas that wouldminimize effort and maximize opportunities and privilege.

Thus the next stage was crude, and included domination and privilege. The **slavery** stage was founded on the accumulation of private property, including humans, allowing for free labor including the ability to force one person to do the work for a few. Accumulation of goods led to privilege. Marriage and patriarchy took over to establish heirs of accumulated property. Healers predominantly served the rulers. Religions tended to worship kings and queens and pharaohs, said to have superhuman powers and some sort of deserved entitlement, validating inequity with superstitious beliefs and mythical stories. Slavery peaked when it became top heavy, as it took too much metal, chains and guards to keep slaves in place.

The slavery stage was overthrown by **feudalism** when authorities figured out people could be managed by ideas or beliefs. "Some are born to rule and others to be ruled," said Aristotle. In European feudalism, religious hierarchy reflected economic hierarchy. The pope was equal to the king. The bishops were equal to the lords. The priests were equal to the knights. The congregation was equal to the peasantry aka pawns. The two power structures were mutually affirming. Those who behaved got to go to Heaven or become reincarnated to greater privilege. In Europe, feudal lords and the Roman Catholic Church became mirror entities, represented by the game of chess. They validated each other's authority and established order.

In an interesting twist of feudalism, having skipped the slavery stage in Northern Europe, the royalty of feudal Europe retained communal peasants within their fortresses as they offered protection to the peasants who farmed their land. Every lord and manner had at least one peasant healer or wild-craft practitioner who served the needs of the royal residents. They were the scientists of the day, and they knew a great deal about the healing qualities of plants and the anatomy of animals and humans. They were philosophers of mental health issues as well, and often regulated unhealthy behavior with adages and fairy tales.

However, the ruling class of nobility and the church were quite superstitious. Paranoia over spells became so pervasive that the authorities thought the best way to solve the problem was to annihilate peasant women in leadership, accusing them of having the ability to cast evil spells. With the advent of feudalism, the Roman Catholic Church was also very jealous of the credibility held by these women who were often chosen by nobility. Two Dominican monks, Kramer and Sprenger, represented the Vatican. They characterized these sages as witches and prescribed witch burnings in their tome, *The Malleus Maleficarium*. This war against influential peasant women lasted a few centuries and the message was strong.

Peasant men didn't have much experience being heads of families. As their women fell under attack, they fled the manors and sought work in the cities. Apprenticeships began to develop. When this labor force opened up, the conditions of feudalism ended and the seeds of **capitalism** were sewn. Thus the Catholic church had won the war for feudalism over communalism, but it lost the war for feudalism to capitalism.

As each economic system was overthrown, so too were its religious system and healers. At some point, progress rewarded innovation and the feudal system broke down. When innovation developed, it served the new economic system of capitalism, and a new religion was born that rewarded the work ethic. In the orient, religions embraced reincarnation as a way of managing class systems. If a person behaved in this life, they could graduate to the next level in their next life. In Europe, that religion was Protestantism. Capitalism was also patriarchal and a new classification of healer was born: the medical doctor.

The practice of patriarchal medicine from the beginning was not about getting at the cause of maladies, but about terminating the symptoms. The same is true today. Causes were thought to be inborn or supernatural, and healing was thought to be about masking the symptoms or driving them underground. It is pro-parent thinking to believe causes of behavior are inborn; that the child is responsible for how he turns out, not his experiences or how he was parented.

The Insane and Poor are Exiled

During the 1500s and 1600s in Europe, it appears those in charge of treating mental illness held pro-parent theories, believing the "insane" were neither curable nor worthy of respect or care. While they believed pathology was inborn, there was no compassion in holding that perspective, just as there would be no compassion for slaves in pre-Civil War America. The broken and "mad" of the cities and towns were kept in "insane asylums" or "general hospitals" to remove indigents from the streets. They were incarcerated until they became sober and industrious citizens. That is, only those who were able to provide for themselves were allowed to return to society. The insane were considered unreachable and uneducable, and thus were never released. They were believed to be less than human and impervious to the weather, so clothing was often unnecessary. They were fed with rotten food, kept in chains in cold, dark, rat-infested dungeons, often lying naked in their own excrement on beds of rotten straw until they died.

John Locke was a spokesperson for the new politics of industrialism and forthcoming capitalism, advocating a strong work ethic. It appears John Locke believed the poor were lazy and could do better if they worked hard enough. He did not adhere to theories of inborn inferiority. People were responsible for their own condition and could work their way out of it. Those who succeeded were entitled to a better life, and those who did not were to blame for their own failures. Childhood experiences were irrelevant.

In his *Two Treatise of Government*, he advocated "masters of workhouses ('houses of correction') be encouraged to make these workhouses into 'sweated labor manufacturing establishments or forced-labor establishments.' Children of the unemployed 'above the age of three' should not unnecessarily 'become a burden on the nation and should be set to work and made to earn their keep.' He wrote of this in 1697 for England's Commission on Trade to answer against the 'relaxation of discipline and corruption of manners'" (McPherson, 1975, p. 222).

Moral Management Retreats are Offered

In the mid to late 1700s, the conditions of asylums were at their worst, and reformers such as William Tuke (1732-1822) of England and Philippe Pinel (1745-1826) of France developed their first therapeutic programs, known as the Moral Management Model, through which they achieved considerable success. "'Moral,' perhaps like 'morale' connoted zeal, hope, spirit and confidence. It also had to do with custom, conduct, way of life, and inner meaning," explains J. F. Calhoun in his book *Abnormal Psychology: Current Perspectives* (1977, p. 173).

The mentally ill were invited to retreat into peaceful settings on quiet rural estates, one of which was named York Retreat of England. They had volunteer companions who would listen and talk with them. They were encouraged to take walks through the countryside, work, pray, or rest until they felt ready to leave.

These Moral Management retreats were so successful that 71% recovered and left within one year. Funding became available in the United States, England, and France for more of these retreats, at which point, in the middle of the 18th century, medical doctors showed an interest in gaining recognition as "experts" in insanity.

"After the takeover by the medical profession, overcrowding became the norm, and asylum living conditions gradually deteriorated once again to pre-moral management levels," wrote Ty Colbert (2001, p. 37), who has written four books to expose the misleading, if not fraudulent, practices behind establishing the psychiatric-medical model, the bad seed or bad genes theory, and the chemical imbalance model of mental health.

Mental Illness Becomes Medicalized

"By the end of the 19th century, when scientific psychiatry was supposedly making great strides, discharge rates had dropped to 20-30%" (2001, p.37), wrote Colbert. The medical community established jurisdiction over the insane by defining insanity as a "medical disease" (p. 37). As a result of lobbying by the Royal College of Physicians, England's 1774 Vagrancy Act mandated only licensed medical doctors could approve the confinement of the insane.

Initially the moral managers refuted the claim that lunacy was a medical disease. Physicians struggled against reformers, fearing the moral management institutions would remain in the hands of laypeople, thereby excluding or diminishing the role of doctors. "Their income, prestige and medical theories were all threatened" (Bynum, 1974, p. 325). In order to completely take healing away from laypeople, the medical profession knew they would have to develop a vocabulary for their publications that laypeople couldn't understand. Further, a newly formed Association for Medical Superintendents of American Institutions for the Insane (AMSAII) published the *American Journal of Insanity*. According to R.T. Fancher in his book *Cultures of Healing*, "...the AMSAII undertook a vigorous, effective—and, we may fairly say, fraudulent—campaign to promote medical control over asylums and to ensure that their own views of care would be promulgated among the public and followed in other asylums" (Fancher, 2009, p. 59). Fancher went on to relate that superintendents published annual reports replete with "consciously manipulated statistics...boasting grossly about inflated cure rates...producing a campaign of fraudulent materials...which were then distributed to libraries, policymakers and journalists" (Fancher, 2009, p. 59).

In the hurry to establish expertise over the insane, doctors believed they had to establish dominance and dominion. They approached this by dominating the mentally ill into submission in order to destroy the symptoms. Further, they considered insolence or rebellious behavior against the doctors to be a form of mental illness. Acting as if inmates were biologically sick, microscopes became a standard part of asylum equipment. Drugs were increasingly used to sedate inmates. Cold baths and showers, isolation, electric shock, rotating chairs and purging procedures replaced the successful treatments of the moral managers. "It is important to understand that psychiatry, at this time, was able to establish itself as a medical profession—not because it identified any true diseases—but because it medicalized a highly successful non-medical program" (Colbert, 2000, p. 37).

The roots of patriarchal medicine were political, arrogant, insensitive and devoid of intuition and empathy. According to Ty Colbert, Dr. Benjamin Rush, a signer of the Declaration of Independence in 1776 and the designated father of American psychiatry, treated George Washington by draining his blood, resulting in the President's death, hence the saying, "The father of American psychiatry killed the father of America" (Colbert, 1996, p. 20). Rush invented the tranquilizing chair:

> I have contrived a chair and introduced it to your Hospital to assist in curing madness. It binds and confines every part of the body. By keeping the trunk erect, it lessens the impetus of blood toward the brain. Its effects have been truly delightful to me. It acts as a sedative to the tongue and temper as well as to the blood vessels. In twenty-four, twelve, six, and in some cases in four hours, the most refractory patients have been composed. I have called it a Tranquilizer (Colbert, 1996, p. 20).

Dr. Emil Kræpelin wrote a medical text in 1883 called *Textbook on Psychiatry* about techniques of his time: "Tobacco smoke was administered in the form of an enema by a special machine in severe cases of imbecility and melancholia attonia [depression]" (p. 60). Kræpelin used other techniques to include "harnessing and tying the patient in a standing position and with arms outstretched for eight to ten hours. This was supposed to mitigate delirious outbursts, encourage fatigue and sleep, render the patient harmless and obedient and awaken in him a feeling of respect for the doctor (Kræpelin, p. 86)." Kræpelin experimented on a catatonic schizophrenic patient, pricking above her eye and all the way through her tongue. He noted: "She does not generally react at all when spoken to or pricked with a needle, but resists violently if you try to take her hand or pour water on her. She obeys no kind of orders" (p. 23).

Medicine did evolve, becoming more scientific even though funding often went to experiments that were whimsical, heartless or mercenary. Nonetheless, medicine improved. Dr. Louis Pasteur discovered germs, milk became pasteurized, the public cleaned up better, medical procedures finally became more sanitary, and life spans lengthened. Other progress was made in medicine, but much of it remained inhumane and patriarchal. As late as 1982 doctors were commonly performing surgery on infants without anesthesia because they didn't think infants felt pain (Hall, 1992). The medical model became the basis for psychiatric medicine. Anything that reduced symptoms could be considered a cure, as long as an "approved" doctor developed it.

When England passed its Divorce Act of 1857, divorce became popular for women. Dr. Isaac Baker Brown concluded wanting a divorce was a biologically based mental disease that somehow correlated with having a defective clitoris. He developed a procedure as an antidote to this trend, performing clitorectomies to cure the problem. "After the operation, they humbly returned to their husbands and there was no recurrence of the *disease* after surgery" (Colbert, 1996, p. 21).

It's hard to say whether this philosophy was nature or nurture. It was, however, the beginning of a perspective that held mental illness was considered cured when the symptoms were eradicated or the behavior acceptable. This philosophy is still apparent when psychiatry favors pharmaceutical interventions rather than cures resulting from empathy and understanding.

FREUD

In the echo of Moral Management Theory, Freud struggled with his own theory that trauma caused psychopathology and ended up reversing himself because he feared being excluded from his peers.

Freud developed a close professional relationship with a rather delusional Dr. Wilhelm Fliess, who came to play an important role in Freud's life as a father figure. Fliess somewhat took an interest in his theories when no one else did. He was not a warm man, but Freud believed he was an extraordinary human being, which may have been rather delusional of Freud.

In 1893, Freud treated a twenty-year-old patient, Emma Eckstein, during which time he regularly consulted Fliess. Although Freud's background was in neurology and he was motivated to study the unconscious, his mentor-colleague was developing a medical theory or "exact biology" of mental illness called Reflex Neurosis based on a "complex set of clinical entities that flowed from the nose" (Colbert, 1996. p. 109).

Freud introduced Emma to Dr. Fliess around Christmas in 1894. Emma's symptoms included stomach ailments, problems with her menstruation, masturbation and difficulty walking. Fliess persuaded Freud, surely against his own causal intuitions, to refer Emma to him for nose surgery, believing that unwed women who masturbated suffered from dysmenorrhea (painful menstruation) and that the only cure was a nose operation to "help them give up this bad practice" (Masson, 1985, p. 57).

In 1895, Fliess operated on Emma using only cocaine to anesthetize her and cauterized spots in her inner nose using a wire heated by a galvanic current.

Severe complications developed following the operation and Freud had to call in another doctor when he couldn't reach Fliess. Freud informed Fliess of the gravity of Emma's condition, reporting he had removed two bowls of pus from her nose. He had to call in another doctor who inserted a drainage tube in Emma's nose and suggested further surgery may be necessary. Freud wrote a letter to Fliess about two to three months after the surgery that ended with, "Please send me your authoritative advice. I am not looking forward to new surgery on this girl" (Masson, 1985, p. 61). A few days later, yet another doctor was called in to treat profuse bleeding. This doctor pulled out twenty inches of gauze that Fliess had erroneously left in. Freud again wrote to Fliess, confessing he believed Emma was not abnormal for masturbating, strongly implying she didn't need the operation in the first place and stating had both done her an injustice.

Nevertheless, Freud began to recant his disrespect toward Fliess, his father figure. He began to modify his own theories on mental illness, in part to protect Fliess and in part to assuage his own guilt, as he sensed Fliess pulling away. He began to blame Emma for her hemorrhaging and to reassure Fliess. He wrote, "It's now time that you forgave yourself for the minimal oversight [of leaving in the gauze]" (p. 68). Freud had begun to explain away his own bad conscience.

Emma's situation worsened and it looked like she might die. She underwent another surgery that left her face permanently disfigured. "I am very shaken that such a mishap could have arisen from the operation which was purported to be harmless," wrote Freud. In another letter he wrote, "Eckstein once again is in pain; where will she be bleeding next?" On May 4, Freud wrote, "So far I know only that she bled out of longing [for attention from me]" (p. 100).

Freud's exchange with Fliess revealed his constant internal conflict with the truth and his deep need for validation. His struggle with blaming Fliess was as likely as anxiety-producing as blaming a parent. He struggled with his own conscience, whether to take responsibility for Emma's conditions and what that would mean to their identities as doctors. He struggled with countertransference, including anger toward Emma who seemed to be putting them through such suffering. Who was to blame for Emma's original symptoms, the patient or the parent? Who was to blame, the patient or the doctor? Or was it the biology or the experience? What to heal, the body or the memory?

Nevertheless, at the time Freud had an excellent theory that survived the problems with Emma for about a year and a half and then promptly folded under social pressure. He had become involved with colleagues also in the process of making sense of the impact traumatic events have on patients. He consulted with Josef Breuer about repressed symptoms of hysteria and their origins in incest trauma, as both practiced "free association" and accepted their patients' recollections.

Freud was also a student and colleague of Pierre Janet and Jean Martin Charcot (Masson, 1984), as he sought to sort out evidence and patterns of behavior leading to causes behind psychological symptoms. Janet, Breuer and Freud hypothesized that abuse impacted the psychology of a child into adulthood, causing adult symptoms. Through these interactions more than from his own patients, Freud came to hypothesize incest and sexual abuse underlie hysterical symptoms. He even wrote to Fliess that he had reason to believe his own father had been "perverse" with his sister. Fliess responded that he believed something similar had happened in his home too (Masson, 1985). Interestingly, Fliess' own son became a psychologist who later reported his father—yes, Wilhelm Fliess—molested him during the period Freud and Fliess corresponded (Miller, 1990a). Apparently the senior Fliess was correct in suggesting it had happened in his home too. Perhaps it happened to him and that's why he reportedly molested his son.

In early April 1896, about a year after Emma's last surgery, Freud wrote to Fliess with excited anticipation of formally presenting his Seduction Theory to his colleagues. On April 21, 1896, he presented his paper to the Society for Psychiatry and Neurology in Vienna, Austria, proposing that psychological symptoms resulted from childhood trauma in the home and specifically, that hysteria was rooted in incest. Convinced he was about to unveil one of the greatest discoveries in history, the amazing Dr. Freud began his speech, "Gentlemen, stones do speak. I have discovered the source of the Nile of neuropathology. I have discovered the origin of human misery..." (Ellenberger, 1970, p. 488). He went on to explain how symptoms of hysteria made sense when understood as symptoms of repressed childhood sexual abuse.

Freud was not well received. His peers rejected him and his theory with a cold shoulder. It devastated him. In a letter to Fliess, he wrote, "Word was given out to abandon me, for a void is forming all around me" (Masson, 1985, p. 185). His colleagues soundly banished him and his proposition that an alarming number of their patients had been molested. They rebuffed the implication that psychiatrists should take on parents and their secrets. The consensus was clear: blame the patient for their biology.

Two weeks after the devastating rejection of his paper, Freud began to formulate and explain his new theory about Emma to Fliess, a theory that would completely exonerate Fliess (p. 186). Robert, Fliess' son, who grew up to become a psychologist, revealed later in his life that his father began to molest him during this time period (Miller, 1990, p. 56). It was one month later in a letter dated June 4, 1896 that Freud wrote to Fliess, "Her story is becoming even clearer; there is no doubt that her hemorrhages were due to wishes."

Nearly six months after his colleagues rebuked him, Freud's father died. The night after the funeral, Freud dreamt that a notice was posted on his front door that read, "One is requested to shut the eyes" (Ellenberger, 1970, p. 445). In a remarkable pro-parent blindness, the otherwise brilliant Dr. Freud interpreted his own dream to mean that he had carried unreasonable hostility toward his father for far too long. By contrast, a pro-child interpretation would have suggested that both the all-powerful peer group, Society of Physicians, and

Freud's father, whose secrets he kept, had requested, demanded and decreed that he shut the eyes.

A little more than a year after the debut of his Seduction Theory and a year after his father died, Freud shut the eyes. He recanted his Seduction Theory in a letter to Fliess dated September 21, 1897, but he did not begin work on a replacement theory for another seven years. He was ostracized for many years but continued to develop his pro-parent theory over the next forty-plus years, explaining, however far-fetched, that sexual fantasies were inborn and resulted from an Oedipal Complex or Electra Complex for the parent of the opposite sex. He presented that it was normal for children to desire their parents sexually or to at least compete with their same sex parent for attention and affection. He also presented a theory of inborn internal drives that propel us away from destruction toward pleasure (rather than the drives to act out denied trauma). Fortunately, he preserved common valuable concepts employed today, such as defense mechanisms, resistance, and repression. In formulating a theory of internal causation to replace the one of childhood trauma, Freud turned "from the repressed to the repressing" (Ellenberger, 1970, p. 517).

This story tells it all, especially because the conditions remain the same today. There is enormous pressure to see any explanation other than the real one in order to spare parents. I call it parental immunity. Experts in the field of mental health cannot see the causes of behavior clearly if they cannot look at childhood. Further, the degree of exclusion and expulsion against those who see and say otherwise is daunting. Psychiatrists and psychologists who tow the line are the considered experts on behavior even though they cannot see cause. They are taught not to see but *what* to see. Then they agree on what they see. It's schizogenic. It's group psychosis. This puts the field of psychiatry under suspicion and renders it potentially dangerous because it has yet to self-reflect.

Freud's Betrayal of the Child: Daniel Paul Schreber

Back up to the late 1860s for some Schreber history... Dr. Daniel Gottlieb Moritz Schreber became Germany's version of America's 1950s parenting expert, Dr. Spock. He was a Christian orthopedist whose own sons were born shortly before he published his treatise on how to raise children. Shortly thereafter, Sigmund Freud was born in nearby Austria, but was probably spared Schreber's pedagogy because his parents were Jewish. Schreber taught Christian parents to beat the spirit out of their children daily and then have them say thank you, Father. This was intended to be the most efficient way to break the child of his or her inherent evil, including the child's alleged drive to manipulate the parent. This way, the parent could eliminate any threat to his or her authority as quickly as possible. Dr. Schreber also said parents should put their children in wooden structures for eating and sleeping, not dissimilar to Rush's aforementioned tranquilizing chair.

Dr. Schreber's techniques did not raise robust children; rather his daughter was reportedly mentally ill, his oldest son committed suicide, and his second son, Daniel Paul Schreber, known in his adulthood as "The Hanging Judge" and "The Paranoid Judge," died in an asylum. While hospitalized, Judge Schreber wrote *Memoirs of My Nervous Illness* in which he described a series of tortures he had to endure. Not only was he tormented, but he was taught his sufferings were "miracles," in my experience a perfect recipe for schizophrenia (lack of touch + intrusive parenting + extreme mental abuse + repression = schizophrenia). In the case of Judge Schreber, torture was included in the recipe as well, resulting in a paranoid schizophrenic (hence "The Paranoid Judge" nickname).

In 1911, six years after recanting his Seduction Theory and proposing the Internal Drive Theory, Freud was challenged to evaluate the junior Schreber via his *Memoirs*, wherein Schreber complained about Dr. Flechsig, his physician-neurologist, claiming he had threatened him with homosexual advances at the asylum. Freud accepted the challenge, probably to prove he had abandoned the Seduction Theory. He assessed Judge Schreber, applying his famous new theories on internal drive and fantasy. Our greatest proof that Freud abandoned the Seduction Theory was his apparent indifference to childhood history, focusing on symptoms as fantasy or inborn drives.

Freud evaluated the judge to be a paranoid homosexual who projected his repressed sexual desires for his beloved father onto the father figure, Dr. Flechsig. In other words, he hypothesized the judge was fixated on unresolved childhood pleasure-bound fantasies of having sex with his father in order to be closer to him. Freud did not consider the paranoia was born of fear or a fear pattern rather than longing.

Freud neglected to consider the impact such an abusive father must have had on the judge-to-be child. He declined to see that Judge Schreber's "projections" of homosexual intent might have been indicative of rape by Dr. Schreber on his son, rather than fantasies of pleasure born of adoring a ruthless father. Neither did he consider the possibility that what Judge Schreber protested in his writings might be true, that Dr. Fleschsig might actually be molesting him.

If Freud had dared to investigate Judge Schreber's childhood, thereupon reporting Schreber's father was a vicious pedagogue who advised Christian parents throughout Germany, he might have been moved to expose Dr. Schreber, discredit his theory and warn German parents. He might have made his case for the Seduction Theory by way of a sister theory on paranoid personality, exposing the long-term effects of emotional and physical abuse, instead of hiding behind his Internal Drive Theory. Yes, he might have further jeopardized his professional standing, but he would have left a greater legacy for himself. He might have prevented the rearing of a whole second generation of German-born Schreber children who grew up without empathy or conscience. He might have prevented the genocide of millions of Jews. One thing's clear: a theory that challenges parenting is insurgent.

Freud's Betrayal of the Child: Adolf Hitler

Adolf Hitler's father, Alois, was the bastard son of a Protestant maid who had lain with her employer, a Jewish businessman who reportedly paid her child support. She eventually married and the family made an attempt to alter the church birth records to disguise the origins of Alois' paternity and give him Protestant legitimacy. That Alois was the bastard son of a Jew was a great disgrace to him and a major family secret. He became a rigid, humorless perfectionist, apparently trying to make up for his imposed feelings of shame and inadequacy. He was a clerk-bureaucrat by profession who wore a starched shirt and suit every day while taking his position most seriously (Miller, 1983).

Alois followed the teachings of Dr. Schreber dutifully. He gave his sons the lash on a daily basis, and many agreed Adolf got the worst of it among his siblings. He was the family scapegoat. Adolf bragged he had developed the capacity to bear the lash without crying (what I call the "sociopathic decision"). He later revealed the worst moment in his childhood was one night when he was taking a bath. Alois came to whip young Adolf, who jumped naked out of an open winter window to flee down the freezing fire escape. Alois looked down on his son, stark naked, shivering under a street lamp in the snow, laughing and jeering at his son (as if it would rid Alois of his own childhood shame).

Adolf had been raised to show nothing but complete respect for his father, and so he had to find a place to put his rage. He resolved his dilemma by hating and scapegoating Jews, who he consciously or unconsciously understood were the source of his father's rage at him.

Hitler's first decree as Führer was to declare that Jews were the enemy of Germany, and anyone of third generation Jewish decent would be included. (Ironically, he would have been included in his own round-up.) He then ordered tanks to desecrate the Jewish cemetery where his grandfather lay buried (Miller, 1983).

After Freud retracted the Seduction Theory and implemented the inborn Internal Drive Theory to spare parents responsibility, there was an outbreak in the search for further evidence that behavior was inborn, while behaviorists carried the parenting banner (on the side of nurture over nature), but recommended dangerous parenting tactics.

Following is a timeline that illustrates how history is a series of causal events, particularly influential in psychological theory.

Three Babies of Germany

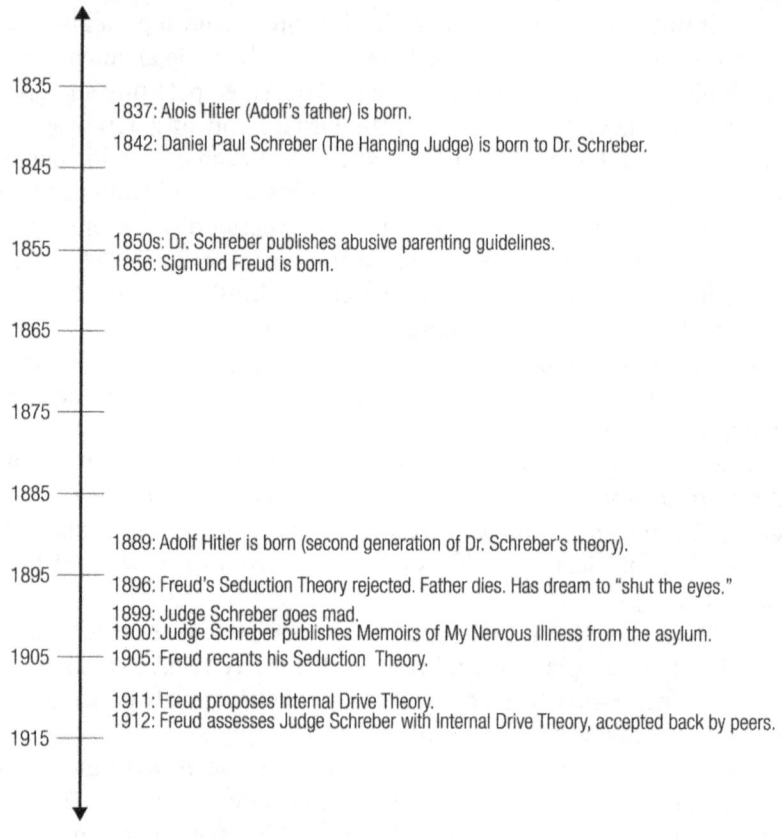

- 1837: Alois Hitler (Adolf's father) is born.
- 1842: Daniel Paul Schreber (The Hanging Judge) is born to Dr. Schreber.
- 1850s: Dr. Schreber publishes abusive parenting guidelines.
- 1856: Sigmund Freud is born.
- 1889: Adolf Hitler is born (second generation of Dr. Schreber's theory).
- 1896: Freud's Seduction Theory rejected. Father dies. Has dream to "shut the eyes."
- 1899: Judge Schreber goes mad.
- 1900: Judge Schreber publishes Memoirs of My Nervous Illness from the asylum.
- 1905: Freud recants his Seduction Theory.
- 1911: Freud proposes Internal Drive Theory.
- 1912: Freud assesses Judge Schreber with Internal Drive Theory, accepted back by peers.

If the misery of our poor be caused not by the laws of nature but by our institutions, great is our sin. —Charles Darwin, Voyage of the Beagle

---

WATSON

While Analytic Theory ultimately came to hold that the source of behavior is inborn drives from within (thereby blaming the child). The father of Behavioral Theory, John Watson, put Behavioral Theory on the map in the mid to late 1920s with his experiments with an orphaned toddler we now know as Little Albert. Watson found the child to be almost fearless and then taught him to be afraid of white fuzzy things. Unfortunately, Little Albert was adopted before Watson could reverse the learned phobia. Today such experiments are unacceptable in our field.

Watson became a parenting expert, applying his concepts in his advice to mothers. Unfortunately Watson, like today's researchers, did not grasp the importance of bonding and attachment. His blindness may have resulted from too much mothering of some sort.

Watson's father abandoned his mother and him when he was a child. They lived on a poor farm in South Carolina. Before the end of his life he destroyed all his notes, journaling and personal correspondence, so we cannot say whether he was an open man (Nance, 1970). From reading his book on childrearing, I have developed a few hypotheses about his personality as well as his childhood. He wrote about parenting as if he was trying to protect the child. He was as adamant about the role of parents in the creation of personality as I am. He had high regard for infants and children. He attributed nothing to inborn traits. He was clear that children should be treated with respect and never be hit. He did not think masturbation was unnatural. He advocated regular conversations between parent and child. Yet he wanted to protect the child from too much affection, which he held in visceral contempt to the extent that he nearly suggested that we replace mothers with professional nannies.

All children need more affection than he realized, so his advice admonishing mothers to relinquish kissing, hugging and holding their infants was actually harmful advice, since most children already don't get enough nurturing. It's difficult to quantify the correlation between lack of affection and his advice to American mothers. I speculate that little John Watson got too much affection because as an adult, he is vigorously defensive against it. His own mother must have been suffocating, or he had Reactive Attachment Disorder, leaving him defensive against minimal affection and intimacy for a lifetime. He could have been a parentified child, stuck in an emotional role as his mother's friend-in-need or her surrogate husband. It's possible that his mother molested him. In any event, it looks as if we will never know the causes behind his adverse reaction to affection. What I think I can safely say is that he suffered substantial feelings of suffocation. Tender maternal gestures came to revolt him and he projected those revulsions onto nearly all the dynamics between mother and child. He saw these dynamics as retarding the growth of children and thought if women really loved their children, they would let them be.

I found some wonderful quotes from Watson's book, first printed in 1928, post-dating Dr. Schreber's theory by sixty years. He proposed to parents that they could have "a doctor, lawyer, artist, merchant chief and yes, even a beggar-man or thief, depending on how they raised a child" (Watson, 1928, p. 6). Watson truly seemed to be pro-child, dedicating his book "to the first mother who brings up a happy child," and it seems clear that this was not his mother. "When the 25 million American homes come to realize that the child has a right to a separate room and adequate psychological care, there will not be nearly so many children born (p. 8)."

Sometimes Watson seemed like a trailblazer. "[I have hope] that some day the importance of the first two years of infancy will be fully realized (p. 9)." He considered parenting a cherished profession. "The oldest profession of the race today is facing failure. This profession is parenthood. Many thousands of mothers do not even know that parenthood should be numbered among the professions. They do not realize that there are any special problems involved in rearing children. For them, all the age-old belief that all children need is food as often as they call for it, warm clothes and a roof over their heads at night is enough. 'Nature' does the rest almost unaided. They argue that parents have been rearing children for a great many centuries, therefore, why bother about learning anything new?" (p. 11). I could have said these words myself.

"No one today knows enough to raise a child" (p. 12), Watson argued. He sometimes spoke like a scientist. "Will you believe the almost astounding truth that no well trained man or woman has ever watched the complete and daily development of a single child from its birth to its third year? Plants and animals we know about because we have studied them, but the human child until very recently has been a mystery" (p. 13). Attempting to persuade mothers, he wrote, "This awakening is beginning to show itself in mothers who ask themselves the question, 'Am I not almost wholly responsible for the way my child grows up? Isn't it just possible that almost nothing is given in heredity and that practically the whole course of development of the child is due to the way I raise it?'" (p. 15)

Watson, the researcher, proposed that the only two things infants naturally fear are loud noises and falling or being unsupported. All the rest we learn by experiences with our parents. "There are no instincts," Watson asserted. "We build in at an early age everything that is later to appear" (p. 38). "Children's fears are home grown just like their loves and temper outbursts. The parents do the emotional planting and cultivating. At three years of age the child's whole emotional life plan has been laid down and his emotional disposition set" (p. 45). Watson said, "The parents' 'don't' is the most potent factor of all in producing both fear and negative responses. Have you as a parent ever stopped to consider how many times a day you use 'don't'?" (p. 57)

"A certain amount of affectionate response is socially necessary but few parents realize how easily they can overtrain the child in this direction. It may tear the heartstrings a bit, this thought of stopping the tender outward demonstration of your love for your children or their love for you. But if you are convinced that this is best for the child, aren't you willing to stifle a few pangs?" asked Watson, as he delivered very bad advice for the good reasons previously cited. Watson appeared to care about babies and parenting more than any clinician of his time. "Mothers just don't know, when they kiss their children and pick them up and rock them, caress them and jiggle them upon their knee, that they are slowly building a human being totally unable to cope with the world it must later live in (p. 44), " said Watson, getting it wrong.

Watson observed the symptoms of broken attachments, or Reactive Attachment Disorder, but did not correctly understand what he saw, because his bias was so strong. "Some of the most tormented moments come when the parents have had to be away from their nine-month old baby for a stretch of three weeks. When they part from it, the child gurgles, coos, holds out its arms and shows every evidence of deepest parental love. Three weeks later when they return, the child turns to the attendant who has in the interim fondled and petted it and put the bottle to the sensitive lips. The infant child loves anyone who strokes and feeds it" (p. 73). Watson did not know he was describing the clues that a child's attachment has been broken and the child will not trust his parents no matter how much they take over his feeding and petting. He will guard his heart, probably for the rest of his life, and he will fear abandonment by anyone he ever lets get close to him. Watson did not recognize a broken heart when he described this fickle child. Neither did he observe that the child would never coo and gurgle in his parents' arms again.

Perhaps the most disturbing words Watson wrote were these: "How about its loves—its affectionate behavior? Isn't that 'natural?' Do you mean to say the child doesn't 'instinctively' love its mother?" Answering, he says, "Only one thing will bring out a love response in the child—stroking and touching its skin, lips, sex organs and the like. It doesn't matter at first who strokes it. It will 'love' the stroker. This is the clay out of which all love—maternal, paternal, wifely or husbandly—is made. Hard to believe? But true. A certain amount of affectionate response is socially necessary but few parents realize how easily they can overtrain the child in this direction" (p. 43).

While I believe touch is critical in the formation of personality, it is not the only thing, and implicit in this paragraph is permission for a mother to stroke her child's genitals in the name of love. If it is not what Watson meant, it is certainly something that could be interpreted that way by readers. It is also a reason why I threw in the possibility that Watson had been molested in the above speculation about why he hated suffocation. I had two clients who became sex addicts because their mothers either stroked or manipulated their genitals to keep them from crying. Both feared their own emotions and masturbated to quell their feelings. I have also known a mother who admitted to me that she couldn't stand her child crying, so she knew a way to stop him. I have heard too many references to this harmful technique. I wonder how much permission Watson gave mothers to do this who otherwise would not have employed this technique. A trend by one parent can be recapitulated for generations to come. I dare say a majority of the African American clients I have seen have experienced whipping. It appears to be disproportionate to whites. I assume this is the legacy of slavery still showing up generations later.

Watson went on to recommend an "ideal formula" for raising children that was not ideal at all. He advocated molding human behavior by strict scientific control, beginning with firm four-hour feeding and sleep schedules, no matter how hungry or tired the child. He said children must be toilet trained early, that six months was not too early and may have even been too late. "Forbid pacifiers, thumb sucking and other forms of coddling. Employ strict discipline at all times. And above all, show no displays of affection. Babies and children can and should be left alone...Never kiss or hug your children. Remember that mother love is a dangerous instrument which can destroy your children's future happiness" (p. 81).

Behavioral Theory came to hold that within the consciousness of a human being is a "black box" that contains the material that influences formation of personality. Unfortunately Watson, who was over-controlled himself and over-controlling, had a caveat that protected parents as well as analytic theory did. He postulated that the material within the black box can never be known. The notion of investigating its contents through reporting forbidden memories or self-examination was considered an inaccurate waste of time and when he destroyed his papers, he suggested something else, possibly his own aversion to self-disclosure or personal histories. Behavioral Theory simply recommends the way to change the contents of the black box is to simply recondition behavior, and cause is unknowable if not irrelevant.

Cognitive approaches to therapy have upgraded this perspective, going beyond conditioning behavior. Cognitive therapists today endeavor to alter faulty beliefs (about anything without much consideration for one's childhood parenting). They lead the patient to explore self-destructive thinking, replacing such thoughts with useful ones. This is a highly regarded type of therapy today, especially since it is supported by research and employs methods easy for scientists to evaluate. Cognitive-Behavioral Therapy (CBT) is the dominant theory and practice, but it still seeks to eliminate the exploration of impactful childhood experiences and effectively stunts exploration into self-awareness. As a result, Cognitive and Behavioral Therapists are generally poor at identifying causes and patterns of behaviors. This is a natural outcome for the theory that holds there is no point in this endeavor. If I were a judge, I would look askance at an evaluation of a therapist by a behaviorist or cognitive behaviorist, such as in a child custody evaluation, a criminal assessment or a standard of care evaluation. CBT therapists are notoriously poor at assessing the causes of behavior and often have the gumption to critique a psychodynamic therapist for the endeavor. A typical cognitive behaviorist would not be able to see the correlation between Watson's childhood, his theory and his recommendations. If I were a behavioral therapist, I would be proud of it, but I would want to study this book and add that I also have a strong understanding of Causal Theory.

Our best theories are not all good. Good theorists are often interspersed with some bad ideas. Today the two leading pioneers in Cognitive Theory are Albert Ellis and Aaron Beck. Last I looked, Aaron Beck was on the board of the False Memory Syndrome Foundation, which indicates that his orientation is pro-parent. Another way to understand the blind spots of theories is by asking fundamental questions about their loyalties. If given a choice between wrongly accusing a father of molesting his daughter or disbelieving the daughter for reporting she was molested by her father, Beck would most likely side with the father because that's what the False Memory Syndrome Foundation is about (2010, Snyder).

4: EVOLUTION OF GENETIC RESEARCH

We carry two genes organized into chromosomes, one from each parent, for every type of instruction inherent in the developing body. When parents make a baby, they each give up one of each gene to the new life for every physical characteristic. In some cases they give up dominant genes, and in other cases they give up recessive genes. Some sons will eventually bald, while others will not. When there is a tie, the dominant gene wins.

Even though we cannot see genetic blueprints—genotypes—with the naked eye, we can see the results of their unique instructions in appearances, or phenotypes. What historic genetic studies have done is look for phenotypes as proof of genotypes. In other words, if I want to prove there is a gene for blue eyes, follow the phenotype—that is, the blue eyes—or the visible manifestations of such a gene over generations. Mendel did this to discover the patterns of recessive and dominant genes in plants, which have such short lives it's easy to follow multiple generations of mating. He found that for every physical property of a living thing, there are genes, some of which are recessive (submissive) and some of which are dominant. He came up with the standard formula for these combinations. This avails many possibilities for heritage, affording an array of possible offspring that look somewhat like the parents. None are exactly alike, except in cases of shared pods or human monozygotic twins of one zygote (a fertilized egg) that subdivides into two separate embryos, both of which share the same genetic structure.

However, some widely publicized theoreticians and researchers have argued genes or inborn character cause behavior (Plomin, 1990; Barkley, 1997) and many of them have used the same model to prove *behavior* is genetically predetermined. They inferred from behaviors (as if they were phenotypes) that genes were responsible for similarities between identical twins, and where there were similarities, there must be genes—not considering environmental factors like systems theory, learning theory or mirror neurons. Then they modified their statistics and wrote up their results to imply they had proven genes create behavior. They had to resort to numerous tricks to produce the desired results for which they had been paid. These scientists convinced genetic researchers that genes created behavior, so the biogeneticists got to work and billions of dollars were spent in search of the illusive genes that cause behaviors.

They attempted to apply the Mendelian Model to prove personality traits were inherited, not learned. We were deceived to justify the expense. New tricks were invented to raise the statistics to something akin to significance. As the results came in, the Mendelian Model for genetic concordance (correlation, statistical agreement or equivalence) initially led to dishonest science. Scientists misled other scientists (Joseph, 2015) at a huge cost to the nation and its children.

In the scientific studies analyzed in this book, we will see historic attitudes of eugenics (inborn superiority vs. inferiority) evolve into scientific hypotheses and research on genetic explanations for behavior. You now have an understanding of pro-child explanations for behavior under your belt, including the childhood impact and implication of attachment experiences, abuse and neglect, as well as family ethics of repression vs. expression and blame vs. personal responsibility. We will soon review the alleged evidence for genetic explanations for behaviors in lieu of environmental explanations, after we take a look at the crude studies that preceded them. Herein I have distilled the predominant genetic studies to briefly and factually present the most significant to my readers.

PEDIGREE STUDIES

The earliest studies were Pedigree Studies, which were similar to theories of breeding. If one wanted to buy a thoroughbred dog, they would either look at its papers or its parents to prove genetic lineage. Likewise, Pedigree Studies were based entirely on whether a person's behavioral and personality traits were also exhibited by other family members, especially traits of schizophrenia, criminality and lower intelligence. If such traits were shared, the presumption was genetic inferiority. The nomenclature "Pedigree Studies" reflects the underlying lens of superiority-inferiority.

The most significant pioneer in Pedigree Studies was the German scientist Franz Kallmann, mentored by the Nazi scientist Ernst Rudin. Kallmann took up the eugenics cause (promoting reproduction by people with positive traits and sterilizing those with undesirable traits) in Berlin in 1938. While he lived in Germany, Kallmann's first research study under the tutelage of Rudin involved the use of hospital records of schizophrenic patients from 1893 to 1902. Kallmann used these records to establish a concordance of these subjects with other schizophrenic family members. The actions taken based on his hypothesis of a genetic link resulted in extermination of 400,000 mental patients and sterilization of another 225,000.

In order to measure or prove a high concordance (correlation) between his schizophrenic subjects and their kin, Kallmann reportedly tried to contact their relatives. Since many of them were deceased or impossible to locate, he claimed the research contended with "formidable difficulties... We were dealing with inferior people... They sometimes escaped our search for years... Quite a few were bad-humored... We had to overcome the suspicion with which certain classes regarded any kind of official activity... Whenever we encountered serious opposition we found ourselves to be dealing with either officials and members of the academic world, or people with exaggerated suspicions, schizoid types, and possible schizophrenics... Our private sources of information were amplified from the records of police bureaus... In making inquiries about people already dead or living too far away, we employed... local bureaus and trusted agents" (Lewontin, Rose & Kamin, 1984, p. 210).

Kallmann's views were not confined to Nazi publications. After his arrival to the United States in 1936, he wrote of schizophrenics as "maladjusted crooks, asocial eccentrics, and the lowest type of criminal offenders. Even the faithful believer in... Liberty would be much happier without those... I am reluctant to admit the necessity of different eugenic programs for democratic and fascistic communities... There are neither biological nor sociological differences between a democratic and a totalitarian schizophrenic" (Lewontin, Rose & Kamin, 1984, p. 208).

In the United States, Kallman continued to pioneer in the study of "identical twins separated at birth," later more accurately known as the "identical twins raised apart" studies in public mental hospitals in 1946 and 1953. He endeavored to locate schizophrenic twins. In 1946 he reported 794 such cases. By 1953, he reported 953 cases. His contribution to this category resulted from the study of schizophrenics admitted to public state hospitals with follow-up on their relatives. These studies had phenomenal results, reportedly proving to the world that schizophrenia was genetic (Lewontin, Rose & Kamin, 1984, p. 208).

Some were identical twins and some were fraternal. Kallmann wanted to demonstrate that identical twins were more concordant than fraternal twins. The assumption was that both were raised in the same environment, but those who shared identical genes would have higher concordance. Fraternal twins, like siblings, would have a high concordance, but nothing as close as identical twins. Yet identical twins have nearly an identical environment, as they are treated as a unit, dressed alike and referred to as "the twins." The fact that they can see themselves in one another is a factor in identifying with one another.

Kallmann attempted to assess the probability that both identical twins would be schizophrenic if one was. In an attempt to improve his statistics he engaged in another process similar to age-correcting (Lewontin, Rose & Kamin, 1984, p. 210). He called this measure the "pairwise concordance rate," which produced different concordance rates for identical twins, monozygotic twins, siblings, and other members of the family. Here's an explanation offered by Jonathan Leo (2003, p. 4):

> Most readers who are not intimately familiar with these studies probably in- terpret concordance rate findings as the percentage of twin pairs who are both diagnosed with schizophrenia within a sample in which one twin of each pair is known to be schizophrenic. For instance if schizophrenia is diagnosed in both members of 50 twin pairs out of a sample of 100 then most people would think that the concordance rate is 50%, but it's not that simple. Schizophrenia researchers refer to this type of reporting as pairwise concordance, yet some prominent researchers prefer to use the proband method of reporting.

In the proband method, the proband is the [diagnosed] member of a twin pair who was used initially to qualify the pair for inclusion in the sample. It is possible for both members of a twin pair to be proband, in which case that pair would appear twice in the sample. The proband method will always produce higher numbers. As an example, if there is a sample of three pairs of twins and in 1 of those pairs both members are diagnosed with schizophrenia then according to the pairwise method of concordance, the rate would be 1/3 or 33%, but according to the proband-wise method, the rate would be 2/4 or 50% (Leo, 2003, p. 4).

No information is available as to how Kallman collected the data on the relatives, and no histories were offered on the patients. He simply wrote, "classification of both schizophrenia and zygosity were made on the basis of personal investigation and extended observation" (Lewontin, Rose & Kamin, 1984, p. 208). The research goal was to achieve a prediction whether or not a co-twin would become schizophrenic if their twin was, and predictions varied between whether twins were DZ or MZ and raised together or apart.

The public and other scientists were led to believe there was a high concordance of 92% for identical twins reared apart, proving that environment is not a significant factor in schizophrenia. Upon closer scrutiny, suspicious scientists discovered that Kallman's criteria for "reared apart" was at least five years of separation prior to the onset of schizophrenia in one of them! When the data was reviewed, scientists discovered that the average age of separation was 10 years old! Further, and perhaps more important, the twins were separated after four years old, which is after the most influential years in the formation of personality (Ross & Pam, 1995, p. 19).

Age-correcting could produce substantially higher results than 100% if they were not careful. In order to come up with convincing data, they would have to use just enough age-correction then stop using it when the desired statistic was reached. This was the antithesis of blind and unbiased research.

Beliefs that behaviors were inborn preceded the discovery of genes. As we've seen in this text, psychology has a history in the 19th century of hiding parenting's impact on development. Acknowledging this impact is the taboo of our field. It seems scientists have been trying to fit that square peg into a round hole long before the discovery of DNA.

Interestingly, Kallmann and other early researchers appreciated the importance of meeting the standards of the classic Mendelian model of 100% concordance for identical twins to prove genes cause behavior. Later it was determined that he manipulated his results to come as close to 100% as possible.

MENDELIAN MODEL REFRESHER

It was beginning to become clear the Mendelian model was failing the geneticists who needed to prove behavior was inherited. The following is a brief refresher in classical genetics to help the reader appreciate the "evidence" in pages to come. According to Mendel's model of genetics, identical twins with the same genes for physical traits would have 100% concordance; that is, their traits would be identical. Twin studies were intended to demonstrate that when we apply the same model to mental development, if one twin has schizophrenia, the other twin should have schizophrenia with 100% concordance. If 95 out of 100 twins shared schizophrenia, that would be 95% concordance and would still prove the power of genetic influence on behavior. The problem was that geneticists could not achieve 100% concordance, or even get close.

Following is a chart by Torrey, Bowler, Taylor and Gottesman (1994) that shows Mendel's model of concordance for various phenomena in identical twins. Note the problem: Identical twins do not have anywhere close to a 100% concordance for schizophrenia. Rather, according to Torrey, et al., their concordance in today's research is only about 28%, which is very low, but Pekka Tienari's more recent research comes in even lower at 15% (not on chart). Both scores are too low to represent genetics as cause at all. Both scores indicate environment, especially since identical twins share the most similar childhood environment of all environments, as they are commonly treated as a unit, and often share far more experiences with each other than fraternal twins do.

Mendelian Model of Concordance in Identical Twins

Variable	Concordance Rate (%)
Race	100%
Eye color	100%
Gender	100%
Huntington's chorea	100%
Cystic fibrosis	100%
Tay-Sachs disease	100%
Epilepsy	61%
Mental retardation	60%
Schizophrenia	28%
Parkinson's disease	27%

As it became evident researchers couldn't prove inheritance of mental illness by the Mendelian model of 100% concordance for identical twins, a new threshold for "significance" in genetic studies emerged, taken from the other scientific model of research and statistics.

The 8% (or thereabouts) model was intended for experimenters to see if a treatment had any recognizable effect beyond chance or if there was any notable result in surveys. If an experiment found a certain treatment worked for 8 to 9% of the population, or she found a certain attitude in a survey in 8 to 9% of the population sampled, she could claim minimal significance above chance. Below 8%, scientists do not acknowledge any meaning other than chance. **Scientists began to claim 8 to 9% as significant proof of genetic influence.** However, the search for identical *personalities* due to identical *genes* cannot be proven with a statistical 8% concordance (correlation) because it is for a different kind of study. Nonetheless, the remaining 92% of behavior *is* significant and proves behavior results from environment. Further, the 8% concordance could also be attributed to the similar environment of identical twins. This huge change in measures shouldn't have convinced anyone of anything. Unfortunately, hardly anyone noticed the sidestep of the Mendelian model, and it worked for public consumption. It turns out altering definitions attracted little suspicion, which seemed to free scientists to venture further into the practice of obfuscation.

ADOPTION STUDIES

There are two primary types of Adoption Studies: Twin Studies and Cross-Fostered Studies. Twin Studies involve identical twins who were adopted away by different parents, allegedly at birth. Cross-Fostered Studies involve tracking and comparing children born to *unhealthy* parents and adopted by *healthy* parents, vs. children born to *healthy* parents and adopted/raised by *unhealthy* parents. This research was designed to prove that parenting is irrelevant, but instead it almost always proved that genes are irrelevant.

Twin Studies "Separated at Birth"

There were five researchers who claimed to study twins separated at birth before 1965 (Shields, 1962), the most recognized of whom were Kallmann and Cyril Burt (1955). Their studies were designed to prove genetics by controlling for environment (*i.e.*, ruling out environment as a causal factor), an issue they anticipated would matter to observers of their work.

Cyril Burt claimed the "largest IQ study of separated identical twins ever reported, supposedly based on fifty-three twin pairs..." (Lewontin, Rose & Kamin, 1984, p. 101). He too held to the Mendelian model of 100% concordance in identical twins. Burt produced research in 1955 with high correlations of .771, or 77%, justifying racism and reportedly proving that whites were more intelligent than blacks by studying "identical twins separated at birth" (Lewontin, Rose & Kamin, 1984, p. 87). Burt had a strong agenda to justify discrimination and even elimination of people of lesser intelligence. In 1903, he wrote in the margins of his undergraduate notebook, "The problem of the very poor—chronic poverty: Little prospect of the solution of the problem without the forcible detention of the wreckage of society or other [sic] preventing them from propagating the species" (Lewontin, Rose & Kamin, 1984, p. 87).

The correlation of separated twin pairs reported by Burt was strikingly high, more so than that reported in three other studies of separated twins. "He alone had been able to measure quantitatively the disparity of the environments in which the separated twin pairs had been reared. The incredible (and convenient) result reported by Burt was that there was no correlation at all between the environments of the separated pairs" (Lewontin, Rose & Kamin, 1984, p. 103), even though their intelligence had remained nearly identical. Thus the public was led to believe that separated twins, raised in quite different environments, still scored with similar intelligence quotients. This would have convinced anyone, even me, had the research been solid.

Additionally, Burt claimed to administer the same IQ test to the biological relatives (including grandparent-grandchild, uncle-nephew and second cousin pairs) by the thousands, and according to Lewontin, Rose and Kamin, "The IQ correlations reported by Burt are the only such correlations ever to have been reported, because achieving such interviews with all the players is nearly impossible. The results conformed to classic [Mendel] genetic predictability by which other scientists were dazzled with the apparent predictability of genetically based IQs" (Lewontin, Rose & Kamin, 1984, p. 102).

Nevertheless, Burt never identified the exact size of the populations he studied or even the test with which he measured IQs. He wrote, "For the assessments of the parents we relied chiefly on personal interviews; but in doubtful or borderline cases an open or a camouflaged test was employed" (Lewontin, Rose & Kamin, 1984, p. 102). In other words, Burt did not even have an objective measure; scores were guessed based on interviews.

Burt's reports of near 80% concordance were presented as hard scientific facts in textbooks of psychology, genetics and education (Joseph, 2006), but some said his survey was too small. As if in response to these criticisms, Burt's research sample began to grow, yet still maintain the exact correlation of 77%. In 1955, he reported having assessed 21 pairs of separated identical twins and found a correlation of 77%. By 1958, the sample size had grown to "over 30," with the same exact correlation of 77%. Then again in 1966, he claimed to have studied 53 pairs with the exact same correlation of 77%. After his death, suspicious researchers reviewed the data behind Burt's statistics and discovered that indeed the data had been manipulated, wrongly interpreted, speculative and implied (Dorfman, 1978). However, for years to come and in the minds of many today, Burt's studies were used to "document" that those who scored poorly on IQ tests did so because they were genetically inferior, not because their environments had failed to stimulate their intellect

(Lewontin, Rose & Kamin, 1984). To date, most people with whom I discuss intelligence believe it is inborn.

The possibility of ever doing a valid study of identical twins reared apart from birth is negligible. In a 1937 nationwide survey, only 19 cases were discovered of twins separated "early in life." None had schizophrenia. Nevertheless, researcher Don Jackson was able to locate two concordant cases of schizophrenic twins "reared apart" in all the world literature. Both cases were studied by Don Jackson in depth (Ross, 2004, p. 23).

Scientists began to use the term "reared apart." One researcher, James Shields, clarified that "reared apart" meant the twins had spent at least five years in different homes from one another during childhood, in some cases having been separated as late as age 15. In another Swedish study (SATSA), "reared apart" meant they were separated before the age of 11 (Joseph, 2004). Most twins have been separated after the primary ages of personality formation, which would be after four, perhaps three years of age. When twins are separated, usually they are cared for by relatives under similar circumstances and allowed to remain in contact with one another.

In my observations as a clinician, there are four, possibly five, primary ingredients in the creation of schizophrenia. They are:

(1) lack of touch in the first year of life (a sensory deprivation, which later leads to a sense that one's body is porous, skin does not contain or mask one's feelings, and others can read their mind or they can read the minds of others, called "thought broadcasting"; followed by
(2) repression of emotions and experiential truth;
(3) intrusive messages from the parent, such as domineering parenting, projections into the child as to his motives and intentions; and finally,
(4) a life-altering, mind-warping, mind-blowing mixed message.

Three out of four of the above causes could create schizophrenia. There is also research that suggests many schizophrenics (5) have been abused.

Also of note, in the 1950s, anthropologist Gregory Bateson and his colleagues observed a "double-bind" factor in the creation of schizophrenia—that is, admonitions to the child to perform in an impossible way. For example Daddy is an alcoholic, but that's a family secret. Mommy teaches the child to always tell the truth. Mommy asks the child, "What do you think of Daddy?" The child cannot answer that question. She cannot acknowledge what she knows, or she will suffer mental abuse and be punished for telling the truth. It's safer to say, "Daddy is a good banana." This has been taken by clinicians to explain the "word salad" or difficulty understanding what schizophrenics mean when they speak incoherently, which is common to those who have chronic schizophrenia. I also take it as evidence they have had minimal true engagement in conversation throughout their life.

The reader will recognize the above-described ingredients in the following case histories for the studied separated twin pairs. I have inserted numbers to represent the ingredients above, where applicable.

Kaete and Lisa

The first of Jackson's located twins were 22-year-olds Kaete and Lisa had a mother who was apparently single (with illegitimate twins), and possibly ashamed, given the time period, financially unable to work and care for two babies, or too disturbed to care for her children [1], so she gave them to her brothers. The exact age of separation is unknown, although they were reportedly "quite young." The probability is high that both suffered insufficient attachment before their mother relinquished them, and both suffered abandonment as well. Both of the mother's brothers to whom the children were gifted were described as "eccentric borderlines" thus creating an ongoing similar environment. Borderline personalities are prone to intrusion [3], abuse [5], and judgmental and blaming behavior [4].

Kaete developed catatonic symptoms after the birth of an illegitimate child [4?] at age 15, where she somewhat recapitulated the circumstances of her own painful origins. Lisa developed increasing "helplessness and emotional indifference," and was placed at age 17 in the same Berlin hospital as her sister with the diagnosis of schizophrenia.

Edith and Florence

Jackson's second found twin pair were Edith and Florence, separated at nine months old after their mother died. We don't know how long she was sick, but this indicates they may both have been insufficiently touched [1] and then abandoned as well.

Edith remained with her father, who was described as a brutal man [3, 5], and a new stepmother until she was eight, when she was placed in a children's home [4] due to "anxious behavior" where she stayed until she was 19. Then she returned to her father until she was 20, when her first paranoid symptoms developed. She left to become a domestic. Edith was more symptomatic than Florence.

After her mother's death, Florence was sent to live in London with her aunt (father's sister?), with whom she lived until her aunt died [4] at 51, recapitulating the death of her mother at a tender age. Twenty-year-old Florence then had to be hospitalized.

Around this time the twins met in the hospital, and Florence developed paranoid thoughts her sister was following her, symptoms that cleared after therapy.

Nicholas and Herbert

In 1965, Niels Juel-Nielsen located two more cases out of seven, which were concordant, tallying four cases of schizophrenic twins separated young, if the other three cases indeed existed. Remember, the other three reportedly came from Kallmann without data.

Juel-Nielsen represented that in one of his two cases, an identical twin developed schizophrenia in childhood and the other at age 18. That's all we know.

The other pair was Nicholas and Herbert, illegitimate offspring of a Chinese English woman whom we only know was another unstable single mother with two babies [1].

Nicholas was in three foster homes before age four, and Herbert lived in two Roman Catholic nurseries until the same age [1, 2]. They met during a Blitz air raid while being evacuated. On their return their grandmother took custody of them for one year. Nicholas was then sent at about age five to a stable foster home, and Herbert remained with his grandmother who had remarried. While Herbert lived with his grandmother, his mother visited the grandmother, so Herbert got to see his mother.

Herbert and Nicholas had occasion to meet again at age 22. Herbert told Nicholas he had been seeing their mother. The fact that Herbert had benefitted from seeing her (while Nicholas had not) [4], sent both of them into an unbearable mental state, and both were hospitalized for schizophrenia two days later. Neither ever recovered. One possibly suffered that he had been given the unlucky life and the other suffered extreme guilt.

Every twin described in these case studies was involved in selective adoptions that paralleled one another's experience. Each shared a similar first year of life, suffering sufficient emotional injuries to produce schizophrenia, especially insufficient bonding in the first year, probably insufficient touch, followed by attachment breaks. They suffered ongoing rejection, possible abuse and emotional trauma, followed by multiple and/or unstable caregivers. All children suffered a mind-blowing experience on top of their fragile identities born of broken and weak attachments.

Tienari (1963)

In 1963, Pekka Tienari published a study reporting that out of 16 identical twin pairs, none of his identical twins were concordant for schizophrenia, while one out of 21 fraternal twins was concordant. That is, Tienari reported a 0% concordance for identical twins with schizophrenia. Other scientists got to work interpreting these results.

Gottesman & Shields (analysis forthcoming) reviewed Tienari's numbers and wrote that it could be due to a small sample size or a failure to use age-correcting, even though Tienari's sample had no subjects under 40 years of age. Tienari updated his figures several times until 1975 when he reported 15% concordance. Another biased researcher Kenneth Kendler then converted Tienari's 15% statistic to 33% by recalibrating using the proband method. Gottesman later represented that it was 36% (Joseph, 2003). Two years later Martin G. Allen revised the figures upward by including some additional twin pairs. The new pairwise concordance rate was 27%, but Gottesman & Shields again converted that number to a proband figure of 43%. To be clear, these scientists deliberately manipulated the data from 0% to 43%.

Heston (1966)

In 1966, Leonard Heston conducted the Oregon Schizophrenia Adoption Study, wherein he identified 47 adopted-away biological offspring of institutionalized women diagnosed with schizophrenia. Their babies had been placed with family members or in orphanages. Children born to schizophrenic mothers in Oregon were particularly unlucky, as Oregon was a state that had historically sterilized 2600 mental patients over 60 years so the public would not have to contend with their genetically-flawed offspring.

Many of these babies waited in orphanages to be adopted for months or even years, and as adults contributed statistically to prove that children of schizophrenics become "neurotics," felons, "sociopaths," or recipients of a schizophrenia diagnosis. Heston himself saw their sadness and withdrawal as symptomatic of their deprivation. Unfortunately after witnessing these children, Heston failed to infer that the lack of early emotional nurturing of his index (symptomatic) group of adults could or would have caused their adult symptoms. Instead, Heston inferred a genetic relationship between psychosocial disability and schizophrenia. In Heston's view, the emotional damage caused by early deprivation associated with institutional care "can be spontaneously reversed by the time adulthood is achieved" (Heston, 1966, p. 819).

Danish Studies (1968, 1971, 1974)

Three studies by Kety, Rosenthal and Wender (1968, 1971 and 1974, respectively) reportedly became the ultimate final results, proving genes create behavior. The former study was of schizophrenic adoptees, the second of schizophrenics adopted away, and the third study was of children adopted by schizophrenic parents (Ross & Pam, 1995).

Kety (1968): Comparing Schizophrenic Adoptees with Biological Relatives

The first of the three famous Danish studies, led by Seymour Kety, attempted to compare adopted children who became schizophrenic with normal children who were undiagnosed. Kety and his team located 33 adoptees diagnosed as schizophrenics in adulthood, and compared them to a control group of 33 adoptees who had never been so diagnosed. They expected to find more schizophrenia among the biological relatives of the adopted children who became schizophrenic. The index group of schizophrenics was separated at an average age of 3.5 months, and the control group of undiagnosed adoptees had been separated from their mother at an average age of 4.1 months. Either group could have had newborns and four-year-olds, even one of which could have skewed the results because the foundation of an unhealthy personality is laid down in the first four years. This is to say, if a child was raised in dysfunction and adopted out at four years of age, their personality would be more reflective of their birth parents than the adoptive parents simply because they lived with their birth parents during their formative years. Further, an attachment break with a healthy parent in the first three years can create life-long trauma or harm to the personality (Bowlby, 1973).

Kety's researchers found 150 biological relatives of the schizophrenics and 156 relatives of the control group. They found only two schizophrenics in all the relatives, one in each group (less than 1%). A fact not spelled out at the time was that none of the relatives who spawned the adopted-out schizophrenics were schizophrenic. The results were meaningless.

So the researchers expanded their definitions to create a result "proving" that schizophrenia is genetic. "Since they were unable to prove that parents and relatives also had schizophrenia, they expanded the study to the extended family and broadened the definition of schizophrenia" (Ross & Pam, 1995, p. 27) to include the following classifications of which I have never heard: "chronic schizophrenia," "borderline states," "inadequate personality," "uncertain schizophrenia," and "uncertain borderline states" (Ross & Pam, 1995, p. 27).

This broadening definition under the umbrella of schizophrenia brought in nine biologically-related families of the index cases from whom the children had been relinquished, increasing the percentage from 1.9% to 8.7%, which was now considered significant, albeit only to data samplers and not to Mendelian geneticists. Without the inclusion of "inadequate personalities" and "uncertain borderline schizophrenia," no significant results existed in the Kety study by any measure.

The Kety study did not prove schizophrenia is genetic. If anything, it proved it was not. The public and other scientists did not hear that there were no biological schizophrenic mothers in the study of the adopted babies who became schizophrenic. By the experimenter's model, only one or two symptomatic children of unhealthy mothers would have been enough to indicate significance. One or two children out of 33 could have suffered a lack of touch while waiting for adoption. As a matter of fact, babies from disturbed mothers have been historically harder to place than babies of healthier mothers and "better families," and they generally wait longer in orphanages and temporary care (Joseph, 2004).

Further, lack of touch is one significant environmental ingredient in the creation of mental illness, especially schizophrenia. It is also quite possible that one or two biological mothers could have neglected their babies before adopting them out, which would have gone unnoted by these scientists. The unique environmental circumstances of each child remain unknown or suspect, meaning the study failed to control for environment in any significant way.

Apparent problems with this study:
- The original results were meaningless.
- A schizophrenic relative was found in both the index group and the control group of normals.
- No identified schizophrenic patient was born of a schizophrenic mother.

- Definitions of schizophrenia were expanded to include vague symptoms, and modifications to the research results were not blind.
- After the expansion, 9% concordance with a close relative was accepted as significant (another shell game).
- There was no consideration given for the age or reason for relinquishment, which could create mental illness.
- It took major public relations, a public that wanted to believe, and a substantial pocketbook, to turn this evidence into "proof" of genetics.

Rosenthal (1971): Schizophrenic Parents Who Gave up their Children

David Rosenthal led the second Danish study in 1971, with Kety as a major player. The Rosenthal study reversed the research design. Instead of finding schizophrenics who had been adopted, then locating their birth relatives, researchers targeted schizophrenic parents who relinquished their children. They compared the biological adopted-away children of schizophrenics to adopted-away children of undiagnosed biological parents. These babies were separated from their mothers at a median age of nearly six months, the average age of separation for both groups. Once again, the median age does not preclude older children above the age of three, which could skew the results in either study, especially if only 8% was considered significant.

Rosenthal also revised the definition of schizophrenia to "the schizophrenic spectrum" and was still not able to achieve statistical significance, even at the revised standard of 8%. Despite having previously insisted that bipolar disorder and schizophrenia result from different genes, Kety, Rosenthal and Wender added bipolar to the mix and finally achieved minimal significance. When asked why, Rosenthal answered that it was "expedient" and because they might learn something about the "genetic relationship between schizophrenia and manic depression" (Joseph, 2004, p. 242). As they increased the spectrum, they sent "blind" researchers to look harder for evidence of potential mental illness (probably in the index group, specifically). Whether genes or environment cause schizophrenia, they would get the same result by seeking family members who also suffered from mental illness, since these family members shared similar environments and family systems. Later, at the end of his career, Rosenthal wrote that both family and twin studies are "confounded" and "One can draw conclusions about them only at considerable risk" (Joseph, 2004, p. 58).

Apparent problems with this study:
- Only one child relinquished by a schizophrenic mother became schizophrenic.
- One child is not significant and only constitutes anecdotal evidence. The age of this child at relinquishment and adoption is not reported. It could have been after the formative age of three.
- Researchers had to expand the definition of schizophrenia again.
- "Blind" researchers were sent to review the data of adoptees to find more evidence of mental illness.

- Results of the extended search for schizophrenic relatives of relinquished children of unstable mothers tripled.
- The ages of relinquishment and adoption for those found to be symptomatic were not reported.
- The experiences of the adopted children in the new homes were not reported.
- After the results of the study were in, researchers revised their results upward by adding more cases.
- Rosenthal found only one schizophrenic born of a schizophrenic mother and still attributed 73% of the variance for schizophrenia to genetic factors. Neal and Oltmanns (1980) stated: "if any doubt remained concerning the importance of genetic factors in schizophrenia, it was abolished by the [Danish] adoption studies (Ross & Pam, 1995, p. 30)"

Wender (1974): The Cross-Fostered Adoption Study

Paul Wender conducted the third Danish study in 1974, and after achieving inevitably disappointing results, he altered the groups to provide the results that helped his cause. His study compared 69 index children born into the "schizophrenic spectrum" and adopted/raised by normal parents, with 28 "cross-fostered" children (born to normal parents and adopted out to symptomatic parents on the "schizophrenic spectrum").

In order to find "schizophrenia," like Kety they expanded the term to "schizophrenic spectrum," which became politically included in the *DSM-V* forty years later in 2015. Let's simply call the schizophrenics from the schizophrenic spectrum "unstable." This is more honest. Really, the only common factor between these subjects was some sort of mental instability.

It can be a complicated study, so I will make it easier to follow by introducing charts. It's important to understand what actually happened, and not be bamboozled by the false information presented publicly at the time. In the charts to follow, the **Born To** column indicates whether the child was born to a normal mother/parents or an unstable mother/parents. The **Raised** column describes the duration and quality of stability of the family within which the child was raised. The **Results** column represents the outcome or results of the adult the child grew to become. Shaded boxes represent instability.

Summary Charts of Wender's Cross-Fostered Adoption Study

My Prediction

Group	Born To	Raised	Results
69 Index	Schizophrenic mothers	Normal families	Normal
28 Cross-Fostered	Normal	"Schizophrenic spectrum"	"Schizophrenic spectrum"
79 Control	Normal	Normal	Normal

Scientists' Prediction

Group	Born To	Raised	Results
69 Index	Schizophrenic mothers	Normal families	"Schizophrenic spectrum"
28 Cross-Fostered	Normal	"Schizophrenic spectrum"	Normal
79 Control	Normal	Normal	Normal

My Prediction of Scientists' Actual Results (Same as my prediction above)

Group	Born To	Raised	Results
69 Index	Schizophrenic mothers	Normal families	Normal
28 Cross-Fostered	Normal	"Schizophrenic spectrum"	"Schizophrenic spectrum"
79 Control	Normal	Normal	Normal

Scientists' Solution (since their results didn't match their prediction)

Group	Born To	Raised	Results
69 Index	Schizophrenic mothers	Normal families	PROBLEM I: NEED THEM TO APPEAR UNSTABLE (They could increase pathological result by "blindly" selecting older adoptees.)
28 Cross-Fostered & 79 Control	Normal	"Schizophrenic Spectrum" + Mostly Normal	PROBLEM II: NEED THEM TO SEEM NORMAL (Dilute this group by adding the normal control group so the resulting group will appear more normal.)

They hoped to show parenting was irrelevant, and the index group of unstable parents would have raised healthier children, while the cross-fostered normal parents would have raised less healthy children. I imagined a different, rather opposite result than the researchers found. I suspected the children born to normal parents and raised by unstable parents would raise less healthy children than those born to unstable parents and raised by normal parents.

When the cross-fostered group of children born to normals and raised by unstables turned out to be unhealthier than the children born to unstables and raised by normals, they had to change their results. In the name of genetics, they apparently had to disguise what they found, that parenting was a more substantial predictor than birth parents.

After the study was completed, scientists decided to dilute the index group of children raised by unhealthy mothers (so they could look healthier) with children raised by normal parents from the control group. Scientists gave an unconvincing reason for altering their results: the group of children raised by unstable parents was too small (Ross & Pam, 1995). Of course if this were truly the case, the research should not have begun until scientists had a large enough group.

Having diluted their results, they said they achieved some significance at 8% in the cross-fostered group, making them seem more normal. I wondered how they could even dilute the cross-fostered group and reach any significance comparing it to the index group of children raised by normal parents. Of course, 8% "significance" is a preferred outcome for these scientists, as opposed to admitting unhealthy parents create more psychopathology. The Mendelian model was completely lost again, as 8% concordance bares no significance, when true genetic theory would dictate they find 100%, or 50%, or even 25% concordance.

With this adjustment, the only maneuver left to prove genetics was find some pathology in the group raised by normals. Given some of the children adopted away from unstable parents were older or in the the critical attachment stage, they could have also suffered life-altering trauma. After tampering with the results, Wender achieved only trace results, which he touted proved "once-and-for-all" schizophrenia was genetic.

Apparent problems with this study:
- Scientists disguised their results by adding normals to the index group of unhealthy parents.
- Scientist explained that decision in an incoherent way.
- So-called blind researchers were sent to review the data of adoptees to find more evidence of mental illness.
- Researchers used the expanded definition of schizophrenia again.
- The public never learned the true results of using the expanded term, so none of the three studies were about schizophrenia after all.
- The ages of relinquishment and adoption for those found to be symptomatic were not reported.

- After the results of the study were in, researchers revised their results upward by adding more cases.
- Researchers were satisfied with 8% concordance/significance, without conceding 92% to environment.
- Results were by interview, so could not be blind by definition.

The designs of the three major Danish studies were brilliant, and if we had ever known the real results, we might have learned environment trumps genes as an explanation for behavior. Even by rigging the results, the scientists failed to come up with anything substantial. Nevertheless, their public relations machine convinced the public that genes instruct behavior. Further, the scientists played along.

Curiously, the jubilant leader of the third study, Wender, boasted, "We failed to discover any environmental component" (Ross & Pam, 1995, p. 30), when they had likely destroyed evidence of an environmental component.

In 1981, Wender and Kleine extrapolated from the Danish adoption data that 8% of the general population are genetically predisposed to develop a personality disorder within the schizophrenic spectrum and only medication could correct the underlying biochemical problem.

It turns out the average age of adoption was about 6 months for each group, but the median ages for the index group in particular, in fact extended between 5 days and 7 years. Those who stayed with their "schizophrenic" parent into three or four years of age spent their formative years with the unstable "schizophrenic" parent, and were probably much more impacted and symptomatic than the younger adoptees, while others may have been adopted away between one to three years of age, creating an attachment break, if they were at all attached. These few children would have had Reactive Attachment Disorder, which would have required special treatment to avoid severe personality issues. These few children were enough to skew the data, especially since they were only looking for about 8% significance.

Additionally, for unknown but fathomable reasons, the measures for the "spectrum" were substituted midway through the design from the previous measure to a "global psychology interview-based scale," and interviewing can produce very subjective results.

Overall the Danish studies were "riddled with serious problems including the sloppy assembly of data from hospitals, poor research design, and even deliberate attempts to skew the data to get the desired results" (Joseph, 2006, p. 60). Psychiatrist Peter Breggin, called by pro-child researchers and clinicians "the conscience of American Psychiatry," wrote later in his book about the Danish studies, "In other words, we have a miracle gene that skips the biological mothers, fathers, brothers and sisters—and even the biological half-brothers and sisters on the mother's side—and strikes only the half-siblings on the father's side." Breggin calls this finding "ridiculous, so clearly an error or a chance finding that Kety, Rosenthal, Wender and the other investigators are reluctant to describe their full data to their colleagues.

Therefore, the actual nature of the alleged genetic tendency goes unmentioned in their reviews and requires deep digging into the original data itself" (Breggin, 1991, p. 100).

In the 1980s, Wender appeared to qualify his once touted results without actually acknowledging the mistreatment of his data:

> Adoption agencies do their best to place their infant charges with normal parents; only an unusual kind of schizophrenic—whom the adoption agency cannot detect—would receive a child for adoption. Such schizophrenic parents might become ill only later in life, long after having adopted a child, or they might be able to conceal their illness from prying adoption-agency eyes. So the group of adopting schizophrenic parents is different from the group of schizophrenic parents who have their own children. Thus the question of what would happen if children born of normal parents were placed in the homes of typical schizophrenics cannot be answered (Joseph, 2004, p. 201).

Veteran Twin Studies: Pollin & Hoffer (1970) and Allen (1972)

There are honest scientists seeking real evidence of genetic instruction for individuals. Pollin & Hoffer, and Martin Allen reviewed, reanalyzed and reported that the evidence behind eighteen earlier twin studies claiming "presence of a genetic factor in pathogenesis of schizophrenia" (Pollin & Hoffer, 1969, p. 599) was almost non-existent between identical (monozygotic, MZ) and fraternal (dizygotic, DZ) twins.

Further, the researchers reported 15% concordance for schizophrenia between identical twins and held that the influence of genes cannot be meaningful, since there is an 85% discordance (Pollin & Hoffer, 1969, p. 599). I add of course, that there has to be some concordance due to the equal and identical environment. It appears to me that 85% proves that environment and only environment determines individual behavior.

The Pollin & Hoffer Study of 1970 and the Allen Study of 1972 are considered two of the most reliable studies, primarily because they did not depend on hospital records and because they reportedly controlled for bias. Combining just the Pollin & Hoffer rate of 15% and the Allen concordance rate of 14%, the concordance rate today is considered by many to be 15%, indicating that 85% of behavior is discordant and therefore environmental, leaving 15% concordance for shared environment. Remarkably, this percentage rate is still said by most to prove that genes cause schizophrenia because in 15% of the cases where one identical twin was schizophrenic, so was the other. Stunning. Again, if genes really caused schizophrenia, identical twins would share schizophrenia virtually 100% of the time.

Gottesman & Shields (1972 & 1982)

Nevertheless, geneticists turned over a new leaf and decided to make their research more respectable and in accord with scientific standards. The higher the standards of research designs, the more necessary it became to reinterpret the data.

Irving Gottesman and James Shields were scientists who worked together on numerous projects wherein they studied identical twins for behavioral concordances. Their results were often affected by how they counted twins, whether by the proband method or the pairwise method. Here's an explanation offered by Jonathan Leo:

> Most readers who are not intimately familiar with these studies probably interpret concordance rate findings as the percentage of twin pairs who are both diagnosed with schizophrenia within a sample in which one twin of each pair is known to be schizophrenic. For instance if schizophrenia is diagnosed in both members of 50 twin pairs out of a sample of 100 then most people would think that the concordance rate is 50%, but it's not that simple. Schizophrenia researchers refer to this type of reporting as pairwise concordance, yet some prominent researchers prefer to use the proband method of reporting.
>
> In the proband method, the proband is the [diagnosed] member of a twin pair who was used initially to qualify the pair for inclusion in the sample. It is possible for both members of a twin pair to be proband, in which case that pair would appear twice in the sample. The proband method will always produce higher numbers. As an example, if there is a sample of three pairs of twins and in 1 of those pairs both members are diagnosed with schizophrenia then according to the pairwise method of concordance, the rate would be 1/3 or 33%, but according to the proband-wise method, the rate would be 2/4 or 50% (Leo, 2003, p.4).

Thus, Gottesman and Shields were able to produce higher statistics in their research by counting proband pairs of schizophrenics.

Meta-Analysis (aka Average Risk Studies)

Perhaps it may have seemed irrelevant to critique older studies, but you cannot understand anything without knowing its history. Older Pedigree Studies influenced the research designs of the studies to follow. They are still often referenced in contemporary studies and have even been averaged into "average risk studies" or meta-analysis. Gottesman produced an "average risk" of 40 studies that included Kallmann's highly biased work, with which we began this section. He failed to mention how discredited these studies have been. The rationale for composite studies has been that there is such diversity in results that the truth must be in an average of all the results. These meta-analyses actually provide another way to raise the statistics because their results are so elevated by the older projects and all the projects that were badly designed or misinterpreted.

Clinical Psychologist Ty Colbert points out that the quality of any scientific research improves as testing instruments are improved (Colbert, 2000). Since the more updated research has fewer flaws and therefore results in a lower concordance rate, it has been a disappointment to behavioral geneticists.

A tried and true way to create a statistical significance is to average the research data with previous and older results, still claiming procedures have improved (Colbert, 2000). The older the studies that get added in, the higher the numbers. To recap, many of the older studies fraudulently alleging to include schizophrenic identical twins separated at birth actually included twins separated at any age, including their twenties.

Franz Kallmann and other subsequent researchers admitted they were not "blind" when evaluating relatives and when they age-corrected for older twins. Nevertheless, a number of more current studies have included a total of all research, inflating results. Colbert makes the inescapable point, "For the sake of accuracy, it does not make sense for biological researchers to average in the older, less accurate studies" (2000, p. 5).

Kendler: Equal Environment Assumption (1983)

A new research design developed in the late 60s, 70s and early 80s wherein identical twins were compared to fraternal twins, and the results were exciting to eugenicists. Some scientists purported that they had found a way to prove genetic causation once and for all by comparing traits of identical twins with fraternal twins, expected to find a high concordance rate. The premise of this design called the Equal Environment Assumption (EEA) was that the environment shared by identical twins should be no more or less similar than the environment shared by fraternal twins, so the higher concordance for identical twins must be due to their genes.

A number of industry researchers criticized this assumption, among them lead Danish researcher Kety, who wrote that the EEA was invalid since identical twins "sleep together; they are dressed alike by their parents; they are paraded in a double perambulator [sic] as infants; their friends cannot distinguish one from the other; In short they develop a certain ego identification with each other that is very hard to dissociate from the purely genetic identity with which they were born" (Kety, 1978, p. 48).

Nevertheless, Kendler and his associates borrowed from the Virginia Twin Registry to prove their point (Kendler, 1983). They began to combat the criticisms by arguing that twins are genetically designed to influence their caregivers to treat them as one entity, thus creating an environmental influence. This thinking came to be known as the Twins Create Their Own Environment Theory. In this theory, even environmental similarities are explained away as being "caused" by genes.

Later Kendler retracted both of his EEA theories. Even so, Human Genome scientist Robert Plomin and his associates defended the EEA as late as 1997.

"The equal environments assumption of the twin method assumes that environmental similarity is roughly the same for both types of twins reared in the same family... The equal environments assumption has been tested in several ways and appears reasonable for most traits" (Plomin, DeFries, Knopik & Neiderhiser, 1997, p. 73).

It seems curious that Kety and Kendler both used the influence of environment to make their arguments against other scientists or on behalf of their own theory. Even they couldn't ignore the influences of environment.

Before ever looking at the most valid of the research, I have predicted that identical twins would have a probable concordance of about 50%. The reason for that prediction is that about half of the monozygotic twins I have known enjoyed their mutuality and validated one another, while the other half seemed to polarize, as if in competition for the limited nurturing available from mother. This typically manifests in one twin becoming dominant and the other becoming submissive or more passive. The inference can be made that in the latter case, these twins have quite dissimilar environments. To a significant extent the dominant twin has a passive sibling for his environment and the submissive twin has a dominant twin for his environment.

Koskenvuo, Langinvainio, Kaprio, Lonnqvist & Tienari (1984)

This study had one of the largest samples of twins. Scientists compared 16,649 MZ and DZ twin pairs (aged 15+ years) in Finland for neuroses, alcoholism and schizophrenia, yet this study is almost never acknowledged by schizophrenia twin researchers in their reviews. Interestingly, they have not explained why it has been left out of their reviews either. In the Koskenvuo et al. study, the concordance rate was 11% for identical twins and 1.8% for fraternals (APA, 2013).

Sherrington (1988)

In his 1991 book, *Toxic Psychiatry*, Peter Breggin remarked on a 1988 research project headed by Robin Sherrington of the Molecular Psychiatry Laboratory of the University of London, which reported locating the gene on the long arm of the human chromosome 5 in seven families from England and Iceland (Breggin, 1991). The researchers stated the exact gene could not be identified, although it was thought to be dominant. "This report," they asserted, "provides the first strong evidence for the involvement of a single gene in the causation of schizophrenia" (Breggin, 1991, p. 99). An editorial in the same issue proclaimed a breakthrough, "New research has shown some schizophrenia to be, in part, genetically determined." The president-elect of the American Psychiatric Association, Herb Pardes, leaped on the promotional opportunity and proclaimed the study to be a "tremendous advance," while in a neighboring article in the same journal another scientist, James Kennedy, tore the study apart (Breggin, 1991, p. 100).

The claim was absurd. When a parent transmits a dominant gene, there is at least a 50% chance each of the siblings will inherit the dominant gene. Hardly anyone has ever claimed a 50% concordance for schizophrenia among siblings. The families used for this study appear to be extremely dysfunctional, and again any decent clinician would strongly suspect severe neglect and abuse. Breggin cited other problems with the study:

> An actual examination of the study brought out more absurdities. Drawing on seven families, it contained 104 individuals. From the family tree reported in the study we find the following examples of extraordinary prevalence for schizophrenia and other disorders among these families: one set of parents had five of seven children with psychiatric disorders, including three who were said to be schizophrenic or otherwise psychotic; another had four out of seven with diagnosed schizophrenia or other psychosis; another had seven out of ten with psychiatric disorders. The typical rate for children diagnosed as schizophrenic in families with a schizophrenic parent usually is estimated to be less than 10%. These families could vie to be in the Guinness Book of World Records for being the craziest family (Breggin, 1991, p. 100).

MISTRA (1990)

The 1990 Minnesota Study of Twins Reared Apart (MISTRA), conducted by Thomas Bouchard at the University of Minnesota, was essentially flawed from its inception. Researchers put out a call to identical twins reared apart. These twins that were called in were self-selected. They already knew one another and together they chose to be part of the research with foreknowledge that they were to be studied specifically for their similarities (Joseph, 2004).

For more than two decades MISTRA gathered interviews with these 74 identical twins who had commonalities that seemed to defy environment. The study was essentially comprised of testimonials by both twins about what they had discovered they had in common. They told stories about marrying women with the same name or liking the same brand of beer, as if these coincidences had anything at all to do with personality. The press had a field day taking photos. Many posed for photographs using the same mannerisms, drinking the same beverage and, as some pairs admitted, planning in advance what they were going to say when interviewed (Joseph, 2004).

The "study" was taken seriously mostly by television programming. The magnitude of confirmation bias (the cognitive tendency of people to pay special attention to details that confirm their beliefs while dismissing or ignoring details that do not) seemed reminiscent of astrology readings. The public seemed highly responsive, especially since many of the twins were interviewed for television and radio. The pairs of look-alikes told their audiences of all the things they had in common, even though they had not known one another during some period of their lives.

The greatest criticism of the study was that the procurers and interviewers refused to share their data. One of the critics of MISTRA suggests that if one hundred of us were together as strangers and we were paired up and asked to find commonalities between us, we would have no problem amazing ourselves (Joseph, 2004). By the same token, this study reminds me of the stories that supposedly prove we have been visited by aliens or how all of us believe the sign under which we were born has meaning, but if we met one hundred strangers and talked to them indefinitely, freely asking questions, we would not be able to guess their astrological sign unless they told us.

For an interesting article about coincidences, even when they are not fabricated, see the link below. These coincidences are not indicative of causality but more of commonality. You may want to include some of this information, as it demonstrates these coincidences, even when they are not fabricated, are hardly remarkable:
http://www.snopes.com/history/american/lincoln-kennedy.asp.

Finland: Tienari & Wynne (2004)

Recent studies still make the same assumptions as the older studies and demonstrate the same blind spots. Pekka Tienari and Lynne Wynne et al. are touted to have reported much more reasonable statistics on children adopted away from schizophrenic mothers who were still symptomatic (1994, 2004). This study is also credited with having assessed the adopting families.

The Tienari and Wynne studies of first degree relatives—biological mother and child—supposedly attempted to control for childrearing practices in the groundbreaking study of adopting families by meeting the adoptive families initially to assess for health and pathology. In this Finnish study, the scientists interviewed, tested and compared two samples. One sample was adopted-away offspring of mothers with schizophrenic-spectrum disorders, compared blindly to adoptees "without genetic risk," meaning these adoptees had "normal" birth mothers.

According to Tienari and Wynne, "Adoptive rearing [techniques were] assessed using family rating scales based on extended family observations at the initial assessment" (2004, p. 216). Adoptees were then independently re-diagnosed after twelve and twenty-one years. The results were supposed to represent that the adoptees from biological mothers with schizophrenic-spectrum disorders were more likely to fall into the schizophrenic spectrum than babies of normal biological mothers who were adopted away.

Tienari and Wynne continued to use the "schizophrenic spectrum," but to be very clear, there were no schizophrenic mothers or schizophrenic offspring in the study. If we take them literally, they are saying they diagnosed mothers in interviews, but when the mothers did not fit the clinical diagnosis of schizophrenia, they were re-categorized into the "schizophrenic spectrum" and they still represented that any significance proved schizophrenia was genetic.

The word "schizophrenia" or "schizophrenic" should not even be mentioned, especially in more modern studies with allegedly tighter controls.

It would be more accurately called a "pathological spectrum" or a "spectrum of mental illness." The definitions are conveniently loose and sloppy, but the word "schizophrenia" has become a catch-all, still implying a specific disorder. Later, results were presumed to prove that schizophrenia is genetically influenced, even though the inclusions within the "schizophrenic spectrum" now include all major symptoms, including bi-polar disorder, which is allegedly caused by different genes.

Once again, the adoptees were not interviewed about how they were raised. The only follow-up after the initial interview was to diagnose them twelve and twenty-one years later.

We do not know at what age the children were adopted since any adoption not at birth and before the age of three could be harmful to personality. Children who waited to be adopted would have suffered attachment trauma, and researchers did not say whether the grown children with pathology (raising the statistics) had lingered alone in hospitals or orphanages for any period of time. Researchers did not say whether the most symptomatic adoptees at age 21 were the exact children who lived longest with their dysfunctional (and unattached) mothers. It was not revealed whether these children were included within the common practice of adopting-out to relatives (who were also in the same family system of learned abuse and neglect) or whether lower functioning parents adopted out to lower functioning families. Most importantly, the study fails to disclose that not one grown child was born of a schizophrenic mother (as opposed to "within the schizophrenic spectrum").

One more thing: Tienari and Wynne reported that they did some age correcting. Tienari writes, "In adoptees at high genetic risk [adopted away from mothers with mental illness to some varying degree] of schizophrenia [note the use of "schizophrenia" interchangeably with "schizophrenic spectrum,"] but not in those at low genetic risk, adoptive-family ratings were a significant predictor of schizophrenia-spectrum disorders in adoptees at long-term follow-up" (Tienari & Wynne, 2004, p. 1).

The translation for the previous quote is that the most significant predictor of how an adoptee turns out is in the adoptive-family ratings. That means the future of a child is most likely predictable by the family who raises that child (not by the [illusive] genes). It appears that modern studies have become increasingly dishonest in their terminology.

Tienari and Wynne state, "The results demonstrate that adoptees at high genetic risk [never proved] for schizophrenia [because they were placed in the "schizophrenic spectrum" without a diagnosis of schizophrenia] are more sensitive to problems in the rearing adoptive family" (Tienari & Wynne, 2004, p. 220). This acknowledgement is framed in the Diathesis-stress model, representing that if a child comes down with a mental illness in a neglectful and abusive environment, it's due to fragile genes. They go on to say, "An alternative way to view the findings is that there appears to be a protective effect in having been reared in a 'healthy' adoptive family" (Tienari & Wynne, 2004, p. 220). They also say, "A similar finding was reported in our earlier report using factor scores instead of raw scores from the Finnish Study. Also in the same report, the age-corrected [!] morbid risk for schizophrenia [they forget to say, 'schizophrenic spectrum'] in high-genetic-risk adoptees reared in 'healthy' families was 1.49%, but 13.04% for high-genetic risk adoptees reared in 'dysfunctional' families, i.e., with both genetic risk and environmental risk present" (Tienari & Wynne, 2004, p. 220).

Despite their careful phrasing, Tienari and Wynne are saying that being raised in a healthy family vs. an unhealthy family makes all the difference, especially if one has weak genes or is at "morbid risk for schizophrenia." However, the truth is that attachment breaks and other early childhood trauma, rather than fragile genes, put children at higher risk of becoming symptomatic in the face of later life stressors or trauma (van der Kolk, McFarlane & Weisaeth, 1996).

Nevertheless, Tienari and Wynne state, "Reciprocal, not unidirectional effects, within family relationships make impossible, and inappropriate, interpretations about simple, unidirectional 'causality' assigned to adoptive parents of the adoptees" (Tienari & Wynne, 2004, p. 222). It appears they're seeking a way to tell the truth about environment while pleasing their colleagues and patrons.

SUMMARY CHART

Despite the clear pattern of behavioral researchers beginning with a pro-genetic conclusion and working backwards, the concordance rates are in fact dropping. I do not think they will drop any further because the 15% concordance represents the similar environment shared by identical twins—not genes—when studying their similarities. Following is a chart that demonstrates the wide variation in concordance rates as research studies become more and more scrutinized.

Comparing Concordance Rates of Schizophrenia in Identical Twins

Year of Study	Concordance Rate (%)	Researcher(s)
1946 (still averaged in with other studies to raise the numbers)	69, 92 (59% uncorr.)	Kallmann
1955-1966	77	Burt
1963	0	Tienari
1966	42	Gottesman & Shields
1968 (edit of his own 1963 study)	15	Tienari
1970	14	Pollin & Hoffer
1971 (edit of his own 1963 study)	33	Tienari
1972 (reassessed P&H's 1970 results)	27	Allen
1972 (review of Danish studies and edit of their own 1966 study)	58	Gottesman & Shields
1974 (edit of his own 1972 study)	27	Allen
1975 (final report on his own 1963 study)	36	Tienari
1982 (reassessed Allen's '72 reassessment)	43	Gottesman & Shields
1984	11	Koskenvuo, Langinvainio, Kaprio, Lonnqvist & Tienari
2004	13.4	Tienari & Wynne

HISTORICAL TRENDS

You have just read about the history of psychology and the two opposing perspectives that have underlied psychological theory from the inception of this profession: genetics/nature vs. environment/nurture. By now you may be able to see how two opposing sides are fighting for dominance. Following is a chart that lays out the critical historic events of our profession. You can trace the swing of the pendulum of historic developments on the chart, signifying opposition and backlashes, rebounding from one side to the other, in the long-standing argument that looks almost like shoelaces, crossing over from side to side. Unfortunately the laces don't hold us together.

Critical Historical Events Showing Nature vs. Nurture

Era	Nature, Bad Seed, Pro-Parent	Blank Slate, Harmful Parenting	Nurture, Pro-Child
COMMUNAL EUROPE 5000 BC - 1700s			Peasant wildcraft practitioners
SLAVERY MID EAST 1500 BC-100 AD		Bible: Spare the rod, spoil the child	
COMMUNAL/FEUDAL 1200 – 1500 AD	Witch burnings		
FEUDAL/INDUSTRIAL 1500s-1600s	Chaining up the mentally ill		
INDUSTRIAL 1600s		John Locke, earning one's keep	Moral Management
Early 1700s-Early 1800s	Medicallizing mental illness, Insane asylums		
Early 1800s		Dr. Schreber	
1865	Mendelian Model		
Late 1800s			Early Freud (childhood)
Early 1900s	Late Freud (inborn)		
Early 1900s		Harsh parenting	John Watson: no inborn pathology
1930s-1950s	Ped Studies, Kallman (false claims), Burt (false claims)		
1960s	Twin Studies, false claims		
Mid 50s to 1960s			Cultural anthropology
Harlow, 30s-60s; Spitz 40s-50s; Bowlby; 60s-70s Ainsworth; 70s-90s			Attachment Studies
1930s-1960s	Twin Studies		
1960s-1970s	Danish Adoption Studies, Twin Studies, Victory of PR selling dominance of genetic influence on personality		Silent victory for environment
1970s			Burt's IQ testing & other ped studies of biodeterminism discredited, silent victory for environment
1980s-2000s			Trauma Studies
2000s	Fragile genes, Diathesis Stress Model		
2002	HGP ends in fanfare without results		
Mid-2000s			Mirror neurons
2004 - present	Epigenetics		

RESEARCH FLAWS IN FAMILY STUDIES

Lack of Rule-Outs

Another focus of research is to find the gene for depression. Ross and Pam have something to say about that:

> It will not be possible to identify a gene for depression, if any such gene exists, until trauma-driven cases, who may be genetically normal, are removed from analysis [ruled out] in family studies. The total dose of depression in the general population driven primarily by genetic factors is swamped out by the contribution of psychosocial trauma, including early childhood loss of a parent. If this is correct, bioreductionist psychiatry dooms itself to a futile search for genes for mental illnesses by retaining too much noise in its pedigrees, in the form of trauma-driven psychopathology (1995, p. 274).

Study authors utilize many popular research flaws to build their cases. In Appendix I the reader can find a list of Research Flaws. To be clear, these are flaws used by researchers again and again, without shame, knowing in advance what objections they may raise, but also knowing from experience they are protected. The flaws enable researchers to get the job done, and nobody seems to mind.

None of the scientifically proven causal factors have been ruled out in this research study, the most significant and invisible of which is quality of attachment and quantity or continuity of attachment. The security of a parent-child bond is a major factor in reducing trauma. Bessel van der Kolk writes that research has shown the more securely attached children do not metabolize war trauma into posttraumatic stress, while the less securely attached children become adults who have multiple experiences with PTSD over their lifetime and constitute the vast majority of soldiers with PTSD (1996).

We now know unequivocally that failed or broken attachments reduce resilience, and many other environmental factors reduce resilience. Probably the most popular flaw is the failure to rule out or to form differential diagnoses. Following is a summary of some of the most common flaws in genetic research.

Biological determinists don't know their confounds. Scientists fail to recognize their responsibility to identify contaminating factors or other explanations for their results. Actually, biogeneticists are generally poorly educated in other explanations for behavior. They are predominantly insulated from them, if not hostile to them, and hold amongst and between themselves myths about environmental factors, such as:

- the equal environments theory held by biogeneticists about identical twins (twins elicit equal treatment due to their genetic instructions and because they are genetically alike)
- fragile genes, not insecure attachments, explain temperament
- blaming parents is unnecessary to research

In logic, it's called Occam's Razor, which is when all else is equal, the simplest explanation tends to be the right one, or "Do not multiply entities unnecessarily."

Scientists make the assumption a behavior is genetic because it runs in families. By contrast, The Causal Theory is clear to explain that behaviors run in families because they are imprinted. What goes in most come out, and what doesn't go in, can't come out. Children imprint behavior especially from their parents. We end up transmitting from generation to generation behaviors which are modeled, a la Albert Bandura, or as Murray Bowen describes, by virtue of the intergenerational transmission process. Giacomo Rizzolatti's recently published work on the discovery of mirror neurons discusses the specialized neurons designed to create in us a drive to experience others' behaviors as if they were us, and ultimately to imitate or replicate the way we have been treated. Thus scientists ignorantly fail to rule out imprints from within the family, and call these mere trends evidence of genetics. For example, when a scientist identifies a behavior that runs in a family, it behooves him or her to rule out all imprinting or family transmission systems or learning via mirror neurons before attributing that behavior to genetics. Genetics should be the last possible explanation.

Most behavioral geneticists have no knowledge of attachment research, that early disrupted attachments lead to a fragile core and lack of resilience. Attachment research has demonstrated consistently that if infants and small children don't have certain experiences at critical and crucial ages, they would develop abnormally. This is demonstrated in identical twin studies where it is alleged when identical twins are separated and raised apart, any correlation in their personalities must be attributed to genetics. However, in many studies, it turns out the twins were separated, but not necessarily at birth, and actually in some cases as old as 15! What researchers don't address is that insecure attachments create the appearance of a fragile core and susceptibility to other trauma. As such, they have begun to reference these susceptibilities as fragile genes. If the researcher of adoption studies doesn't address the fact that the earliest experiences are the most formative, then the researcher has once again failed to rule out obvious confounds for twins not separated immediately at birth.

Failure to Replicate

Research that cannot be replicated is invalid. R.C. Lewontin, Chairman of the Research Department of Biology at Harvard, points out the study of schizophrenia has a history of so-called discoveries being made and reported to the press that scientists are "on the trail of the gene," only to be disproved later, often because the studies cannot be replicated. Thus reports to the press linger in the collective mind of the public of success after success after success, while the follow-up reports these studies are no longer valid are not made to the public or reported as news. Lewontin describes a series of claims which supposedly indicate schizophrenia is genetic, only to be discredited later:

Among the claims for causative factors in schizophrenia made since the 1950s we may point to: abnormal substances secreted in the sweat of schizophrenics, injection of the blood serum of schizophrenics into other, normal subjects inducing abnormal behavior; and the presence of abnormal enzymes in red blood cells and blood proteins. Between 1955 and the present day, conflicting research reports have claimed that schizophrenia is caused by disorders in serotonin metabolism (1955); noradrenaline metabolism (1971); dopamine metabolism (1972); acetylcholine metabolism (1973); endorphin metabolism (1976); and prostaglandin metabolism (1977). Some molecules, such as the amino acids glutamate and gamma-amino-butyric acid, came into fashion in the late 1950s, fell into neglect, and now in the 1980s, have come back into fashion once more." (Lewontin, Rose & Kamin, 1984, p. 205).

While geneticists continued to produce research to support headlines progress was being made toward finding genes for behavior, the studies could not be replicated, which was essential to good science. If another scientist cannot replicate a study, then it failed.

Researcher and clinician Erik Turkheimer and his colleagues describe "an extended period of frustration as most of the reported discoveries either turned out to be very small or failed to replicate at all" (Turkheimer, Pettersson & Horn, 2014, p. 534).

Highly-cited psychologist Stephen Faraone and his team wrote, "It is no secret that our field has published thousands of candidate gene association studies but few replicated findings" (Joseph, 2014, ch. 8). Yet another scientist explained, "Although twin, family and adoption studies have shown that general cognitive ability [GCA] is substantially heritable, GWAS [genomewide association study] has not uncovered a genetic polymorphism replicably associated with this phenotype (Joseph, 2014, ch. 8). Scientists are basically admitting we've been misled.

Revisions of Language

Another one of the most developed flaws in genetic research has been obfuscating language, which requires interpretation. If one is sane and carefully follows the words, they may begin to see how the trickery is done. Slowly we will be persuaded something that is causal is only incidental. Something that is obvious is irrelevant. Something that is formed by genes or caused by genes (neurotransmitters) is taken to be the gene itself. This is a critical flaw because it enables researchers to infer genetic causes as if they were facts.

There are lots of explanations why the research didn't turn out as planned. One explanation that shows up frequently is "incomplete penetrance," which apparently means the effect of the gene wasn't strong enough, again perhaps due to a contrary environment. According to Ross and Pam, "The 'incomplete penetrance' complicates the genetic effect, without any basis for this assertion other than conjecture and the plotting of graphs for the hypothetical distributions" (Ross & Pam, 1995). Even Rosenthal found this explanation problematic: "Although the concept of [reduced penetrance] could and perhaps should be useful, many geneticists feel that it is too often used to make ignorance respectable, and that in human genetics, it has been abused to the extent that it is in danger of falling into disrepute" (Rosenthal, 1970, p. 29). Pro-child researcher Dumont added, "Incomplete penetrance is an 'apologetic compromise' to hold onto a genetic approach that is unsupported either by data or by the science of genetics…To assume the structure [of a gene] can 'cause' the structure [of behavior] is an error of such magnitude as to be something like a thought disorder itself" (1984, p. 332).

Molecular and behavioral genetic researchers have adopted an updated explanation for their failed results, "missing heritability." It is an assumption the genes that underlie phenotypes exist, but they cannot be found for unknown reasons. Clinical psychologist, researcher and author Jay Joseph writes, "They had no doubt that the problem is missing heritability, as opposed to non-existent heritability because a 'substantial proportion of individual differences in disease susceptibility is known to be due to genetic factors…'" He continues, "The real issue confronting researchers is not "missing heritability," but missing genes." Scientists do not consider that the missing genes do not exist (p. 214).

Joseph points out how rhetoric can belie reality. **Scientists can turn a failure into a win**. Hudziak and Faraone claim while "no causal DNA variant has been discovered using" genetic linkage analysis, "this has led to the important discovery that, if common variants exist, their genetic effect sizes must be very small" (p. 731). "Thus, in rhetoric but not in reality, gene-finding failures are transformed into an 'important discovery.' An alternative interpretation, unmentioned by the authors, is that researchers have discovered that no such genes exist" (p. 731).

Another generous explanation is that environment plays some part in the pathogenesis, but as Ross and Pam point out, "this glibly slips in the presumption that genetic factors account for the rest" (1995, p. 18).

It was assumed identical twins create the same environment genetically, as they are prone to solicit the same treatment by their behaviors or because they look alike. Therefore, researchers conclude, the degree to which they have the same behavior is genetic. Well, identical twins do have a similar environment, but the biggest contributor to their environment is the other. Some identical twins polarize. Others become like one another because they think of themselves as a unit while they are treated as a unit. The concordance rate for identical twins is actually closer to 50%, which proves environment creates behavior, not genes.

In some cases identical twins have primary caregivers who can meet the needs of two babies. Identical twins are at much higher risk for weaker attachments with their primary caregivers, who may not have enough inner strength (from their own early attachments) to nurture two babies as well as one. Sometimes they bond to each other instead. Sometimes they rival for mother's attention. In some cases one twin becomes the dominant twin, while the other becomes the passive twin. Sometimes, one becomes the domineering twin, and the other becomes the unprotected twin. In cases of extreme inequality there is a higher likelihood of schizophrenia, due to the mind-warping circumstances of unfairness.

So, while these studies are looking for similarities to prove they are the same behavior genetically, they are also failing to look at how polar opposite many sets of twins turn out to be. Actually, these studies prove more that behavior is *not* genetic. To reiterate, if behavior were genetic, then the twins would have identical personalities 100% of the time. Most twin studies for schizophrenia show a concordance rate of a low of 15% (Tienari, 1963/75) to a high of 69% (Kallman, 1946). Averaged together the studies show a rate of 43%, according to the standard pairwise method (Colbert, "The Four False Pillars of Biopsychiatry: One Hundred Years of Medical Nonsense,"2000). The evidence proves twins who are in a similar environment still turn out so differently that 57% of twins who are schizophrenic still have a twin who is not.

Thus scientists prove environment, while thinking or suggesting they are proving genetic cause. No two people have the same environment, and that applies to twins as well.

Data Tampering

The public, clinicians and laypeople still remember a famous study, the Kety Study from Copenhagen which expanded to a Denmark Study which claimed it looked at sets of identical twins wherein one was schizophrenic. They supposedly showed genetic causes of schizophrenia by identifying a significant number of relatives in the extended family who were also schizophrenic. The study reportedly demonstrated 8.7% of "schizophrenics" had relatives who were also schizophrenic. Incredibly, this was considered significant (Kety, 1984) proof there was a recessive gene for schizophrenia. Of course, more ridiculous is that "schizophrenics" in this study were not schizophrenic.

Researchers have broadened definitions to prove the un-provable. "Originally there were only 1.9% of relatives [of schizophrenics] had schizophrenia," reported pro-child researchers Colin Ross and Alvin Pam (1999). "Since they were unable to prove parents and relatives also had schizophrenia, they expanded the study to the extended family and broadened the definition of schizophrenia" to include the following classifications of which I have never heard: "chronic schizophrenia," "borderline states," "inadequate personality," "uncertain schizophrenia," and "uncertain borderline states." This broadening of the definition under the umbrella of "schizophrenia," brought in nine biologically related families of the index cases, upping the percentage from 1.9% to 8.7%, which was considered "significant," and would not have reached that mark without the inclusion of "inadequate personalities" and "uncertain borderline schizophrenia" (Kety, Rosenthal, Wender & Schulsinger, 1968).

Scientific significance has dropped from Mendel's 100% concordance to a measly 8.7%, a measure borrowed inappropriately from experimental research.

Researchers have actually tampered with their data. The famous Scandinavian researchers, Kety, Rosenthal and Paul Wender actually pulled a switch-a-roo. In one study, the researchers, after finding they proved environment over genetic inheritance, diluted the results that parenting influenced behavior more in adopted children than the their biological parents, so they added the control group of normals to the group of children raised by unhealthy families, but adopted from healthy families. This rendered the study insignificant, which was better for the researchers than having to report children born of healthy parents but raised by unhealthy parents were less healthy than children born of unhealthy parents and raised by healthy parents.

Interviewing researchers have skewed results in their interviews, especially in studies where the subjects are hospitalized. These studies were not "blind" studies and were susceptible to confirmatory bias. It appeared the schizophrenic patient wanted to be perceived as identical to his or her healthier (fraternal) twin, while the healthier (identical) twin wanted to be perceived as different from her unhealthy twin. Researchers were requested to locate the alleged identical twin, but many could not be located, and some were dead. Researchers encountered twins who were reportedly identical, but claimed to be a fraternal twin. Thus researchers had to make judgment calls. When the twin appeared to be unhospitalized, the researchers often concluded they were fraternal twins (Lewontin, Rose & Kamin, 1984).

Scientists have skewed the meaning of their results to imply genetic explanations where the research clearly proved environment caused personality. According to Ty Colbert, "A supplementary basis for the distortion is major methodological research flaws in the earlier MZ [monozygotic or identical twin] studies. The Tienari study (1963/75) and a study by Hoffer and Pollin (1970/83) are considered two of the most reliable primarily because they did not depend upon hospital records." According to the most ethical of the twin studies by Tienari, there was only a concordance rate of 15% between identical twins where one was schizophrenic, and Hoffer & Pollin produced a higher rate of 18% the concordance. The rate today is considered to be 16.5%, which is not used to prove that, despite the most equal environments, 83.5% of identical twins do not share schizophrenia, when one was diagnosed with it. One could assume it would be fair to report, at least, that their environments account for the 83.5% lack of concordance. One could easily assume then the 16.5% could result from a shared environment.

Early research was the most faked, as early researchers sought to prove 100% concordance between identical twins. That research is now averaged in with current studies to inflate the statistics. Colbert points out it is a common practice of researchers to inflate their results by averaging results with previous research, which has been found to be significantly flawed. While the more updated research may have fewer flaws, it has a lower concordance rate, and the only way to create a statistical significance is to average the results with previous results. "The quality of any scientific research positively evolves over time as the methodological problems associated with testing instruments and procedures are recognized and corrected. For the sake of accuracy, it does not make sense for biological researchers to average in the older, less accurate studies; but by including them, they raise the concordance rate and buttress the inheritance [false] pillar of [biopsychiatry] (Colbert, p. 5)"

Further, if the nature of the data had been shared with the public, even a layperson could have seen the deck had been stacked with the inclusion of this unique family, and it would be evident the study did not avoid the issue of a shared family environment, since the six brothers all shared the same family. If I had had contact with this family, I would have suspected major neglect and severe abuse, beginning at least with the father's childhood, long before I would have hypothesized some illusive genetic cause, especially since the gene shows up nowhere else in the father's lineage.

5: THE HUMAN GENOME PROJECT

More recent research in twin studies comes closer to admitting it's difficult to prove genetics, that environment is showing strongly in the formation of behavior. We can find an actual warning to take scientific claims lightly from two spokesmen for The Human Genome Project (HGP), Joseph McInerney and Mark Rothstein (retrieved from the original project website):

> Traditional research strategies in behavioral genetics include studies of twins and adoptees, techniques designed to sort biological from environmental influences. More recently, investigators have added the search for pieces of DNA associated with particular behaviors, an approach that has been most productive to date in identifying potential locations for genes associated with major mental illnesses such as schizophrenia and bipolar disorder. Yet even here there have been no major breakthroughs, no clearly identified genes that geneticists can tie to disease. The search for genes associated with characteristics such as sexual preference and basic personality traits has been even more frustrating... more than any other aspect of genetics, discoveries in behavioral genetics should not be viewed as irrefutable until there has been substantial scientific corroboration...
>
> No single gene determines a particular behavior. Behaviors are complex traits involving multiple genes that are affected by a variety of other factors. This fact often gets overlooked in media reports hyping scientific breakthroughs on gene function, and, unfortunately, this can be very misleading to the public (2008).

Adoption studies made boundless headlines by misrepresenting their findings. It is psychologist and researcher Jay Joseph's opinion the results of the twin studies and adoption studies have had long-term, far-reaching ramifications. The lure of proving genes cause behavior was exciting and infectious to psychiatric researchers, but the ramifications of their claims became fuel for the fire in The War of the Researchers. Their "evidence" misled molecular biologists and biogeneticists into setting goals of the multi-billion-dollar Human Genome Project, which was funded to find the genes that instruct behavior as well as disease.

No patient, not a single one, has ever benefited from genetic research into mental illness, although many have been indirectly harmed by it (because it has discouraged the development of adequate services for patients and, during one shameful period, was used to justify their slaughter). No effective treatments have so far been devised on the basis of genetic information and, given what we now know, it seems very unlikely that further research into genetics of psychosis will lead to important therapeutic advances in the future. –Bentall, 2009, p. 145

SUMMARY

Lisa Gannett summarizes the history of The Human Genome Project for the *Stanford Encyclopedia of Philosophy*, first published November 26, 2008, which I've further narrowed and organized for you here.

In the mid-1980s, three scientists independently came up with the idea of sequencing the human genome ("all the genetic information in a person" (WebMD, 2008, p. 175)). They were:
- Robert Sinsheimer, then Chancellor of the University of California at Santa Cruz, who had $30 million to repurpose;
- Rene Dulbecco of the Salk Institute, who sought to understand the genetic origins of cancer and other diseases; and
- Charles DeLisi, with $4.5 million from the Department of Energy, who wanted to find a way to detect radiation-induced mutations as opposed to evolution's mutations.

Below is a compilation of statements from Gannett's (2008) summary:

They found supporters in prominent molecular biologists and human geneticists Walter Bodmer, Walter Gilbert, Leroy Hood, Victor McKusick and James D. Watson (Gannett, 2008). Senator Pete Domenici from New Mexico introduced a bill to Congress that awarded the Department of Energy (DOE) another $10.7 million and the National Institute of Health $17.2 million, which they combined to initiate The Human Genome Project. It would begin in 1990 and end on April 12, 2003, commemorating the 50th anniversary of the discovery of the double-helix by aforementioned Watson and Crick. Still they were short of funds; the founders estimated a total cost of $3 billion. Fundraising began on an international level. A number of molecular scientists were critical of the endeavor. "Caltech's David Botstein referred to the initiative as 'DOE's program for unemployed bomb-makers.'"

Geneticist Walter Gilbert was quoted to say, "sequencing the human genome is like pursuing the holy grail" (Lee, 1991, p. 9). Nobel Prize winner James D. Watson who, with Francis Crick discovered the molecular structure of DNA in 1953, and founded The Human Genome Project, wrote, "The Human Genome Project is much more than a vast roll call of As, Ts, Gs, and Cs: it is as precious a body of knowledge as humankind will ever acquire, with a potential to speak to our most basic philosophical questions about human nature, for purposes of good and mischief alike" (Watson & Berry, 2003, p. 172). The Salk Institute's Rene Dulbecco wrote we would discover "our human essence in the genome..." and declared "the sequence of the human DNA is the reality of our species" (1986, p. 1056). Some discussion about manipulating genes for the better of human kind brought on criticism of playing God. One evangelical Christian scientist, Francis Collins along with David Galas, responded in the Los Angeles Times to say, "God is not threatened by all this. I think God thinks it's wonderful that we puny creatures are going about the business of trying to understand how our instruction book works because it's a very elegant instruction book indeed" (Gosselin, 2000).

The intent of The Human Genome Project was to:
- identify all genes of the human genome estimated to be over 100,000;
- sequence the approximately 3 billion nucleotides of the human genome;
- develop databases to store information;
- develop tools for data analysis;
- address ethical, legal and social issues; and
- sequence a number of model organisms, including the E. coli bacterium, the roundworm, and the fruit fly.

Geneticists expected over 100,000 genes in the human genome because the fruit fly genome consists of 13,000 genes and the roundworm consists of over 18,000 genes.

Gannett (2008) continues:

> Unfortunately, the claims made by the adoption and twin studies were like methamphetamine to the biogeneticists. Scientists acted as if they had just been invited into an untapped gold mine, and the National Institute of Health's head Bernadine Healy advocated gene patenting. Then Director of the National Center for Human Genetic Research (NCHGR), Watson disagreed with her decision to approve patent applications where there was lack of knowledge of function. Watson resigned. The Christian scientist Francis Collins was eventually named as his replacement at the NCHGR.
>
> Francis Collins established an intramural research program at the NCHGR to complement the extramural program of grants for university-based research that already existed. Their goal was to map and sequence genes by increasing the number of groups working on the project.
>
> At the same time, J. Craig Venter's privately held The Institute for Genomic Research partnered with Michael Hunkapiller's company Applied Biosystems because Hunkapiller offered a gene sequencing machine.
>
> The race to sequence the genome was on and the countdown to fulfill promises began. The publicly funded scientists downplayed the race and their fears that funding would dry up, since the private sector was willing to take over the sequencing endeavor. The project was more staggering than scientists anticipated, so a strategy to map first and sequence later was established in order for the deadline to be met. The contest appeared to end in 2000—three years ahead of schedule— with a tie for the prize, "But it was more an arranged truce" between

two adversaries who no one predicted would remain together in the same room.

Neither side completed the goals of the HGP, but the private sector was acknowledged to be further along. In 2000, the Celera Corporation—also owned by J. Craig Venter—announced the completion of the "first assembly" of the human genome with 99% coverage. President Bill Clinton was joined at the White House by Francis Collins, J. Craig Venter, Ari Patrinos from the Department of Energy, and UK Prime Minister Toni Blair (via satellite), for a press conference to announce the human genome had been sequenced (Stanford, 2008).

An anonymous author for *Nature* described "the fanfare of 26 June as an 'extravagant' example—one reaching 'an all-out zenith or nadir, according to taste'—of scientists making public announcements not linked to peer-reviewed publication, here to bolster share prices (Celera) and for political effect (the HGP) given the 'months to go before even a draft sequence will be scientifically useful'" (Anonymous, 2000, p. 981).

It turned out no genes were isolated for behavior, or for any physical diseases. The human genome had no more than 34,000 genes, as opposed to the 100,000 they expected. Scientists were stumped because they anticipated genes responsible for an infinite number of behaviors (Lipton, 2001, p. 3).

Since the right hand never knew what the left hand was doing, MISTRA adoption researchers Bouchard & McGue wrote in 2003, "the search for specific genes in personality is likely only to intensify as additional behaviorally relevant genes are identified through The Human Genome Project" (p. 4). Then without further factually supportive information they wrote, "We conclude that there is now strong evidence that virtually all individual psychological differences, when reliably measured, are moderately to substantially heritable" (p. 4).

PLOMIN IS THE FACE OF HOPE

Behavioral geneticist and advocate for molecular biology Robert Plomin began cheerleading and writing optimistic reports that dominated the field for nearly three decades beginning in 1983. In 1991, he and Richard Rende said the "pace of development" in molecular genetics is "breathtaking" and the HGP "will lead to the identification of many more genetic markers" (p. 171). They wrote:

> We predict that in less than ten years—perhaps by the time of the Annual Review of Psychology chapter on human behavioral genetics scheduled for the year 2000—molecular-genetic techniques will have revolutionized human behavioral genetics (Plomin & Rende, 1991, p. 176).

Jay Joseph (2015) detailed Plomin's progression of reports in journals that often reached the media. I am borrowing from his survey some brief examples of the resilience of genetic researchers in the face of failures to discover, isolate or formulate the null hypothesis, such that no such genes for behavior exist. Joseph said the history of scientific refutation is that "adherents of established theories construct ever more elaborate or unlikely explanations to fend off their critics" (p. 213). Take special note of the reference years as you read in order to grasp the vast span of time researchers spent searching for (and never finding) the non-existent single gene isolated for behavior.

The same year the HGP came to a close without discovering any gene for behavior, Plomin announced genetic variants were being found for personality and reading disabilities (Plomin, 2000). Plomin, McGuffin and Riley wrote in 2001 that gene linkages had been discovered for aggression, schizophrenia, ADHD, male homosexuality and dyslexia. In 2003, Plomin, DeFries, McClearn and McGuffin wrote, "Molecular genetics has come on center stage in behavioral genetics much faster than anyone anticipated" (p. 231).

In 2003 and 2004, Plomin began to tone down predictions. Plomin and McGuffin admitted that progress in identifying genes that influence behavior "has been slower than some experts expected" (Plomin & McGuffin, 2003, p. 205). He acknowledged the genes for schizophrenia "remain elusive" (p. 213)..."and the story for major depression and bipolar depression is similar to schizophrenia" (p. 214). However, Plomin continued to believe, claiming within the next decade genes will be identified and used to predict risk.

Plomin's frustration began to become more palpable, when he wrote, "Being an optimist, my response [to when we are going to be there] is soon" (Plomin, 2005, p. 1030), yet in the same year, he and Asbury wrote that "the future of genetic research on behavior lies in molecular genetic studies of DNA that will eventually identify specific DNA variants responsible for the widespread influence of genes in behavioral development" (Plomin & Asbury, 2005, p. 93).

Plomin claimed a few years later behavioral sciences remained "at the dawn of a new era" of forthcoming gene discoveries (2008, p. 90), and again predicted, "Many genes responsible for the widespread genetic influence on behavior will be identified and used in research and clinics to assess genetic risk with the next decade" (2008, p. 118) and reaffirmed researchers' claims that genes had been discovered for ADHD.

Plomin and Davis wrote, "[T]he speed of discovery in genetics is now so great that it would be impossible to predict what will happen in the next five years, let alone the next 50 years" (2009, p. 66). Yet when he teamed up with Haworth, they wrote, "It seems highly unlikely that most of the genes responsible for the heritability for any complex trait will be identified in the foreseeable future" (Haworth & Plomin, 2010, p. 783). Still, molecular biologists Hudziak and Faraone wrote, "Although we are only in the infancy in our field, the pathway to discovery is clear. One can only imagine the incredible progress that will be made in he next decade" (2010, p. 734).

Commenting on the outrageous yet unsubstantiated claims of behavioral geneticists, Jonathan Latham and Allison Wilson wrote, "The dearth of disease-causing genes is without question a scientific discovery of tremendous significance" (Joseph, 2015, p. 212).

Researcher Turkheimer commented, "It was widely thought that the Human Genome Project would deliver the vindication of behavioral quantitative genetics... Everyone assumed that once the human genome was sequenced the 'genes for' the phenomena that had been demonstrated to be heritable would be just around the corner, but it hasn't happened" (2011, p. 231). Plomin and his associates fell back on the problems of "missing heritability" for molecular biologists, and blamed and explained the lack of results on the "missing non-shared environment" (Plomin, 2011, p. 585).

A publication by the American Psychiatric Association began to show a weakening of faith, "In the future, we hope to be able to identify disorders using biological and genetic markers... Yet this promise, which we have anticipated since the 1970s, remains disappointingly distant. We've been telling patients for several decades that we are waiting for biomarkers. We're still waiting" (Joseph, 2015, p. 209).

Along with two colleagues, Maciej Trzaskowski and Philip S. Dale, Plomin acknowledged a lack of evidence for genetic causes of behavior in a paper written for a developmental psychology publication. They wrote, "Childhood behavior problems have become the target of genome-wide association (GWA) studies that attempt to identify the genes responsible for their heritability. As in other life sciences, these GWA expeditions have come up largely empty-handed" (2013, p. 1048). His comment seems to discretely point to adoption studies as misleading or as another branch of science that has also failed to produce similarly projected results. Ironically, Plomin wrote those words the same year he wrote for another journal that the potential for discovering the influences of genes on behavior is exciting (Trzaskowski, Dale & Plomin, 2013).

Joseph wrote, "The numerous assumptions, decisions, predictions, and claims by Plomin and leading behavioral genetic and psychiatric genetic researchers have been put to the ultimate test under the microscope of molecular genetic research—and the results are now in" (2015, p. 234). Cheerleader and trailblazer Robert Plomin finally gave up his post, writing, "The truth is that next to nothing is determined by genes and our environments are hugely powerful" (Asbury & Plomin, 2013, p. 96).

NOT ONE GENE HAS BEEN ISOLATED FOR BEHAVIOR

No gene has ever been isolated that can be said to cause human behavior or personality; researchers work by "phenotypes." To be fair, it is possibly not necessary to isolate a gene to show evidence for a genetic predisposition. Some scientists claim isolating a gene may be impossible, while it is still possible to prove such a gene exists by phenotype; that is, by observing its manifestations (*i.e.,* blue eyes, red hair) from generation to generation. This is something that has only been successful with the physical body, not the personality.

Joseph wrote, "15-20 years of molecular genetic studies of childhood and adolescent psychiatric disorders have produced an important finding: The imperative that the scientific community reexamine genetic interpretations of the twin (and adoption) studies that compelled researchers to look for genes in the first place" (2015, p. 200)... "The historical crimes committed by the 'racist hygienist' founders of psychiatric genetics such as Ernst Rudin in Nazi Germany have been documented at length... The massively flawed research produced by this field has also been documented... This leads to the following question: Has the field of psychiatric genetics contributed anything positive to the human condition in its roughly 100 years of existence?" (p. 201). "Ironically," says Joseph, "The only positive contribution that the field of psychiatric genetics has ever made to the human condition is its finding that genes for major psychiatric disorders do not appear to exist" (2015, p. 202). Reiterating, "Researchers rarely give serious consideration to the possibility that years of negative gene-finding results indicate that genes for behavioral differences and psychiatric disorders do not exist" (2015, p. 214).

Critical behavioral genetic researcher Douglas Wahlsten (2012, p. 475) declared, "In human behavior genetics...powerful new methods have failed to reveal even one bona fide, replicable gene effect pertinent to the normal range of variation in intelligence and personality." After conceding that environment is nearly everything (Wahlsten, 2012); after offering critical feedback to the behavioral scientists who produced the misleading twin and adoption studies (Joseph, 2014); after criticizing the revisionism of terminology by epigeneticists to misrepresent genetics (Keller, 2000; Dupre, 2004); molecular geneticists have apparently been persuaded to rebound. There are two new tracks available to them to come on board. One is to join the epigeneticists, and the other is a fragile new shell game of an argument (Plomin, 2014).

The newest argument to promote genetic explanations for behavior is there is no single gene to create schizophrenia or any other malady. Instead, they say, it is the combination of *statistically insignificant* genes that—even though their impact was proven irrelevant by research—when combined together, are now said to create *predispositions* to psychopathology. The reason it works is because significance, proof and replicability no longer seem to be relevant in the genetic research field.

But just to entertain the theory, let's do the math. Say each "insignificant gene" necessary to create schizophrenia occurs 5%, or 1/20 of the time, and say schizophrenia is caused by the combination of four of those insignificant genes. Illustrating the math, $1/20 \times 1/20 \times 1/20 \times 1/20 = 0.00000625$, or 0.000625%. The more insignificant genes it takes to combine to create a phenomenon, the more rare is the phenomenon. Let's say schizophrenia affects only 1% of the population, but the genetic combination to create schizophrenia manifests 0.000625% of the time. Mathematically, that would mean 0.999375% of schizophrenics are created by environment.

Some may argue it's not a *particular* combination, but there are many permutations that can create schizophrenia. The problem with that argument is it has no predictive value. It is more meaningful to say four insignificant genes can combine .000625 percent of the time to create schizophrenia than to say there are many random and unknown combinations that can combine often enough to create schizophrenia.

♦ ♦ ♦ ♦ ♦

To this point in the text, there have been two major bodies of scientists trying to prove genes create behavior: The Adoption Researchers looked for common phenotypes (similarities in the families), for which the results had to be generously doctored in order for them to claim success. Molecular Geneticists have been looking for genotypes, attempting to isolate the gene(s) responsible for behavior, with zero sucess to-date. A third body of scientists has begun looking to prove some combination between inborn genetic instruction and environment, whether via the 50/50 Genetic Assumption, or via Epigenetics. After so many adoption studies promised genes were behind behavior, the molecular biologists determined there was gold in "them thar hills." When that didn't pan out, epigeneticists took their turn at selling fools' gold.

6: THE 50/50 GENETIC ASSUMPTION

When I taught Developmental Psychology at California State University, Northridge (CSUN), I took a poll on the first day of class for two semesters (Snyder, 2006, 2007). I asked my new students the percentage of behavior they attributed to genes vs. environment—most specifically, parenting. I also rephrased it by asking them what percentage of a serial killer's crimes they would ascribe to genetic instruction. I only offered two blanks for them to enter splits totaling 100%. Out of 107 students, 104 entered 50% in the blank for genetics and 50% in the blank for environment.

Now what do we do with that? What are the ramifications of this perspective that 50% of behavior is caused by genes and 50% by parenting? This increasingly popular view seems more oriented toward political correctness and bet-hedging than factual accuracy, as it grants both geneticists and childhood advocates equal legitimacy. In effect it minimizes the responsibility of those in our field to determine what is factually true. Even though we can prove that given childhood experiences produce given behaviors while no genes have been found to produce any specific behaviors, society continues to believe behavior is genetic. Imagine how this belief informs us in a therapy office or in the home.

How would we discern which percentage of the evaluated behavior comes from genes and which percentage is a product of environment? This consideration has made forensic evaluations completely up for grabs with loosely constructed forensic interpretations. With this perspective, an observer cannot say anything about the causes of behavior. They will look for childhood causes tentatively, if at all. This is the current standard, and it's what the profession expects for a therapist to be considered legitimate. You have to think this way to pass a licensing exam. Cognitive behavioral therapy—which avoids looking at childhood causes—and pharmaceutical interventions are at the top of the list of best practices.

It was only a little more than a decade ago that most genetic researchers believed nearly all mental illness was attributable to genes. Most biogeneticists believe today that no genetic instruction will be activated without environmental influences. More and more geneticists reframe their position, simply saying genes predispose behavior, but environment still triggers genetic instruction (Plomin, 1990). The 50/50 Genetic Assumption holds that even though we can't prove genetics and haven't found any genes causing behavior, we know certain environments will trigger those genes we haven't found.

The illiterate of the 21st century will not be those who cannot read and write, but those who cannot learn, unlearn and relearn. —Alvin Toffler

As we have seen, the nature/nurture debate preceded the debate spawned by twin research studies and other studies of relatives, but the adoption studies led to the imperative of the HGP to find the genetic structures of human beings. The nature/nurture debate brought out comments by other scientists, updating The War of the Researchers. Many researchers fought this war as if they were protecting parents, and a few even admitted they were.

Yet as the search for genetic explanations for behavior dwindled, the motives for legitimately positive results have remained. From the ground up, parents have continued their need to believe in genetic explanations for behavior, and the pharmaceutical industry continues to need ever-growing profits from psychotropic drugs. Public relations continue to generate "public education" and pay scientists who can generate a headline, if not a new strategy, while veteran behavioral geneticists have begun to recant.

If one says something definitive about the causes of behavior based on childhood experiences, they are often accused of overstating their case, bias, ignorance, or "parent-bashing." Spending time reviewing childhood experiences to understand the genesis of a depression or anxiety disorder is often considered frivolous by health maintenance organizations (HMOs). More and more we are expected to refer out to a psychiatrist or a pediatrician for medications that would harness behavior immediately, as the history of psychiatry is to treat the symptoms more than the cause. This works well socially because most of us are loathe to "blame" anyone's parents, especially our own. Unfortunately, while their family, friends, teachers and employers become relieved, the patient is sacrificed to a chemical lobotomy, an effective term coined by Peter Breggin (1991).

When someone avoids facts to spare "blaming parents," they have developed internal blind spots around their own experiences, and anxiety about an authentic representation of themselves. These blind spots lead to unconscious bias and difficulty seeing clearly. It's something that happens even in researchers. This is particularly significant when that person is a therapist or a parent, in charge of someone else's behavior and quality of life.

Even so, there are variations on the 50/50 Genetic Assumption. The Department of Psychology at CSUN was a strong advocate of the Diathesis-Stress Model when I taught there. **The Diathesis-Stress Model theoretically maintains that the more symptomatic a person presents, the more evidence exists that their genes are fragile**. That is to say the most symptomatic child or adult is not the recipient of the worst abuse and neglect, but rather has fragile genes that render them more *susceptible* to abuse and neglect. Likewise, this model would suggest the more resilient a person is, the more evidence exists not that they had great parenting, but that their genes are strong. This is a way of camouflaging information right in front of us. We are likely to dismiss symptoms of child abuse, or overlook the products of excellent parenting.

We appear to have formulated an assumption that has no bell curve for parenting. Extremely bad parenting and extremely good parenting do not seem to be acknowledged. Most if not all parents are doing their best we suppose, but there are very bad parents and very good parents, and it's usually due to their own childhoods that their parenting is bad or good. It's a shame because we have so much more control over our children's destiny than we acknowledge. We learn little under this shroud. With clarity, we would understand the best and worst of us are the results of parenting. Parenting makes all the difference.

The perceived virtue of the 50/50 Genetic Assumption is that it is open-minded and reasonable but it ends up being a kind of paralysis. It allows our thought processes to remain vague and uncritical, potentially blinding us to the clues that a child needs help.

We look at a child with symptoms of neglect or abuse, and we modify the degree of her suffering in our own mind because we believe parents couldn't be *that* bad, and children are resilient and don't notice or remember their devaluing experiences. So we don't respond because "it's probably genetic." There are children walking around in schools who are quirky, odd, withdrawn, bullying, fake, secretive, failing, sullen, depressed, anxious or otherwise displaying abnormal symptoms, and they pass our scrutiny because we prefer to think they have fragile genes or their behaviors are at least in part, inherited.

I am proposing that insecure attachment and other factors create unstable temperaments, personality issues, depression, anxiety and behavioral problems. These issues are often responded to as if the subject's affect were a phenotype. We often think 50% is the constitution of the person, but constitution comes from security of attachment. This paradigm never fails me. When I see a client look uncomfortable within himself and with others, I start wondering about his life and experiences. Those who think in terms of fragile gene theory look at the same discomfort and think of it as a genetic predisposition. Any reminder that babies were evolved to need their mothers now seems like a political trick against women, a concept I too once believed. I am quite accustomed to recognizing issues and asking the right open-ended questions. I am often credited with being psychic or highly perceptive when it is simply my ever-so-useful cognitive model: follow the clues.

People get angry and defensive over this issue. To challenge genes and infer environmental cause or parenting from how someone appears or acts is blasphemy to many. Immediately, it's as if we are blaming parents instead of genes, rather than seeking to understand and recognize important formative events. It's as if we are saying there is no God. The parallel is reasonable since both require faith, and those we trust to lead us treat the unknown or unknowable as fact. Unfortunately, the 50/50 Genetic Assumption is effectively just as blinding as the 100% genetic model.

THE CASPI STUDY

In 2002 Avshalom Caspi with his associates published a highly cited study, "Role of Genotype in the Cycle of Violence in Maltreated Children," that is typical of how most behavioral genetic research is presented. I have elected to autopsy the Caspi study in order to show the reader the maneuvers found in most similar studies. The study supports the 50/50 Genetic Assumption, touting that a specific gene interacts with a person's childhood to cause a given personality. I'll review applicable parts of the study and analyze its flaws in outcome, specifically how it does not actually prove any genetic explanation of behavior. [For ease in reference, from this point forward, "Caspi" includes all contributors to the study: Caspi, A.; McClay, J.; Moffitt, T. E.; Mill, J.; Martin, J.; Craig, I. W.; Taylor, A., Poulton, R.]

Caspi's data was pulled from another body of research, the Dunedin Study, which sampled 1,037 children born in the same hospital in Dunedin, New Zealand, in 1972 and 1973. Caspi undertook to measure levels of Monoamine oxidase A in the 1,037 study members, assessed at ages 3, 5, 7, 9, 11, 13, 18, 21, and 26, representative of the general population. Note these children were first interviewed at age three. The issues of secure or insecure attachment were never addressed. Caspi evaluated the data and made his own interpretation, which in addition to the 50/50 Genetic Assumption, also presumes and supports the Diathesis-Stress Model, and seems to be considered by otherwise reputable clinicians as scientific evidence that genes affect behavior.

Caspi opens strong:

> Childhood maltreatment is a universal risk factor for antisocial behavior. Boys who experience abuse—and, more generally, those exposed to erratic, coercive, and punitive parenting—are at risk of developing conduct disorder, antisocial personality symptoms, and of becoming violent offenders. The earlier children experience maltreatment, the more likely they are to develop these problems. But there are large differences between children in their response to maltreatment. Although maltreatment increases the risk of later criminality by about 50%, most maltreated children do not become delinquents or adult criminals (p. 851).

And then he continues into the abyss with nothing but an unproven theory. [All **bolded** items are my emphasis unless otherwise noted, representing key points for the reader.] "The reason for this variability in response is **largely unknown**, but **it may be** that vulnerability to adversities is **conditional**, depending on genetic susceptibility factors" (Caspi, 2002, p. 851).

The reason some abused children do not become criminals is not "largely unknown." It is *well*-researched and *well*-known. Babies who are insecurely attached are at far greater risk when harmed than securely attached children who are resilient (Bowlby, 1980). One can speculate vulnerabilities born of genetic predispositions, or of one's experience as an infant. The former is pro-parent, Tulip Theory. The latter is pro-child, Causal Theory. Our little baby blobs have all sorts of formative experiences happening while we are thinking—incorrectly—that nothing is going on in there until he or she can talk.

The Caspi subjects were measured four ways that were mutually confirming: personality checklists, clinical diagnoses, criminal records, and at age 26, a questionnaire answered by someone "who knows you well." The subjects were also tested for MAOA levels, although it is not known if that was just at age 26 or beginning at age three. Each subject was assigned a score for how much child abuse they suffered, although it is not known what measure was used to assess child abuse, since it is often a sworn secret.

Monoamine oxidase A (MAOA) is an enzyme created under genetic instruction of the MAOA gene, aka the "warrior gene," located on the short arm of the X chromosome. The enzyme functions as a neurotransmitter that facilitates a calming response to stress or abuse. There have been two diverse correlations between levels of MAOA and the impact of child abuse. High levels of MAOA tend to reduce violent responses to provocation, and low levels of MAOA tend to support violent responses to provocation. The general inference from this correlation is when the levels are low, child abuse hits deeper and leads to criminal behavior; when the levels are high, child abuse is not as detrimental and does not lead to criminal behavior even half as often (Caspi, 2002). The real question is: which comes first, the levels or the abuse?

Caspi represents:

> Based on the hypothesis that MAOA genotype **[the inherited map it carries within its genetic code]** can moderate the influence of childhood maltreatment on neural systems implicated in antisocial behavior, we tested whether antisocial behavior would be predicted by an interaction between a gene (MAOA) and an environment (maltreatment)" (p. 852).

The question arises again why some abused adults have high levels of MAOA and do not become as symptomatic, while others have low levels of MAOA and become diagnosable for behavioral issues. The rule-out or probable answer is it is far more likely those with low levels suffered more unidentified trauma, including attachment trauma, than the others. As we have said before, there are other causal factors, including how old the child was when the abuse took place, as well as how chronic and/or severe it was, followed by how open the child was allowed to be about his or her experience.

This study repeats the same presumptions throughout, so my bolded commentary may seem redundant. I have considered whether or not to avoid redundancy for the reader's sake, but have concluded it would cheat the reader out of the recurring logic and an academic experience of reiteration and reinforcement of revised logic and critical thinking.

Habituation

According to Caspi, levels of MAOA affect how poorly or well the subject will react to chronic abuse over time. It is my contention the MAOA levels result from previous trauma, especially attachment trauma, and are the result of experiences, not the cause or evidence of genetic predispositions.

Caspi continues on his path however, speculating that high MAOA levels lead to habituation (learned tolerance)—considered a good thing—and lower levels lead to hyperreactivity:

> Maltreatment has lasting neurochemical correlates in human children, and although **no study has ascertained whether MAOA plays a role**, it exerts an effect on all aforementioned neurotransmitter systems. Deficient MAOA activity may dispose the organism toward neural **hyperreactivity to threat**. As evidence, phenelzine injections, which inhibit the action of monoamine oxidase, prevented rats from habituating to chronic stress. Low MAOA activity may be particularly problematic early in life **[indicating early life stressors vs. inherited low levels of MAOA?]** because there is insufficient MAOB (a homolog of MAOA with broad specificity to neurotransmitter amines) to compensate for an MAOA deficiency. Based on the **hypothesis** that MAOA **genotype** can moderate the **influence** of childhood maltreatment on neural systems implicated in antisocial behavior, we tested whether antisocial behavior would be predicted by an interaction between a gene (MAOA) and an environment (maltreatment) **[rather than predicting that insecure attachment followed by childhood maltreatment would be predictive of antisocial behavior]** (2002, p. 851).

MAOA levels do respond to stressors. Stressors take place first and then MAOA levels drop, not vice versa. Paranoia or anticipation of a recurrence of trauma may raise MAOA levels or lower them. The nature of PTSD causes an ongoing anticipation, fear or anxiety that another assault is imminent. Sometimes this anxiety is valid, and other times it is simply conditioned, thus the levels probably remain low after attachment trauma until therapy is sought.

There are multiple reasons early childhood stress and trauma cause levels of chemical adaptation to become lasting. If the stress or trauma is not resolved—acknowledged, revealed and expressed—the body forms a defense against future similar experiences, anticipating them in a form of expectation or paranoia. Subjects may adopt a hair trigger.

According to Harvard Professor of clinical psychiatry Judith Herman (2013, p. 61):

> Stress initiates adaptive processes that allow the organism to physiologically cope with prolonged or intermittent exposure to real or perceived threats. A major component of this response is repeated activation of glucocorticoid secretion by the hypothalamo-pituitary-

adrenocortical (HPA) axis, which promotes redistribution of energy in a wide range of organ systems, including the brain. Prolonged or cumulative increases in glucocorticoid secretion can reduce benefits afforded by enhanced stress reactivity and eventually become maladaptive. The long-term impact of stress is kept in check by the process of habituation, which reduces HPA axis responses upon repeated exposure to homotypic stressors and likely limits deleterious actions of prolonged glucocorticoid secretion. Habituation is regulated by limbic stress-regulatory sites, and is at least in part glucocorticoid feedback-dependent. Chronic stress also sensitizes reactivity to new stimuli. While sensitization may be important in maintaining response flexibility in response to new threats, it may also add to the cumulative impact of glucocorticoids on the brain and body. Finally, unpredictable or severe stress exposure may cause long-term and lasting dysregulation of the HPA axis, likely due to altered limbic control of stress effector pathways. Stress-related disorders, such as depression and PTSD, are accompanied by glucocorticoid imbalances and structural/functional alterations in limbic circuits that resemble those seen following chronic stress, suggesting inappropriate processing of stressful information may be part of the pathological process.

It's questionable whether habituation is a good or bad thing, unless it indicates the subject is more securely attached, or that the public will be safer. Some subjects have habituated to trauma when it is chronic, like daycare at an early age. Habituation does not necessarily indicate a predisposition, nor does it indicate a healthy response because those who habituate tend to develop more medical issues, as demonstrated profoundly by the mega-research project at Kaiser: The Adverse Childhood Experiences, or ACE, Study (Felitti et al., 1998). Of course, as a society, we'd prefer the victim of child abuse to habituate to the abuse so we don't suffer the consequences of their neglect and abuse. It appears to an educated observer that scientists who cannot recognize the role of experience and trauma as cause for behaviors, have habituated themselves.

MAOA reduces reactivity to stress. Subjects who experience acute stress and recover are not as likely to develop criminal responses to stress, whereas subjects who suffer chronic stress and habituate to stress also may not develop criminal behaviors. Scientists apparently consider habituation to stress desirable. The focus seems to be on adaptation to stressors rather than prevention or removing the stressors. Ultimately, the solution of researchers is chemical injections. Unfortunately, the more a person learns to live with stress, the more they are at risk for other illnesses. For example, a child who is *insecurely attached* and molested is more likely to become a sexual predator than a child who is *securely attached* and molested. The securely attached child will not become a violent personality, no matter how much abuse he or she experiences. The securely attached child will have empathy, no matter how badly treated as an older child, while the unattached child will not have empathy, and will be prone to manipulation and scapegoating others. And so forth.

Caspi explains, "The MAOA gene...encodes the MAOA enzyme, which metabolizes catecholamine neurotransmitters, such as norepinephrine, epinephrine, serotonin and dopamine, rendering them inactive" (2002, p. 851). In other words, when MAOA is high, the alarming neurotransmitters are low—a good thing—and when MAOA levels are low and alarming transmitters are high, the body is defensively or aggressively responding to abuse. Is that as it should be? Scientists write as if **they assume a healthy individual will not respond aggressively to abuse**, although there are "lasting neurochemical correlates" (Caspi, 2002, p. 851). I predict these observations by scientists are oriented toward generating a pharmaceutical solution rather than an educational one wherein parents learn how to better treat their children, or a therapeutic solution wherein clinicians facilitate clients in processing original injuries.

These durable levels are thought to be inborn because some subjects habituate to abuse or do not develop low levels of MAOA and criminal behavior. **Is a failure to become non-symptomatic from abuse ever evidence of healthier genes? Is there another explanation?**

Lissek and Grillon, PTSD learning experts, address the issue of habituation:

> Evidence for a variety of PTSD-related abnormalities in basic learning processes have been found, the most promising of which include slowed habituation **[failure to adapt to abuse]**, heightened sensitization **[reactivity to abuse and symbols of abuse]**, failure to retain extinction learning **[failure to heal from behavioral therapy]**, overgeneralization of conditioned fear **[PTSD]**, heightened contextual anxiety **[paranoia or fearful anticipation of more assaults]**, and deficits inhibiting fear to safety cues **[an ironic failure to recognize warning signs]** (Beck & Sloan, 2012, p. 187).

The authors also represent that habituation is considered a healthy response and reactivity is unhealthy. As such, they have begun to look at habituation as evidence of resilience and good genes, while reactivity is evidence of fragile genes. Perhaps habituation is evidence of chronic trauma, as some scientists suggest, or stronger attachment, as other scientists suggest. Further, it is difficult to discern from overall research whether scientists have concluded that habituation is considered a good or bad thing, or a normal or abnormal response.

Poor Resiliency

Early in the Caspi study we are persuaded the cause *and* the solution of criminal behaviors are largely chemical. The authors go on to say, "**Circumstantial evidence** suggests the **hypothesis** that childhood **maltreatment predisposes** most strongly to adult violence among children whose **MAO is insufficient** to constrain maltreatment-induced changes to neurotransmitter systems" (Caspi, 2002, p. 851). Translation: Although we have no direct evidence, we infer maltreatment may result in violence when MAOA is insufficient, and when MAOA is sufficient, maltreatment probably will not result in violence. Therefore, a rise in MAOA reduces aggression, something medication could do as well.

As I have previously discussed, the most fundamental ingredient in resilience is a secure attachment. Nevertheless, geneticists seem to be searching for the unholy grail, turning over every rock within their wheelhouse, but never venturing outside to see what is known by other researchers—especially trauma and attachment scientists—about environmental or parenting sources of resilience. This is because they are searching for a genetic explanation for behavior. Period.

A number of pro-child researchers report children in daycare have high levels of cortisol and the younger the child enters daycare, the higher the cortisol levels (Belsky, 1986) and lower levels of MAO activity result from emotional deprivation and/or assaultive experiences. Defensive activity is often aggressive, as we have all learned about the fight or flight response. After enough assaults, a child will become self-destructive or aggressive, regularly and naturally.

A *pro-parent* way to look at it, similar to the fragile gene theory, is when MAO is low, whether or not trauma has taken place, the child (young or grown) needs medication to boost adaptability. A *pro-child* way of looking at this phenomenon suggests that when MAO is low, attachment was insecure so the child would not be resilient to trauma that may also be taking place. The patient should be treated for trauma, and parents of young children with propensities for violence should take parenting classes to learn what they never learned at home when they were young.

Stress

According to pro-child theory and science, when MAO levels have dropped, it indicates one has insufficient attachment, experienced continuous aggression and/or stress, and/or has developed PTSD in anticipation of ongoing repeated experiences, however realistic. The scientists infer children who are abused and don't calmly respond lack MAO according to genetic instruction. A minor correction in the Caspi study follows, "[A]lthough no study has ascertained whether MAOA plays a role, it exerts an effect on all aforementioned neurotransmitter systems. Deficient MAOA activity may dispose the organism toward neural hyperactivity to threat" (Caspi, 2002, p. 851). In other words, **without sufficient MAOA, a subject may react or overreact to threat**. Actually, the way it works is the child, who cannot fight or flee will freeze, repressing their reaction until they can't anymore. One wonders if at any point in their research the pro-parent scientists wonder even for a second if they are discounting abuse. How do we avoid seeing what is in front of us to see, unless we do it willfully?

Scientists concluded, "Maltreatment groups did not differ on MAOA activity, suggesting that genotype did not influence exposure to maltreatment" (Caspi, 2002, p. 852). **This is a definitive statement lost in the text that discounts genetic influences.** Nevertheless, it's a remarkable concept to have ever been considered. To put it another way, the scientists are saying children predisposed to react to abuse violently did not appear to foster their own abuse or "influence exposure to maltreatment." While one would like to think we don't blame children for their own abuse, and while this statement clarifies the children did not cause their own abuse, the very suggestion they didn't cause it is remarkable. Who needs such clarification? The underlying implication is the child is inherently the cause of his/her own abuse, as well as his/her behavior.

It is also interesting that scientists represent extreme responses of reactivity are pathological, even when causal experiences were unusually young or severely and/or chronically abusive. The assumption is no matter how badly we are treated we need to respond appropriately. Extreme responses are not thought to be indicative of suffering and a need for rescue, but of fragile genes.

Nevertheless, pro-parent, genetic scientists seem to prefer habituation to stress as a healthy response, and they are looking for chemicals that can allow a person to habituate to stress, rather than react to it. In other words, rather than spend funds to study ways to avoid stressors, to educate and to prevent child abuse, scientists are looking for medications so subjects can better adapt to their environment without becoming symptomatic. I find this endeavor to be harmful to children.

It seems rather remarkable some scientists focus on the impact events have on body chemistry, while other scientists focus on how body chemistry impacts experiences.

RESEARCH FLAWS OF THE 50/50 GENETIC ASSUMPTION, WITH CASPI AS EXAMPLE

Lack of Rule-Outs

Genetic scientists typically fail to rule out other explanations for their findings. It's as if pro-parent researchers do not read any pro-child research. It's as if they think they are inventing the wheel, reporting their own discoveries with enthusiasm or intended meaning, infusing environmental explanations into their own work, as if they prove genetics. Behavioral geneticists seem so naïve.

Scientists need to rule out confounding effects of trauma before proposing cause, or even before formulating the research design. Some trauma is chronic. Some trauma is acute. Some trauma becomes habituated and some trauma leads to PTSD, and cannot be metabolized. These complicating factors evidently have not yet been worked out by neurobiologists.

The most important or dramatic finding was that those who had higher levels of MAOA generally committed fewer crimes. Those who were abused but had lower levels of MAOA were more than twice as prone to criminal activity (Caspi, 2002*)*. To reiterate, these scientists inferred the MAOA levels were a cause rather than an effect, and higher levels of MAOA activity mitigated abuse, while lower levels made the subject more susceptible, supporting the fragile gene theory. Abuse + high MAOA = less crime. Abuse + low MAOA = more crime. Again, which came first, the levels of MAOA, or the impact of the quality (attunement) and continuity (consistency) of attachment?

The evidence presented to "prove" genetic instruction is once again tied to symptoms that could be caused by environment. Which environmental factors that exacerbate or mitigate stress should be ruled out before drawing genetic conclusions?

Rule out insecure attachment. The main problem with pro-parent or biogenetic behavioral science is that these scientists are uninformed about the pro-child research in attachment and trauma. Neglect in the first years of life produces chemical activity in children that may continue in anticipation of more such events and may set up a sort of posttraumatic stress predictor since children who suffered early attachment trauma are more susceptible to future trauma even into adulthood (van der Kolk, McFarlane & Weisaeth, 1996).

The subjects followed by Caspi from ages 3 to 11 had already formed secure or insecure attachments, which caused resilience—or lack thereof—creating a strong core or a fragile core. There was no information offered as to the security of attachment for these subjects in the first three years. This was a major hole in the study, and there should have been differentiations and comparisons between children with secure vs. insecure attachments. Subjects with high levels of MAOA might predictably have had more secure attachments and suffered less trauma in their earliest years, and subjects with low levels of MAOA might predictably have suffered failed attachments or abandonment trauma, and could have been more susceptible to other types of trauma as well (van der Kolk, McFarlane & Weisaeth, 1996).

Rule out repression ethics in the home. Researchers do not likely know what most clinicians hopefully know: the more aggressive a person is, the more likely they are expected to defend their parents and deny abuse. It is common for people who have been abused not to reveal their abuse. Further, the more protective a person is of abusive parents, the more likely they are to act out and scapegoat others.

The freedom to express one's feelings and thoughts about a trauma mitigates trauma and can even cause healing. Children who have the freedom of expression will be able to rebound, while children who are expected to continue honoring abusive or neglectful parents, will not be able to rebound from trauma. Further, a repressed child will be most inclined to scapegoat others, especially as he grows into adulthood and finds his own power. So, the correlation that some people were not abused but had lower levels of MAOA can be explained by repression, a factor that should have been ruled out before the study began. These conditions would show up as a form of underground living, secret keeping, shallow self-awareness, and protecting parents in particular and in general.

Rule out imprinted content via mirror neurons. No two abuses are the same. Some happen younger, some more frequently, and some are more severe. The more these combine together the worse it is for the child, especially when they cannot reveal their thoughts or express their feelings. All experiences at the hands of our parents are metabolized by mirror neurons as automatic responses later in life. In order to transcend these automatic responses, a person would have to become self-aware to the degree they can will themselves not to react, but to become vulnerable instead. That's a huge feat that turns out not to be hard once we achieve it. Usually it requires therapy.

Some children who are abused witness their parent drink away their pain and turn to alcoholism. Other children who are abused witness their parent apologize afterwards and discover self-reflection (raising MAOA). Some children who are abused learn to abuse lest they be further abused (lowering MAOA). Some children who are abused are allowed to cry and complain about their abuse (raising MAOA), while others would be punished for complaining (lowering MAOA).

Mirror neurons provide the simple explanation. While mirror neurons were discovered mapping activity specifically in the motor cortex (Ramachandran, 2000), it appears these special neurons may actually be found *throughout* the brain working in conjunction with other neurons, enabling us to identify with one another's actions and learn by modeling. Mirror neurons may be the most adaptive mechanism in life. We may imprint empathy, or not. We may imprint self-reflection, or not. We may imprint self-expression, or not. Mirror neurons probably work in conjunction with neurotransmitters. They may be found recording trauma in the amygdala, leaving us with a drive to hurt back. They may be found in the prefrontal cortex, enabling us to reason as we have seen reason modeled. And so forth.

Molecular biologists Hudziak and Faraone exemplify how geneticists fail to use rule-outs in their studies. They write, "We went on to discuss candidate gene studies that have helped us understand the role of the environment in a child's outcome" (2010, p. 731). Citing Sugden et al. (2010), they explain that some children when victimized by bullies who have "a particular genetic variant," as compared with children who don't have that variant, "were at greater risk to have emotional problems at age 12 years" (Hudziak & Faraone, 2010, p. 732). The solution seems to be to find the right pharmaceutical rather than produce efforts to decrease bullying.

Well-known researcher Jay Joseph asks:

> But didn't we already know, long before candidate genetic studies that bullying harmed children and that interventions aimed at reducing or preventing bullying would help alleviate the suffering of the victims and help prevent 'childhood psychopathology'? ... Simply put, we do not need molecular genetic research to teach us that bullying harms

children any more than we need it to demonstrate that the harmful psychological effects of other obvious environmental adversities... But focus on genes does serve as a diversion from noticing the harmful psychological effects of those and countless other adverse environmental conditions and events. It actually helps those harmful conditions to persist, which is the exact opposite result that Hudziak and Faraone claimed for molecular genetic research (2010, p. 199).

Revisions of Language

Caspi's languaging begins representing correlations as phenotypes early in the study and escalates to actual characterizations of MAOA levels as evidence of genotypes. The Caspi authors suggest reduced MAOA lead to criminal behavior, although "[A]ntisocial behavior is a complicated phenotype" (Caspi, 2002, p. 852) and thus, a genetic predisposition. They also write, "the **association** between maltreatment and antisocial behavior is conditional, depending upon the child's MAOA genotype," even though the study does not represent actual genes were identified. Further, "maltreated males (including probable and severe cases) with low-MAOA activity genotypes were more likely than non-maltreated males with this genotype to develop conduct disorders by a significant odds ratio" (Caspi, 2002, p. 852). **The languaging progresses from phenotypes to genotypes without any actual study of the subjects' genes.** "Maltreatment has lasting neurochemical correlates in human children" (Caspi, 2002, p. 852). Children do become conditioned by trauma, but it doesn't follow that this conditioning is genetically predetermined.

Apparent Research Motives

Growing the backward reasoning, the scientists hold, "Knowledge about environmental context might help gene-hunters refine their phenotypes" (Caspi, 2002, p. 854). In other words, scientists believe knowledge of the subjects' environments and experiences would help them define gene-driven personalities! I would have thought it makes more sense to say, "Knowledge of the environment will help scientists understand how pathology is created and to clarify the lack of genetic determinism." I cannot even force myself to make sense of the statement. The detour from logic continues, "[K]nowledge about specific genetic risks may help to clarify risk processes" (Caspi, 2002, p. 854). In other words, if we know which children are at risk genetically, we can what? We can protect them from abuse? No, they intend to protect those who have low MAO not from abuse, but by giving them drugs, perhaps even in advance of the abuse.

Scientists write, "[M]ales with low-MAOA activity genotype who were maltreated in childhood had significantly elevated antisocial scores relative to their own low-MAOA counterparts who were not maltreated" (Caspi, 2002, p. 853). Of course they did. If they were maltreated, they were stressed at least at critical and pervasive periods of their lives. "In contrast, males with high MAOA activity did not have elevated antisocial scores..." but scientists add, "even when they experienced child maltreatment" (Caspi, 2002, p. 853), implying the experiences of maltreatment of both groups were comparable.

Other questions needed to be raised and answered: When were the MAO levels taken? Were they taken on children the researchers knew were being abused? Were levels taken on adults sitting in prison with little to do but maintain their tough persona? Did any of them have therapy (to lower their MAO)? Which males did not have an elevated antisocial score when their MAO level was low? I would like to meet them to ask questions about their childhood. Then we might learn some *real* redeeming factors.

We have a clue. Scientists write, "[A] functional polymorphism in the MAOA gene moderates the impact of early childhood maltreatment on the development of antisocial behavior in males" (Caspi, 2002, p. 853). Who were the abused children who had low amounts of MAO and did not become abusive? I suggest they were probably securely attached in the early years; they may have had more permission to express their truth and feelings; their abuse probably took place predominantly after the age of four or five and it is was less frequent and less intense than those whose levels of MAO diminished as a result of the abuse.

The paper finishes with the sentence, "Both attributable risk and predictive sensitivity indicate these findings could inform the development of future pharmacological treatments" (Caspi, 2002, p. 853).

7: EPIGENETICS

If you can't explain it simply, you don't understand it well enough. —Einstein

Science writer Ethan Watters writes:

> We commonly accept the notion that through our DNA we are destined to have particular body shapes, personalities, and diseases. Some scholars even contend that the genetic code predetermines intelligence and is the root cause of many social ills, including poverty, crime, and violence. 'Gene as fate' has become conventional wisdom. Through the study of epigenetics, that notion at last may be proved outdated. Suddenly, for better or worse, we appear to have a measure of control over our genetic legacy (2006, para. 7).

A fresh concept has emerged to explain behavior in terms of inborn traits. Epigenetics alleges that environment tips pre-existing genetic instructions toward expression or toward over-riding genetic instruction. Apparently no one accepts that we never found any genes that created behavior in the first place. So how is it these never-found genes are *influenced by environment*, rather than *environment itself is the influence*? There continues to be a sort of convoluted effort to attribute genes to behavior, this time via "environmental triggers." Clearly, we still don't understand that all experiences create a fabric of personality, woven in and out of our histories, defining our view of the world and ourselves.

As biogeneticists have begun recanting and reframing their results to acknowledge there is more evidence environment causes behavior than they previously acknowledged, new researchers have ponied up to fill the void. The new researchers introduced epigenetics as a large re-frame, suggesting environment couldn't influence behavior if genes didn't have a plan for these events and further, events alter genetic instruction for future generations. Well, almost. They say genes themselves are not modified they say, but the instructions are intercepted or ushered along for a few generations to come. It was a face-saving and ideal *theoretical* model for genetic mental health research, even though it didn't seem necessary or accurate in the fields of physical medicine. Epigenetics remains an unproven theory, but it is being treated as fact, just as genetic theory is still treated as fact by many. Epigenetics applied to mental health, especially trauma, is the ticket to admitting environmental influence while crediting behavioral genes. It appears all the techniques of double-think have been preserved and refined.

Epigenetics used to mean dynamic or adaptive. Now it means inborn or preformed, but modifiable by environment, given the yet-to-be-discovered gene has a pre-existing planned response to any given experience. Without that convoluted genetic inborn response, they maintain or strongly imply there would be no such adaptation to the environment. **Epigenetic theory represents that genes have preformed multiple ways of expressing themselves for various environmental triggers. It implies environment throws a sort of proverbial genetic switch, a switch that theoretically pre-exists.** Thus there is a new way to credit genes for the influence of environment, still calling it nature.

Evidently, genes have to plan for the eventuality of things that never happened before. By inference, genes had to plan for the daycare phenomenon, even though evolution never had a role in preparing for daycare. Genes would supposedly have had to plan for the impact technology would have on hospitalized infants or on families that disperse. I don't think evolution works that way.

Epigeneticists claim to have modernized genetic theory by recognizing environment, without recognizing the other research that has been explaining behaviors according to environment for decades. Pioneering epigenetics researcher Randy Jirtle declared, "Before, genes predetermined outcomes. Now everything we do—everything we eat or smoke—can affect our gene expression and that of future generations. Epigenetics introduces the concept of free will into our idea of genetics" (Watters, 2006, para. 8). Still, there is no recognition of the researchers on the other side of the divide who have been explaining specific behaviors according to environment and parenting for decades.

A HISTORY OF EPIGENETICS

You may recall that Psychiatrist Irving Gottesman led and influenced other researchers to modify their research results upward? Well the revised concept of epigenetics was his idea. He appeared to fight the statistical decline of concordances of identical twins, first by inflating his data with proband analysis, then convincing other scientists to reassess their results by applying the proband method, and then by terming environmental influences as epigenetic influences. He reportedly introduced the term "epigenetics" in his book, *Schizophrenia: The Epigenetic Puzzle,* co-authored with James Shields (1984), ever searching for genetic explanations for behavior when traditional genetic studies of twins failed to produce the data he needed and further, consistently demonstrated the power of the environment.

The breakthrough in a new approach to an old problem came when a scientist strapped an icepack on the back of a brown rabbit, which caused the fur under the pack to turn white (or black or brown in other studies of different species) (Gilbert, 2005). Scientists understood this phenomenon was due to pre-existing genetic instructions. It was a rare type of condition, but they took the phenomenon and ran with it, inferring genetic instructions everywhere await changes in environmental conditions, especially in the area of mental health issues. It was quite a leap, but it solved everything, and just about everyone loved it.

In another study, scientists demonstrated changes in a pregnant mother's diet affect whether her grown child is susceptible to cancer (Gilbert, 2005). This effect was presented in the context of epigenetic research and was considered to be a modification of DNA [shocking and exciting], best explained by epigenetic theory. While we look for modifications in genetic structure to understand behavior, the rest of medical science is beginning to recognize the causal factors in environment without formulating an epigenetic explanation. The World Health Organization is on top of environmental influences:

> The cancer research arm of the World Health Organization (WHO) has determined the consumption of processed meats like hotdogs, ham, sausages and meat-based sauces causes colorectal cancer, while eating red meat like beef, pork and lamb is "probably carcinogenic to humans" (October 26, 2015).

In the old days we used to simply say, "You are what you eat."

Attachment Research Called Epigenetic Research

According to science writer Lizzie Buchen (2010), almost all the scientists citing epigenetics for explanations are behavioral scientists and pharmaceutical researchers. They are working for the pharmaceutical companies and seek results that support medications rather than depth therapy (which seeks original causes and catharsis to remedy them). As such they ignore the vast replicated research that precedes them.

Epigenetic pioneers, pharmacist Moshe Szyf and behavioral researcher Michael J. Meaney, found nurtured rats more resilient than non-nurtured rats, but theirs was not an attachment study. Both groups of rats were confined in an acrylic tube, creating states of high stress, then tested for chemical changes presumed to affect their DNA. The rats that had been more nurtured by their mothers recovered quickly, while the ones who had poor mothering during infancy remained traumatized (Issa, 2008).

Frances Champagne of Columbia University introduced another study that was not represented as attachment research, although that's what it was. They evaluated the mating behavior of rats and discovered the female rats who experienced affection in the beginning of life were more discriminating about who they allowed to have sex with them, while the ones who lacked affection were less discriminating and even promiscuous (Kuchment, 2009).

The effects of mothering and lack of mothering were established by scientist Harry Harlow during the 1950s in his studies of baby monkeys. It was simply reported at the time that babies who were nurtured became nurturing mothers; unnurtured babies become aggressive. Learning theory and the discovery of mirror neurons better explains how the experience of being nurtured fortifies the grown child to nurture.

Scientists failed to acknowledge previous research demonstrating victims of early attachment trauma are less resilient to later traumatic events. Until recently, scientists have been calling lack of resilience a genetic personality trait, as indicated in the Caspi study we reviewed in previous pages, while other scientists have proven in many replications that early attachment trauma changes personality and diminishes resilience (van der Kolk, 1994b; Issa, 2008; Kuchment, 2009). In other words, the above research proves environment, not epigenetics.

What plausible epigenetic instructions would there be for the human body or psyche? Biogeneticists are suggesting the vitamins women take during their pregnancy affect DNA with epigenetic instructions. One researcher writes some vitamins may be wrong or too much for pregnant women (Watters, 2006). This argument about using supplements seems to serve multiple purposes: (1) the competitive goal of the pharmaceutical industry to discredit natural cures; (2) to suggest epigenetics can apply to humans too; and (3) to demonstrate clearly what epigeneticists mean to address in environment are chemical modifications. Of course we are absent a discussion of allergies and dosage, one that could apply to foods as well, or that we have known for centuries the quantity and quality of what we ingest affects our health.

The bottom line is that reframing environmental influences in genetic terms leads to pharmaceutical interventions. Funding for epigenetics is ample, as behavioral geneticists have renewed high hopes of breaking the code for bad mothering and providing the pharmaceutical antidote.

Excitement in the Air, Again

Szyf claimed from his lab at McGill University in Montreal, "People used to think that once your epigenetic code was laid down in early development, that was it for life..." (Watters, 2006, para. 11). Which people used to think this? They did also think the genetic code was from conception, for life? This appears to be a deliberate attempt to conflate the two. There is no epigenetic code. There are genetic codes, but there is no epigenetic code.

"...But life is changing all the time," says Szyf, "and the epigenetic code that controls your DNA is turning out to be the mechanism through which we change along with it" (Watters, 2006, para. 11). Thus, according to Szyf, an epigenetic code *controls* DNA. What a stretch! This is a complete reframe. There is no epigenetic code and DNA does not control behavior. This is purely a theoretical construct that will not pan out, but is constructed to support further medical interventions for emotional suffering.

Emotional and physical nurturance simply keep the body well or not so well. The correct representation would be that once genes have designed the body, environment—which is "changing all the time" and different for everyone—determines behavior. Szyf, speaking like a consummate politician, continues, "Epigenetics tells us that little things in life can have an effect of great magnitude" (Watters, 2006, para. 11), when the truth is that *environment* tells us little things in life can have an effect of great magnitude.

The Way It Works This Time

Epigeneticists claim environment can alter the expression of yet-to-be-discovered genes. They assert "DNA instructions" can be modified or switched off by exposure to certain chemicals. Champagne explains that life experiences alter the DNA *expression,* although not necessarily its sequence. Rather, the "chemicals that decorate it and how tightly it winds and packs" surround "proteins inside the cell" making genetic instructions "easier or more difficult for the cell's protein-making machinery to read" (Buchen, 2010, p. 146).

These altered expressions are believed to result from "the attachment of methyl groups to specific nucleotides in DNA, which can completely silence the expression of nearby genes" (Buchen, 2010, p. 146), although to reiterate again, there is no evidence of any gene expressing itself such that it instructs behavior. Since all substances in reality are chemicals and everything we experience or ingest is either life-sustaining or toxic, that almost makes sense. All we have to do is reverse it so what was cause is effect and then it makes sense: Bad treatment or bad air, food or water will modify the chemicals in our body such that our brain will respond with emotions and selected behaviors.

Scientists began to refer to such changes as epigenetic modifications or **methylation**. Methylation becomes the key unifying concept for whether or not a person takes vitamins, eats well, or is traumatized in early life. The chemical changes in blood samples (cortisol, adrenaline, MAO levels, *etc.*) become characterized as epigenetic factors *causing* differences in behavior. In this way, experiences become reframed such that pharmaceutical interventions seem logical.

According to Buchen, Champagne proposes her neglected rats *"might* have less methylation near the oestrogen receptor gene. And such differences occur specifically in regions of the hypothalamus known to be involved in sexual behavior. Less methylation (nurture) leads to increased expression of the oestrogen receptor throughout life… making the adult daughters more responsive [histrionic] to the hormone's influence when sizing up suitors" (Buchen, 2010, p. 146). Translating this into pro-child attachment language, nurtured babies develop a capacity for intimacy and learn to feel secure, while deprived infants become desperate for attachment and fearful of abandonment.

Buchen calls the concept the new "middle ground in the centuries-old debate over nature vs. nurture. Yet without the new "middle ground," geneticists might have finally been conceding that behavior and personality are environmental, as no evidence was ever established for genetic programming. The "middle ground" is a variation on the 50/50 Genetic Assumption.

Buchen reports:

> Instead, epigenetic changes are represented to be the conduit through which environment elicits life-long biological change. Many behavioral scientists have latched onto the idea, searching for epigenetic explanations for a number of differences in behavior,

including homosexuality, intelligence and conditions such as autism, bipolar disorder and schizophrenia. Although experience has been connected to altered methylation for only a handful of genes, epigenetics has become one of the hottest areas of behavioral science... But it is also one of the most hotly contested (Buchen, 2010, p. 146).

Criticisms of Epigenetic Theory and Research

Needless to say, funding of epigenetic explanations for behavior is ample, as pharmaceutical sales efforts have renewed high hopes of breaking the code for bad mothering and providing the antidote. "This is a big public health issue," says Champagne (Kuchment, 2009, p. 5), yet these scientists seek funding for chemical antidotes instead of parenting classes that teach pregnant women about attachment. However, Miller suggests, "There is very little evidence in humans that epigenetics connects early life experiences to behavioral or health problems later in life" (Miller, 2010, p. 27). Even so, I wonder if he knows there is a great deal of evidence that life experiences create behavior and health problems later in life (Felitti et al., 1998).

Buchen spoke with Columbia University geneticist Timothy Bestor, who told her behavioral epigenetics "is a field that has a lot of deep problems" (Buchen, 2010, p. 146). In paraphrasing his position, Buchen writes, "The evidence supporting it [epigenetics] is weak and grossly over-interpreted and the mechanisms by which it works remains unclear. To prove the field's worth to the hardcore molecular biologists, the behaviorists will have their work cut out for them" (Buchen, 2010, p. 146). Behavioral psychologist Gregory Miller admits, "I think there's been a lot of putting the cart before the horse...This work is still ongoing, so I think it would be premature to conclude anything definitively, but we've had less success than we'd hoped and imagined" (Miller, 2010, p. 24).

According to Buchen:

> Even if researchers can work out how methyl marks are removed from a gene, they have to show the mechanism by which a life experience such as maternal care would cause that change. [M.J.] Meaney has proposed that mother rats' licks increase levels of the neurotransmitter serotonin, and that this increase *could* [emphasis mine] result in methylation changes, but no experiments have provided evidence that would *explain how this link would work* [emphasis mine]... Meaney had found that the type of mothering a rat receives as a pup calibrates how its brain responds to stress throughout its life. Rats raised by less-nurturing mothers are more sensitive to stress when they grow up...
>
> Can this proposed phenomenon of methylation be considered a cause more than an effect? If a mother rat licks her pups she might create a chemical response in the brain similar to serotonin. Would we then study serotonin as a cause, rather than bonding? Champagne admits, "The question always becomes, how do you transduce a social

experience to the level of DNA methylation? Right now it's very speculative. We don't know. To really study that, you have to go back to a dish, ultimately (Buchen, 2010, p. 146).

According to cancer researcher Steve Cole at the University of California, Los Angeles (UCLA), who collaborated on the Proceedings of the National Academy of Sciences (PNAS) study, **there is too much emphasis on epigenetics being the link between environment and genes**. Cole told science journalist Greg Miller (no relation to previously quoted psychologist Gregory Miller), "The big-picture story is that clearly social interactions can regulate gene expression, but they do so in different ways in different tissue" (Miller, 2010, p. 27). According to Cole, epigenetics as a field, represents only one aspect of all the available mechanisms that alter gene activity. Numerous factors can bring about long-term changes in gene expression without help from DNA methylation or other epigenetic mechanisms. "Lots of people have spent lots of time and money and are now a little grumpy about this," Cole told Miller (Miller, 2010, p. 27). Miller reflects, "The main criticism of molecular biologists is that behavioral neuroscientists' data is highly correlative and the underlying mechanisms remain largely unknown" (Miller, 2010, p. 27).

Darlene Francis of University of California, Berkeley, one of Meaney's former students, also remains skeptical:

> Too many researchers are embarking on 'undirected' searches for epigenetic alterations in human populations without a solid rationale. What some people take away from the rodent work is that methylation is now the cause and solution to a lot of life's problems... I get frustrated with the over-extrapolation of the animal findings, and some of it is my work, so it's ironic (Miller, 2010, p. 27).

Epigenetics calls behaviors "gene expressions" since it's about which genes will be expressed at which times, despite there being trillions of unique permutations in the adventures of humankind. Epigenetics calls responses to environment or experiences "phenotypes." Actually, the definition of epigenetics varies from scientist to scientist. It claims methylation simultaneously represents environment and gene expression. "Environment" can be replaced by "methylation." Methylation can include pharmaceuticals. Methylation may someday claim to include a pharmaceutical that can replace "mother love."

Multiple adaptive instructions cannot possibly cover all permutations of experience. Such a phenomena would limit our adaptability. It makes so much more sense that our brain adapts to experiences, period. The new field implies if the behavior is there, the predisposition will also be there. If the behavior were not there, the genetic instructions for the behavior must not be there, whether or not there have been environmental influences. The assumption remains that the alleged—as yet unidentified—genetic instructions account for behaviors as well as physiology. Thus we are led or directed to presume whatever exists indicates there was a gene for it, as well as the designated environment. If it doesn't exist, but could have, then they infer it means the "methylation" overrode the genetic instructions. Thus, they reason, however much environment creates behavior, there will be no behavioral phenomenon without previous genetic instructions. To be clear, according to epigeneticists, the absence of a behavioral phenomenon does not mean there was no gene for the behavior; it may have just been turned off.

This begs the question: Would a clone of Jeffrey Dahmer, The Milwaukee Cannibal, have the same genetic instruction to become a cannibalizing serial killer even if loving, attentive, vegan parents raised him? Would we surmise Dahmer had a pre-existing drive to kill and eat flesh, or that all of us have a pre-existing drive to kill and eat flesh, given our childhood experiences? Forgetting there is no gene isolated or identified for any behavior, just what genetic instructions would science expect to be turned off and on? Are there enough experiential permutations to cover every conceivable experience? Or are we talking about universal instructions regarding basic needs like touch, affection, interaction, regard, understanding, validation, safety, *etc.*?

PREPARING TO STUDY A STUDY

The following review of the heralded Yehuda study gives us another chance to see the theory applied to research and its interpretation. Fortunately, by reviewing behavioral research in chronological order we are more prepared to deal with how scientists write and represent.

Epigenetics became the liberal, compromising 50/50 Genetic Assumption, replacing the Diathesis-Stress Model, represented with lots of scientific explanation, documentaries, animation and polish. It seemed to solve everyone's problems because we learned environment is essential and pulls the trigger, yet the solution is still pharmaceuticals.

With this study I have endeavored to model how scientists could write better as communicators. I have interpreted their words in the process and rebutted some of their presumptions. *If* I have misinterpreted epigenetics—a hypothetical process, not a thing—then I challenge these scientists to do a better job explaining their work and updating themselves on research from the other side I suspect if they were forced to explain it more clearly, they *might* have an ah-ha moment.

I am providing two "aids" to support the reader through the study: (1) **a list of known communication tricks** for which we need to keep a lookout, and (2) after every paragraph written by the researchers that is technically convoluted or "over our head," my own interpretation and/or commentary follows. You may want to skip ahead and read my interpretation before you struggle with any of these opaque paragraphs. In my opinion there is no excuse for writing something so influential in such an obscure manner that only a few can follow it, and even fewer can evaluate it. I have each type of vagary numbered [1, 2, etc.] in order to easily identify them where applicable. This list is also available in the Appendix, formatted to tear out from the book for convenient reference while reading.

(1) fails to rule out alternative explanations
(2) confuses cause and effect with vague languaging (ex. "associated with")
(3) tends to be over-technical, failing to explain invented terminology for other laypeople or scientists to follow
(4) tends to be sloppy with language, like substituting "genotype" for "phenotype"
(5) key sentences over-state the value of the study
(6) key sentences over-state the results of the study
(7) key sentences reveal bias, with the assumption in the hypothesis
(8) key sentences reveal the hypothetical and unfounded nature of the study, buried amidst other text
(9) terminology implies existence of something that is speculative (ex. "epigenetic mechanisms")
(10) assumes facts not in evidence
(11) uses terms that imply proof, but actually represent a circular logic (ex. "demonstrated")
(12) language designed to distance from or mitigate failed results
(13) overgeneralized language
(14) key sentences promote the use of pharmacological interventions
(15) proves the opposite (pro-child) research and theory
(16) erroneous
(17) relevance not clear

THE YEHUDA STUDY

In 2015, Rachel Yehuda and her associates produced a reportedly groundbreaking research study, "Holocaust Exposure Induced Intergenerational Effects on KFBP5 Methylation." Their research was designed to prove trauma symptoms could be inherited from parents by "genetic" transmission, though they were not claiming the DNA had been permanently modified. Thus the transmission would only affect a few generations and then fade.

Yehuda and her colleagues believe they were the first to discover a phenomenon of epigenetic intergenerational transmission of unprocessed trauma [ahem, unprocessed emotions]. They have considered the phenomenon could only be epigenetic [ahem, genetic], as that is the only lens allowed on their side of the divide.

♦ ♦ ♦ ♦ ♦

They introduce the study to us, explaining:

> *The involvement of epigenetic mechanisms [9] in intergenerational transmission [1] of stress effects has been demonstrated [11] in animals [13] but not in humans [10].*

In other words, the authors represent a single model of intergenerational transmission, but note there are at least three divergent types of studies in the realm of intergenerational transmission. First, it has been demonstrated that some rare physical traits have been dually-programmed genetically, wherein for example, the color of a rabbit's coat will change by strapping an ice pack to its back. Second, it has been represented by epigeneticists that when tortured animals physically show stress, it can only be explained as an epigenetic phenomenon. Third, pro-child researchers have shown that humans and animals can transmit attitudes and coping styles developed under stress to offspring by how they treat their offspring. The most recent scientific explanation for this is mirror neurons. In pre-existing research, we have seen stress conveyed as experienced coping styles from one animal to another, and from one human to another (Harlow, 1965, 1971; Milgram, 1965, 1974; Zombardo, 2007). This is actually what anthropology and sociology is about—the transmission of norms from one generation to the next. However, this is reportedly the first study to represent transmission of trauma or vulnerability to trauma via epigenetics in humans.

◆ ◆ ◆ ◆ ◆

Yehuda and her team describe their methods:

> *Cytosine methylation within the gene encoding for FK506 binding protein 5 (FKBP5) was measured in Holocaust survivors (n=32), their adult offspring (n=22), and demographically comparable parent (n=8) and offspring (n=9) control subjects, respectively. Cytosine-phosphate-guanine sites [3] for analysis were chosen based on their spatial proximity to the intron 7 glucocorticoid [3] response elements [3, 9, 11].*

They have selected three groups: (1) survivors of the Holocaust; (2) Holocaust survivors' offspring; and (3) a control group. They indirectly inform us the body produces enzymes when suffering takes place. These enzymes reside in the body to tend to the suffering self. Biochemists can locate how these enzymes can be observed. They can determine whether proteins are present to help the enzymes become metabolized or degraded in the body. Researchers presuppose the rescuing event within the body took place before the suffering and then contributed to the suffering, which constitutes confirmatory bias in anticipation of a causal genetic explanation for the event or the intensity of the experience.

Detour for Definitions and Background Info

In case the reader would like to be apprised of some basic definitions commonly used between scientists dabbling in epigenetics, I have pulled some standard definitions from Wikipedia. These definitions appear to be generally accepted and I would imagine epigeneticists would complain if they were not accurately representing that body of science, even though they commonly modify definitions as they go. Epigenetics is so flakey they keep putting articles up and taking them down. This is how they're defining their terms today. It's all gobbledygook.

♦ ♦ ♦ ♦ ♦

According to sources on Wikipedia (search term: cytosine):

> Cytosine can also be methylated into 5-methylcytosine by an enzyme called DNA methyltransferase or be methylated and hydroxylated to make 5-hydroxymethylcytosine [6]. The implications of deamination [removal of an amine group from a molecule] on 5-hydroxymethylcytosine, on the other hand, remains less understood [12].

Clearly I don't profess to specialize in nuclear biology, but a motivated reader can wade through some of the basics in the above paragraph. I can tell that a chemical can be changed by interaction with another chemical, which is something the body does all day long as we eat, drink, sleep, and have experiences that include thoughts and feelings. These chemicals act on one another. Experiences are ongoing and complex and unique. Our genetic instructions for these processes are universal and not particular to any specific person, but may become unique due to unique experiences. Just as the piano has keys to an eight-note scale, those keys can be played in such a way as to create an incomprehensible number of different songs, most of which have yet to be written. In the last sentence, we are told some of these processes, especially a process of degradation, are not yet well understood.

♦ ♦ ♦ ♦ ♦

Wikipedia authors explain (search term: FK506):

> FK506 is a binding protein [2], which is encoded by the FKBP3 gene... facilitating immunoregulation and basic cellular processes involving protein folding and trafficking... FKBP5 has been established to have a chemical role in anxiety, especially posttraumatic stress disorder, as well as depression.

Methyl is a chemical that is represented to be in contact with genes, but is actually an aspect of nutrients, toxins and body chemistry. It's more like a synthesizer working in the blood chemistry, helpful or harmful to metabolizing another (chemical) substance such as milk, water, air, fear (i.e., cortisol), or anything in nature, including insults and their resulting hurt or sadness (i.e., noradrenaline). We appear to be discussing synthesizing and metabolizing of environments, most specifically physical and chemical properties, some of which are toxic and some of which are nurturing. Why can't they just speak English? They seem to just be trying to dazzle each other.

Of course, we already know from other arms of behavioral science that emotional suffering produces immeasurable changes in our brain and body chemistry, and links events in the brain facilitated by chemical neurotransmitters such as serotonin, MOA, epinephrine and norepinephrine. We have spent a whole generation seeking pharmaceuticals to "balance out" these neurotransmitters, rather than identifying the recorded experience(s) causing the suffering (Breggin, 1991, 1994, 1998, 1999, 2000, 2001, 2008; Galves, 2002; Glasser, 2005; Hubbard & Wald, 1999; Karon, 2008; Kresser, 2008; Leo, 2000; Mitzberg, 2006; Petersen, 2008; Turner, 2008; Valenstein, 1988; Whitaker, 2002).

♦ ♦ ♦ ♦ ♦

Wikipedia also informs us FKBP5 is a binding protein (search term: FKBP5):

Genetic studies have identified a role [9, 11, 13] for FKBP5 in posttraumatic stress disorder, depression and anxiety. For example, single nucleotide polymorphisms (SNPs) in FKBP5 have been found to interact [2] with childhood trauma to predict [4] severity of adult posttraumatic stress disorder (PTSD). These findings suggest [5] that individuals with these SNPs who are abused as children are more susceptible to PTSD as adults [2]. FKBP5 has also been found to be less expressed [2, 4, 11] in individuals with current PTSD. The FKBP5 gene has been found to have multiple polyadenylation sites[1] and is statistically associated (2) with a higher rate of depressive disorders [2].

As Wikipedia's information is aggregated from geneticists and epigeneticists, we have another opportunity to wade through the above paragraph to find the obscuration of a hypothesis' validity. Here's how I would rewrite the above paragraph: Pro-parent scientists will surmise that the appearance or over appearance of these single nucleotide polymorphisms predict that child abuse will be suffered more harmfully as a result of this temporary inborn predisposition to child abuse. (It is interesting that they failed to explain how this works. Do they know?) A pro-child interpretation, on the other hand, would be that these SNPs are the result of trauma from child abuse or neglect.

They identify a role for FKBP5 in PTSD, but do not say what that role is. SNPs in FKBP5 "interact" with trauma to "predict severity." Are they produced by trauma? Are they the result of trauma? The implication is that they predate the trauma, so as to interact with it and predict it. It can be inferred the role is to stabilize the body during trauma because when it is deficient, the symptoms of PTSD seem to be worse, or predictive of deficient resilience. It makes more sense to say individuals who are abused as children are more susceptible to PTSD as adults. By saying this pre-existing condition makes a child more susceptible to abuse, it diminishes the responsibility of the abuser and puts it on the child or her inheritance.

Back to Analyzing the Yehuda Study

Yehuda reports as a result of their investigation:

Holocaust exposure had an effect on FKBP5 methylation that was observed in exposed parents as well in their offspring. These effects were observed at bin 3/site 6 [17]. Interestingly, in Holocaust survivors, methylation at this site was higher in comparison with control subjects, whereas in Holocaust offspring, methylation was lower. [2] Methylation levels for exposed parents and their offspring were significantly correlated. [2] In contrast to the findings at bin 3/site 6, offspring methylation at bin 2/sites 3 to 5 was associated with childhood physical and sexual abuse in interaction [2] with an FKBP5 risk allele previously associated with vulnerability [2, 4, 5, 9, 10, 11, 13] to psychological consequences of childhood adversity. The findings suggest the possibility of site specificity to environmental influences, as sites in bins 3 and 2 were differentially associated with parental trauma and the offspring's own childhood trauma [10, 11], respectively. FKBP5 methylation averaged across the three bins examined was associated with wake-up cortisol levels, indicating functional relevance of the methylation measures [15]...

This is the first demonstration [1, 6, 10, 11, 13] of an association [2] of pre-conception [2, 5, 6, 7, 9, 10, 11], parental trauma with epigenetic alterations [4] that is evident in both [2, 5, 16, 13] exposed parent and offspring, providing potential insight [11] into how [16] severe psychophysiological trauma can have intergenerational effects.

This study has taken a phenomenon that has been rigorously studied in multiple scientific venues, claiming to have been the first to study it from an epigenetics perspective on humans. Certainly these are not the first scientists to study the transmission of behaviors, attitudes or injuries from moment to moment and lifetime to lifetime (Baillargeon, Needham & DeVos, 1992; Baillargeon & Wang, 2002; Bandura, 1963; Bullock, Gelman & Baillargeon, 1982; Craighero et al., 2007; Felitti et al., 1998; Harlow, 1965, 2009; Herman, 2013; Hickok, 2014; Jacobson, 1979; Jones, 1967, 2009; Lissek & Grillon, 2012Markman, 2011; Meltzoff, 1999; Milgram, 1965, 1974; Perry, 2001; Ramachandran, 2000; Rizzolatti, Fadiga, Gallese & Fogassi, 1996; Umilta et al., 2001, 2004, 2005; van der Kolk, McFarlane & Weisaeth, 1996; Zombardo, 2007).

We need to include that the first generation experiences of abuse for subjects in this study were experienced directly by strangers. The experiences of the offspring were different. They were of neglect by a parent and included internalizing the parent's pain as more important than their own pain. This interferes with the offspring's ability to become authentic, a huge loss to self. Both would be registered in the body, although differently. I call the former a first generation experience and the latter a second generation experience, wherein the child senses and internalizes the parent's needs and perspective. This is an issue of cause and effect, and which comes first. Which event causes? Which event results?

♦ ♦ ♦ ♦ ♦

Yehuda describes how trauma is transmitted:

> *FKBP5 single nucleotide polymorphisms have additionally been shown to interact [2] with early trauma to predict [2] both PTSD and major depression, possibly [8] through involvement of allele-specific, environmentally dependent changes in methylation of specific cytosine-phosphate-guanine (CpG) sites.*

Scientists use the term "interact" and "predict" rather than acknowledge environment influences change in the body. Cause and effect have not been demonstrated or proven here, only speculated in the wrong direction. The epigenetic premise is that effect precedes the cause. This study also presumes the manner of transference is from chemistry to genes rather than from the parent's treatment of the child by virtue of the parent's impaired ability to be appropriately responsive.

♦ ♦ ♦ ♦ ♦

According to Yehuda, transmission can be predicted biologically:

> *Post trauma exposure is associated with greater risk for posttraumatic stress disorder (PTSD) and mood and anxiety disorders in offspring. Biological alterations associated with PTSD and/or other stress-related disorders have also been observed in offspring of trauma survivors who do not themselves report trauma exposure [2] or psychiatric disorder. Animal models have demonstrated that stress exposure can result in epigenetic alterations in the next generation, and such mechanisms have been hypothesized to underpin [2] vulnerability to symptoms [2] in offspring of trauma survivors.*

Yes, of course. Anyone who has already been traumatized is more susceptible to trauma than someone who has not. That's different from someone who has inherited trauma in his or her blood chemistry.

One of the factors that inhibits healing from traumatic experiences is the expectation that one should not express or reveal their experience. When one has a fragile parent, there is a tendency not to lean on that parent, and in fact, usually it is the parent who creates the second generation of injury by neglect, as a result of their preoccupation with their own unhealed injuries.

Again, the assumption is made that the "biological alterations" precede and "underpin" the second-generation symptoms, when these children of Holocaust survivors were probably traumatically neglected in infancy, as it takes a fairly healthy parent to nurture and attune to an infant.

◆ ◆ ◆ ◆ ◆

Yehuda claims it's difficult to disentangle the parent's trauma from the child's experiences:

> *Since parental trauma exposure has been linked [2] with offspring trauma, particularly childhood emotional abuse, it has been difficult to disentangle effects of parental exposure from those potentially conferred by the offspring's early experiences [8]. A major gap in the clinical literature is that parents and their adult offspring have not been studied in tandem, making it difficult to understand the origin of changes [2, 8] in association with parental exposure. Furthermore, whereas some aspects of the offspring phenotype are similar to those observed in parents, offspring also show a range of responses reflecting multiple contributors [8].*

The parent's PTSD is certainly registered in the body by chemical fallout from trauma. However, to say it was transmitted before birth and before experience is another story. Here, scientists write that in truth it is difficult to distinguish what exposure to the offspring stems from environment or childhood emotional abuse and "multiple contributors," and what results from biologically inherited trauma (if any). Scientists couldn't possibly believe they can find chemical changes that indicate the source, as if the body will report, "Mom hurt me here," or, "My teacher hurt me here," or, "I was born with Mom's injury here." Please tell me they are not talking about reading particular injuries in the blood.

◆ ◆ ◆ ◆ ◆

Yehuda used self-reported questionnaires to measure symptoms:

> *Thus we investigated epigenetic changes in FKBP5 methylation in Holocaust survivors, offspring, and demographically matched Jewish parent-offspring pairs from peripheral blood samples to determine whether Holocaust exposure and/or PTSD symptoms and offspring's own experience were associated with changes [2] both PTSD and intergenerational effects in FKBP5 methylation in the Holocaust offspring.*
>
> *The Childhood Trauma Questionnaire (CTQ) was completed by the F1. Holocaust F1 completed the Parental PTSD Questionnaire, which asks offspring to rate parental PTSD symptoms and severity of Holocaust exposure. The Beck Depression Inventory and Spielberger*

State-Trait Anxiety Inventory were used as measures of symptom severity.

To answer their own good question, they resorted to checking changes in methylation at the FKBP5 sites to identify which changes were inherited, and which changes resulted from direct experience. I cannot imagine how this can be done. How can they look at any physical matter, whether methyl or any other substance and tell what caused it? One must look at history to see cause.

How did scientists attempt to distinguish environmental factors from inherited factors? They used self-report, not blood. There is no questionnaire more ticklish and unlikely to be answered with candor than an evaluation of one's parents and one's own parenting. Given that second-generation subjects have most likely had to swallow their own experience in order to support their injured parent, it is unlikely their self-reports were authentic and reliable. Additionally, due to memory limitations, self-reports would not include any memory of attachment trauma and cannot be considered objective, since these types of factors are usually invisible to the subject.

Further, if these scientists are actually saying they can determine origins of trauma by sampling blood, then I'd like to see this method replicated, especially at birth. Further, to use blood work, scientists would be assessing general types of injuries, recorded in general ways across cultures. This is another way—an indirect way—of acknowledging that the only way impact can be inherited is by a universal type of injury leading to universal experiences such as assault, rejection, betrayal, and neglect, rather than a particular experience leading to a particular genetic explanation.

◆ ◆ ◆ ◆ ◆

In search of an opportunity to characterize and generalize the impact of trauma on DNA expression, Yehuda writes:

Future prospective, longitudinal studies of high-risk trauma survivors before conception, during pregnancy, and during postpartum may [9, 10] uncover sources [2, 9] of epigenetic influences. In addition, it would be of interest to replicate our findings on FKBP5 intron 7 methylation in other populations with substantial trauma exposure. For example, peripheral blood from female survivors of the Tutsi genocide who were pregnant at the time of exposure and their adolescent offspring was analyzed for NR3C1 and NR3C2 promoter methylation. Interestingly, in that study, exposure effects were identified at specific sites in both exposed mothers and offspring, and mothers' methylation correlated [2] with offspring methylation. It is also necessary to investigate multiple generations to differentiate among exposure effects, epigenetic inheritance, and social transmission. Animal models can provide further mechanistic understanding of how extreme stress effects mediate changes in offspring.

The scientists speculate they may find distinctions between inherited trauma and environmental trauma in the blood. Since children who have insecure attachments have already been traumatized and are thus vulnerable to future trauma, scientists will have to get the blood before a child has a chance to experience attachment trauma if they want to show the changes are inherited. They would then have to get the blood before the child experiences trauma. Of course the collection of blood from a newborn is traumatic, and would set the child up with an initial and long lasting impression of how safe the world is. Is it worth this to prove something that can't be proven when a better explanation already exists?

I am betting scientists cannot prove the child is *born* with this alteration, and thus, this "result" can't be replicated. However, if this can be done it still doesn't prove the DNA "expression" has been altered. It proves the physical and emotional conditions of the mother affect the physical and emotional conditions of the infant, and scientists have been tempted to attribute them to genes. Blood samples may show evidence of impact, but it does not prove the nature of the source. It does not prove the source was a non-event, but rather a pre-existing condition predisposing the child to future trauma transmitted in the blood and tissue, instead of by neglectful parenting. It is true early trauma predicts a fragile constitution, further susceptibility to trauma and later depression, anxiety, or insensitivity. It is important to be clear that early trauma—say, if the mother has postpartum depression—is not the same as inherited biological predictors.

◆ ◆ ◆ ◆ ◆

Yehuda's team finally gets honest in their following discussion:

> *It is not possible to infer mechanisms of transmission from these data [1, 8]. It was not possible to disentangle the influence of parental gender, including gamete or in utero effects, since 21 of 22 Holocaust parents were survivors. Epigenetic effects in maternal or paternal gametes are a potential explanation for epigenetic effects in offspring, but blood samples will not permit ascertainment of gamete-dependent transmission [1, 8]. What can be detected in blood samples is parental and offspring experience-dependent epigenetic modifications [5]...*
>
> *To our knowledge, these results provide the first demonstration [8, 9, 10, 11] of an association of pre-conception [2, 3, 4, 5, 6. 7] stress effects with epigenetic changes in both exposed parents and their offspring in adult humans. Bin 3/site 6 methylation was not associated with the FKBP5 risk allele and could not be attributed [2, 4, 12] to the offspring's own trauma exposure, their own psychopathology, or other examined characteristics that might independently affect methylation of this gene. Yet it could be attributed [2, 4, 12] to Holocaust exposure in the F0.*

What they are detecting is environmental reactions to parental neglect, most likely attachment trauma, not second-generation stored trauma. Scientists acknowledge they cannot learn pre-conception transmission information, which is possibly the only way to prove intergenerational transmissions can take place independent of chemical changes that could have been caused by experiences after birth. Since pre-conception changes cannot be shown, the only chemical changes to take place after birth are after attachment has begun. It is predictable that victims of the Holocaust would not thoughtfully attach and attune to their offspring. Rule-outs of other explanations are critical in good science.

♦ ♦ ♦ ♦ ♦

Yehuda presents graphics that indicate no results:

The following unremarkable bar chart from the Yehuda study represents the almost indiscernible difference between survivors and the control group, and between offspring and the control group. The difference is so minimal that it appears attributable to chance. There was no distinction except the measure of methylation barely increased for survivors, and barely lowered for offspring at bin 3. Further, if this "correlation" could possibly be considered meaningful, then it could just as well represent the difference in the body between the effects of abuse by strangers and neglect by one's own parents. These are related experiences, but not the same, the former born of abuse and the latter born of neglect. Scientists' assumption that these results represent anything predetermining is an ongoing causal error that shows a failure to rule out other explanations. Since these correlations were close to insignificant, it is a misrepresentation of the facts to make such major proclamations about such a discovery.

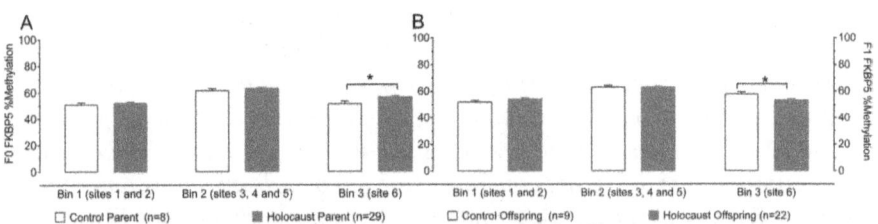

*Methylation at FKBP5 intron 7, bins 1, 2, and 3 for Holocaust survivors (A), Holocaust survivor offspring (B), and their respective comparison subjects. The percent methylation (mean 6 SEM) is represented by red bars for Holocaust survivor parents (F0) and their offspring (F1) (F0: n=32, F1: n=22) and by white bars for F0 and F1 control subjects (F0: n=8, F1: n=9). Division of sites into bins is indicated. *$p < .05$.*

> The main finding in this study is that Holocaust survivors and their offspring have methylation changes [6] on the same site in a functional intronic region of the FKBP5 gene, a GR-binding sequence in intron 7, but in the opposite direction.

Perhaps it is possible they have discovered a location at which trauma is registered in the blood and on molecular sites. Perhaps different types of trauma register in different ways in multiple places in the body and brain—resulting from different chemical adaptations. It would be wonderful to consider this discovery, were it not for the hocus-pocus and slights of hand in order to prove ulterior agendas:

> *Despite the potential limitations of our cross-sectional approach, a significant effect of severe parental trauma was observed in both generations at the same site of a transcriptionally relevant region of a stress-related gene... The directional difference in bin 3/site 6 methylation between Holocaust survivors and their offspring was unexpected but may reflect an intergenerational biological accommodation [2].*
>
> *Further analysis indicated that the effect was driven by a physical abuse induced site 3 demethylation in FKBP5 risk allele carriers.*
>
> *Perhaps there is something to this site having a role in processing abuse and trauma. These results partially replicate previous findings in which bin 2 demethylation was associated with physical and sexual abuse, the FKBP5 risk allele, and their interaction in two separate large cohorts...*
>
> *However, this minority contributed clinically relevant variance to CTQ scores for physical and sexual abuse. Klengel et al. and other investigators focusing on early childhood trauma effects and the influence of the gene 3 early life environment interactions on methylation did not assess the contribution of parental experiences, particularly trauma exposure.*
>
> *Our findings suggest that it is important to assess parental exposure characteristics since they may exert profound influences. Although different sites may be involved in mediating parental vs. offspring's own early trauma, it is possible that the effect of offspring abuse may be an indirect consequence of parental trauma. Indeed, parental trauma exposure has been shown to result in an increased prevalence of childhood abuse, most strongly emotional abuse, in offspring.*
>
> *Although we were unable to disentangle functional effects of methylation... there is reason to believe that methylation at individual sites in the FKBP5 gene may contribute to transcriptional and functional effects. Indeed, for the NR3C1 gene, associations of individual sites with exposures to several types of adversity are increasingly recognized.*

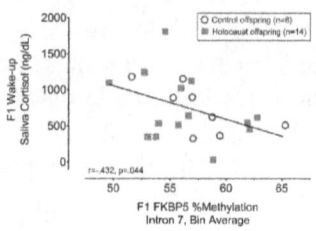

Relationship between FKBP5 intron 7, bin average percent methylation, and wake-up salivary cortisol (ng/dL) in first generation (F1). Holocaust survivor offspring (n=14) are depicted by red squares and control subjects (n=8) are depicted by blue open circles. Significance was set at p < .05.

In summary, our data support an intergenerational epigenetic priming of the physiological response to stress in offspring of highly traumatized individuals. These changes may contribute to the increased risk for psychopathology in the F1 generation. Two sites anticipated to operate similarly to regulate FKBP5 gene expression were demonstrated to have different environmental influences. The mechanism of intergenerational transmission of epigenetic effects at bin 3/site 6 is not known but does not appear to be mediated by childhood adversity, as is the case for bin 2. From a biological perspective, accommodation to multiple environmental influences at distinct and potentially redundant sites on genes central to stress regulation would facilitate maximal stress responsivity and adaptation. Future studies should focus on assessing the effects of trauma at various developmental stages, as well as potential differences in maternal and paternal effects. Additionally, the mechanism of intergenerational transmission of trauma and functional importance of site specificity remain to be explored. Early detection of such epigenetic marks may advance the development of preventive strategies to address the intergenerational sequelae of exposure to trauma.

It actually seems preposterous such a big deal could be made of something that appears so insignificant. In the graph above, we see insignificance represented as significant once again.

The significance is represented at only 5%, which qualifies for nothing. Rather it is irrelevant in the realm of science. It is remarkable this "finding" supports any hypothesis at all, as there seems to be no real trend, and most scientists would attribute such a "pattern" to randomness.

♦ ♦ ♦ ♦ ♦

Yehuda acknowledges possible motives for the study:

> This work was supported by National Institute of Mental Health R01 MH 64675-01 "Biology of Risk and PTSD in Holocaust Survivor Offspring" and 1RC1MH088101-01 "Identification of an Epigenetic Risk Marker for PTSD" and, in part, by a Grant (5 M01 RR00071) for the Mount Sinai General Clinical Research Center from the National Institutes of Health.
>
> RY [Rachel Yehuda] and FH [Florian Holsboer] are co-inventors of the following patent application: "Genes associated with posttraumatic stress disorder," European Patent #EP 2334816 A1. FH and EBB [Elizabeth Binder] are co-inventors of the following patent application: "FKBP5: A novel target for antidepressant therapy," European Patent #EP 1687443 B1. All other authors report no biomedical financial interests or potential conflicts of interest.

RESEARCH FLAWS OF EPIGENETICS, WITH YEHUDA AS EXAMPLE

Lack of Rule-Outs

John Greally of Albert Einstein College of Medicine wrote an article entitled, "Over-Interpreted Epigenetics Study of the Week" (2015). Expressing reluctance to criticize fellow scientists, he stated that such over-interpretation of research was only going to hurt the credibility of epigenetic research in the long run. Greally wrote:

> The starting hypothesis is not explicitly stated, but can be inferred to be as follows – people who have survived the trauma of the Holocaust are distinctive for having cells in their bodies that change DNA methylation, and their offspring, not having been exposed to the Holocaust, also have changes in DNA methylation in their cells, making them distinctive compared with other people who are not offspring of Holocaust survivors. What is assumed based on the shared change in DNA methylation is that the parent changed DNA methylation, that this occurred in somatic and germ line cells, and that the offspring inherited the DNA methylation change, a trans-generational inheritance of this epigenetic regulator.
>
> So what exactly did they find in this study? Fundamentally, they found that while the first two bins of DNA methylation values measured for >1 CG showed no difference between groups, the DNA methylation values of the single CG in the third bin were different in the Holocaust survivors themselves compared with controls, and in their offspring compared with controls.
>
> So does this prove the starting hypothesis? The answer is no, the study is pretty typical of all epigenetics studies today for being uninterpretable for the following reasons:

> a. Confounding molecular processes are not studied... Without knowing the effects of these influences, you can't assume the changes of DNA methylation are independent of these influences in a way that addresses the starting hypothesis.
>
> b. The influence of cell subtype composition is unstudied.
>
> Without wishing to beat this study to death, the fact that the DNA methylation difference that characterizes the exposed parents is an increase while that characterizing the offspring is a decrease is difficult to reconcile with any sort of heritability mechanism.

I am wondering if Greally has in mind the influences of mirror neurons, in his comment (a). He appears to be searching for rule-outs, alternative explanations for the results. And in (b), is he reminding scientists that other aspects of cells work to metabolize or fend away environment, such as the cell membrane?

Greally offers some criticisms and sane suggestions as to what real research needs to be done to produce credible results that would contribute toward medicine. Apparently that would be the branch of medicine involved in finding true cures, rather than the branch of medicine invested in medicating children for profit. He apparently has not followed the history of genetic research is not inoculated to good research. His standards remain high, like the kind of scientist we used to believe in.

In conclusion, Greally writes:

> Unfortunately, the story is typical of many in the field of epigenetics, with conclusions drawn based on uninterpretable studies. While there have been high-profile reviews that emphasize the weakness of the evidence for transgenerational epigenetic heritability, especially in humans, they have not been enough to steer people toward the rigorous studies needed to test this attractive but poorly-founded idea. Every week there are uninterpretable epigenetics studies published, the Holocaust study is merely one of many. These authors are merely following prevailing beliefs in over interpreting their data. However, every such study damages the 'brand' of epigenetics a little more. If we want human disease epigenetics to be sustainable as a field of research, we have to start to do substantially better in designing, executing, interpreting, reviewing and funding these studies.

The environmental explanation includes internalizing an entire gestalt of discrete experiences by the child recorded in the brain and body, unfolding throughout the relational process with his or her parents and siblings. There is observed the results of an ongoing daily process that is complex, more like the weaving of palpable and perceivable experiences into a unique mental and emotional fabric of memories and learned lessons. Every aspect of this explanation is supported by replicable science, and the most critical aspects of environment can be somewhat quantified in the Predictor Score Sheet (see my book, *The Predictor Scale: Predicting and Understanding Critical Childhood Experiences*). Such an expedient assessment would be illuminating to the scientists, but it would also improve their rule-outs. Ultimately, I doubt human experiences can be any better assessed, identified and ruled out than this.

Failure to Replicate

It is the gold standard that valid research must be replicable by another researcher who follows the same research design. When research claims cannot be replicated, they become discredited. In the case of genetic research, this appears to not be the case, or rather, it appears we've withheld that standard for an agonizing period of time.

However, in the field of epigenetics, failure to replicate may not be as big of an issue, at least not until the research designs improve. Regulations and standards for quality research are so irrelevant and loosey-goosey that we don't even reach the point of questioning ability to replicate. Interpretations are accepted so far afield from valid and acceptable measures that the problem of replication may actually be irrelevant.

Revisions of Language

Now we observe epigeneticists playing with terminology as well. The very term was taken from epigenesis, a legitimately recognized phenomenon in cellular biology. These embryonic cells are able to cooperate with other cells and take on different shapes and roles, depending on their location assignment in the body. The same types of cells, all sharing the same DNA instructions, could work with other cells to form the heart, the brain or any other functioning organ or part of the body. The phenomenon is real and verifiable.

There is no such phenomenon in the world of epigenetics. It is theoretical and speculative, and shown by inference, absent rule-out alternative explanations. Thus we are left to visualize some sort of pre-existing dormant state, and a switching apparatus whereby the environment triggers a sort of Plan B for the genes.

This is a template that has been stretched and reinterpreted by scientists. Some of them speculate an actual switch from Plan A to Plan B, while others suggest environmentally spawned chemicals have attached to the DNA, enhancing or retarding its expression, with no specific Plan B. In both situations, scientists acknowledge the DNA is not changed, but they imply it, using language such as "gene expression" or "epigenetic mechanisms," linked to other terms such as "modified" or "mechanisms of transition," all together referring to non-mechanical chemical changes in the body that result from impactful, somehow pre-existing experiences.

Rather than concede that temperament, personality and behavior are fashioned by interaction with environment, these biodeterminists have made another play to represent psychological nurture and parent-child interaction as genetic, using the revised terminology, beginning with "epigenetic." The public hears the term "epigenetic" and assumes genes are responsible for how environment becomes metabolized, so accepting a pharmaceutical solution seems logical. Thus the new terminology is borrowed from the study of biomedical genetics.

As we have seen, behavioral geneticists moved the goal post of significant concordance from 100% to as low as 8%, borrowing from the research model. They introduced terms such as "twins separated at birth," which later had to be revised to "twins reared apart," in order to include twins separated as late as 15 years of age. We have seen them introduce a term, "incomplete penetrance" to imply the directing gene was there, but its influence was not evident, a purely theoretical construct treated as fact. We have seen them introduce "age correcting" and the "proband method" of counting schizophrenic twins to elevate their data (counting the non-diagnosable twin as half-schizophrenic because he or she still has until the age of 50 to have a schizophrenic episode). We have seen them change the definition of schizophrenia to multiple variables, including bipolar and homosexuality, in order to achieve some semblance of significance, even by their own watered down terms.

Then scientists imply a number of things. It gets very confusing, probably even for the scientists. They seek out explanations that suggest: (1) the fragile or resilient condition pre-existed; (2) said condition was handed down from a previous generation (rather than created solely by parenting); (3) environment is at best a co-conspirator; and/or (4) the best intervention is pharmaceuticals.

Epigenetic scientists imply: (1) the genetic instructions pre-existed the environment's influence on the body, and environment simply flipped the switch; (2) the modification in the body took place at the same time the experience took place, such that they "correlated," "corresponded," "cooperated" and/or "interacted with" environment, and even "predicted" a change in "genetic instruction" [although they finally acknowledged this change is always temporary]; (3) these conditions pre-existed in the body, so when the experience took place, the body was prepared with a Plan B, which was probably Plan A; (4) these pre-existing phenomena actually influenced the experience to take place, and caused the new behavior; and (5) the phenomena took place simultaneously with the environment, but never *after* the environmental influence. Scientists conflate genetic instructions between individuals with universal instructions to all humans. Different studies appear to be trying to find ways to fit into the previous elastic definitions and requirements of epigenetics.

It is clear epigeneticists must not acknowledge there are other, more dominant areas of the body recording and directing the impact of these experiences, such as the brain. Neither do they acknowledge that environment can create a simple Ockham's Razor-like explanation for cause and effect... simply that the event took place and the body responded within and without. Such a simple explanation induces insight.

Just as definitions of "schizophrenia," "significance" and "concordance" were modified to meet the needs of scientists in adoption studies, so has become the meaning of "gene" in epigenetic studies. Scientists have now taken to redefining genes, probably so they can continue their attempt to support genetic interpretations via epigenetics, a branch of behavioral biology that has begun to loosely refer to turning genes on and off for behaviors, even though such genes have never been found.

Physicist and author Evelyn Fox Keller has weighed in, writing, "[I]t seems evident that the primacy of genes as the core explanatory concept of biological structure and function is more a feature of the twentieth century than it will be of the twenty-first" (2000, p. 9). Given this context-dependence in what genes are considered to be and do, it seems that pluralism has become the order of the day, for genes as for species. According to Stanford's Encyclopedia of Philosophy report on The Human Genome Project, Keller "pointed out an irony which has ensued from the HGP's successes: even though gene-talk is more pervasive than ever in the popular and scientific presses, the concept of the gene, whether defined structurally or functionally, has been 'radically undermined'" (2000, p. 5). She is quoted, "As we listen to the ways in which the term is now used by working biologists, we find that the gene has become many things—no longer a single entity but a word with great plasticity, defined only by the specific experimental context in which it is used" (2000, p. 69).

Science philosopher John Dupre advocated that a gene is "any bit of DNA that agrees that anyone has reason to name and keep track of" (2004, p. 332). Molecular biologists have jealously guarded the term, but other scientists have disregarded its original referent, referring to it as the "preformationist gene" (Moss, 2004) and the "instrumental gene" (Griffiths & Stotz, 2006).

Paul Griffiths and Karola Stotz characterize a broader definition of genes as "nominal molecular genes," referring to specific DNA sequences annotated by researchers (2006). Lenny Moss refers to other uses of the term as the "Gene-D," or "developmental resource," providing a template for RNA and protein synthesis but is "indeterminate with respect to phenotype," since this depends on other developmental resources and the cellular and extracellular contexts (2004) This works well for epigeneticists to frame their references to environment in terms of a genetic resource and serves the pharmaceutical industry's focus on chemical explanations that can be treated with chemical interventions, aka medications.

Incentives (Patents and Grants)

In the wake of The Human Genome Project, a trend developed wherein researchers began to patent their "discoveries." According to the *Stanford Encyclopedia of Philosophy*, "universities and other nonprofit institutions were allowed to apply for patents on such research, and tax incentives were provided to the private sector to encourage investment" (Gannett, 2008). Following the lead, multinational corporations began to apply for patents on any such research claims. The Yehuda study concluded with notification that three of the seven researchers have related patents pending. Specifically, Yehuda and her superior filed for the patent "Genes associated with posttraumatic stress disorder," which is about as valuable as a patent that proves chalk changes the nature of a chalkboard. The money tree and its gardeners are nevertheless proliferating. It's astounding that anyone would stake a claim to have discovered this association, especially as if methylation of genes explains the disorder when mirror neurons explain it better.

Underscore that the National Institute of Mental Health (NIMH) provided Yehuda's grant; it is their frequent practice to provide grants to studies designed to prove genetic causes and pharmaceutical interventions. While I do not know their level of funding in the arena of epigenetics vs. genetics, I am speculating rather advisedly that they may have largely transitioned over to the new model. Epigenetic researchers may be winning grants from the pharmaceutical industry as much as geneticists, if not more; they continue to provide fuel for public relations campaigns of pharmaceuticals that treat inborn mental health issues.

Fixed Research Designs

While the research designs of the twin studies and adoption studies were actually excellent, the problem with those designs from a scientist's point of view was that they didn't prove what they wanted to prove. The problem from the beholder's point of view was the fraudulent interpretation of results. Many of the studies were too well designed to produce pro-child or truthful results, although some honest scientists attempted to report honest results.

However, in the case of epigenetics, the research designs appear to be more for effect than to create real insight into reality. Champagne's rats were tested to prove epigenetics influence behavior because the rats had chemical changes in their bodies resulting from stress. However, that did not prove epigenetic causes, but rather chemical stress effects from mistreatment. If the results are so incorrectly interpreted that an experiment of neglect and torture turns into a justification for an epigenetic explanation, design doesn't matter, since the interpretation can be anything.

INTERGENERATIONAL TRANSMISSION

Understanding the intergenerational transmission process is enlightening and is particularly poignant in the homes of schizophrenics. My very first patient, Ronnie, was a schizophrenic man whose mother survived the Holocaust. She was so extremely depressed she was unable to mother her children. He recalled numerous occasions when she was picked up and taken away in an ambulance because she was suicidal, and he felt invisible and irrelevant. As many times as this happened, no one spoke to him about it. The only person with whom he could discuss his life was his 15-minutes-a-month psychiatrist. He didn't know what to make of it, as she barely acknowledged his existence. He felt so invisible that he fixated on any evidence he existed. His mom was so traumatized she could not mother her sons, and his childhood was traumatic too, not because she transmitted her trauma in her genes, but because of the way she thought of herself, how she felt, how she related (or didn't), and how she mothered, all while keeping it bottled up inside.

To be clear, it appears we have two bodies of science theoretically vying to explain the same phenomenon different ways. One is pro-parent and the other is pro-child. Only one appears to know about or acknowledge the other. It's rather schizogenic itself. In the Yehuda case, we are looking at how behaviors are transmitted from one generation to the next. Epigeneticists see it as almost a mystery to be understood only on a molecular level, whereas neurologists see it as a natural process appearing not just among humans but throughout the animal kingdom. When a little gosling hatches, it will follow a human instead of its mother if it sees the human first. It is so clearly cause and effect; those who see it as a mystery would have denied the effect of parenting and environment their entire life, including their childhood, thereby creating their own blind spot.

Children swallow their feelings so as not to violate the needs of their parents (Miller, 1983). We get our very identities from how we are treated, especially before the age of five. By then, our personalities are significantly formed. Whatever is denied that we have experienced is transmitted to the next generation unconsciously, often via scapegoating. What is acknowledged can be transcended. The great scientific breakthrough of our time was the discovery of mirror neurons, not changing genes.

In the case of Ronnie, it is sometimes harder to handle emotional abuse and neglect by one's very own parent than by strangers who are more violent. His trauma was quite different from his mother's trauma, but both were devastated. I suspect his mother was not resilient due to her own early childhood neglect. Perhaps she was a small child when she first entered a concentration camp.

I wrote earlier in this book, but it bears repeating:

Genes do enough to deliver a miraculously designed body—fashioned brilliantly by evolution—but they do not do everything. They instruct our stem cells how to set us up for survival and success. They regulate the physical structure of the body. The microorganism within the human body that makes decisions on behalf of the body appears to be the cell membrane, which determines which chemicals are toxic and which chemicals are beneficial, and as a gatekeeper makes decisions of inclusion or exclusion. The misunderstanding by geneticists of the role of genes is based on an assumption that behaviors are pre-programmed, not adaptable. The brilliance of the human organism is that we are adaptable to environmental demands. We are flexible. We are able to learn from experiences and history. These experiences inform our choices reflexively, unconsciously and consciously.

8: ANALYSIS

> We cannot expect the leaders of behavioral genetics to recognize that the historical positions of their field are mistaken, that their prized research method and "landmark" studies are massively flawed and environmentally confounded, and that family, social, cultural, economic, and political environments—and not genetics—are the main cause of psychiatric disorders and variations in human behavior. Because most leaders of the field will not allow themselves to see this, it is left to others to show that the pillars of behavioral genetics are crumbling before our very eyes. –Jay Joseph, 2015, p. 235

PSYCHIATRY AND THE RAMIFICATIONS OF GENETIC THEORY

A Review of The Tulip Theory

This book is about the nature/nurture debate today. It's been going on probably as long as there has been language. Now that we have science and technology, this debate is renewed with the possibility of being settled.

The human design is to attach first and individuate later, with license to be authentic. Therein lies the rub. At an early age most human beings are confronted with a choice and necessary decision. Many of us learn that complaints against our parents are unacceptable because our parents can't handle it. We then formulate an assumption, which becomes a life-long belief, that we must sacrifice our own feelings and understanding in order to protect our parents' needs. We do this in order to be loved or safe. This belief may then develop a need for agreement. We want others to appreciate and follow our assumption with us. Together we will all agree parents are not responsible for how we turned out. Together we will agree to parent by The Tulip Theory on an unconscious level. We agree to apply it in rearing our own children.

We can surmise The Tulip Theory may be the oldest type of parenting in human history. It is so old and pervasive that it is practically invisible, like water to a fish. We have been debating inborn sin and forgiveness, karma, issues of good and evil, and where bad behavior comes from, for as long as history has been recorded. It's a debate that had to take place, but since the real option is a forbidden consideration, multiple explanations are invited. I imagine it was debated in the Communal Stage but established as a dominant theory by the advent of the patriarchal Slavery Stage. In more recent years, that is the Dark Ages of Medieval Times in Europe, the feudal Roman Catholic Church believed in inborn evil. Following those feudal years, the capitalist revolution was born of a new philosophy one could work hard and earn their way up the ladder of social privilege. Those who succeeded were deserving and those who didn't succeed were undeserving. We looked at the insane as inhuman, unfeeling, a burden on society and unworthy of protection.

Men dominated the healing profession and the new standard was to find treatments that eliminated symptoms even if it meant mistreating the patient. Society firmly established the notion that worthwhile and respectable citizens deserved better treatment than those who were insufficiently productive. This enabled an easy transition into exploitation and systematic abuse during slavery, and the subordination of women, children, laborers and ultimately, the mentally ill.

There have been a few pivotal moments in the history of behavioral science that changed the course of events, redirecting progress into a major regression the equivalent of genocide. These events probably have greater ramifications than the assassination of President John Kennedy, Martin Luther King and Robert Kennedy combined. The first event was the devastating rejection of Sigmund Freud's presentation of the Seduction Theory to his colleagues, which established that childhood issues were not to be explored. After that, adoption researchers tried to prove genetic inferiority akin to the Mendelian model and they were willing to lie and cheat to prove it. It's still happening. Sometimes the powers-that-be simply put a lid on what we are allowed to know or think for their sake, not ours.

A Failed Opportunity to Clear It Up

Theory calls for research. If scientists really were objective in their studies and experiments, we could have been remarkably enlightened by now, as a society and a world community. Funding facilitates the research from which it will benefit. The results of research direct practice. We were misdirected and our misdirection has been "scientifically" confirmed in "research." In an era that requires clinicians to demonstrate evidence-based practices more and more, we have been taught lies. We are expected to promote only evidence-based practices, and we are required to acknowledge the genetic theories of the medical model. This is known as a double-bind. It is a rather schizogenic autocratic structure, in the name of mental health.

Unfortunately, in the early stages of psychology, researchers attempted to apply the Mendelian model to prove superiority and inferiority on behalf of the powers that be. Psychologist and researcher Jay Joseph, writes:

> The historical crimes committed by the "racist hygienist" founders of psychiatric genetics such as Ernst Rodin in Nazi Germany have been documented at length... The massively flawed research produced by this field has also been documented... This leads to the following question: Has the field of psychiatric genetics contributed anything positive to the human condition in its roughly 100 years of existence? (2015, p. 201).

What we have seen is a grave betrayal of trust by scientists. What we come to believe is true has affected how we treat our patients and our children. As long as we continue to believe in The Tulip Theory, we abandon responsibility for steering our lives, guiding our children and healing our clients. We have been led to believe black is white and up is down. **We have been taught to see what is not true, and not see that which is true.** Given the mental health of millions of people has always been at stake, this is our own responsibility and serious failure. Correcting it is our mandate.

How did we, in the field of mental health, tolerate these harmful and self-serving beliefs? I suggest we believed the researchers because we wanted to believe them for a multitude of our own reasons, and because we have been taught that scientists are objective, the same way we have been taught to trust our children with all priests, that capitalism is self-monitoring or the judicial system is fair. We have trusted their research is done in our best interests and the results are correct. Our experts and leaders have authenticated them, and we have believed. Silly us. On the other hand, many of us were raised to be compliant and to support authority, right or wrong.

Researchers write like they're writing to each other, as if they understand what they write and the others will too. They write to deceive or mislead. They write to imply they have come up with something when they haven't. They certainly intend to write over the layperson's head. I have tried to sum up and/or clarify their reports in a way that is easier for more people to understand. I have also attempted to confront the theory of epigenetics on my own, as it is difficult to find trailblazers ahead of me or even beside me. I dearly hope this book will encourage more critical thinking so we can stop being fooled.

Denial and Pro-Parent Motives

The pro-parent side of The War of the Researchers has had to fabricate information to remain true to their original cause, thereby ignoring the critical needs of children, probably unknown to them. Metaphorically, if I want to prove my car runs on honey, I will have a lot harder time proving it than if I want to prove it runs on gas. Pro-parent researchers have a much harder job than pro-child researchers. I often wonder what it does to them to hold true to their denial, and whether their dream life tries to awaken in them some insight into their own self-deception and dangerousness to entire populations of children. It certainly affects and affirms their ongoing inability to see clearly or objectively. The pro-child side can do the most rigorous research, which can be replicated (a test of good research). They are on the side of reality.

Jonathan Latham and Allison Wilson, who run the Bioscience Research Project, attribute the misperception of genetic influences to the twin studies and other relative studies, but propose that believing in the studies despite their flaws suggests these convictions must be perceived as necessary to the underlying social order, especially politicians and corporations. Such beliefs support the medical model, thereby reducing responsibility for society's mental health. The history of scientific refutation is that "adherents of established theories construct ever more elaborate or unlikely explanations to fend off their critics" (Joseph, 2015, p. 213).

Pro-parent arguments seem illogical compared to the attachment/pro-child arguments. Psychologist and journalist Robert Karen, who has extensively explored the motives of geneticists, represents the pro-child/pro-parent debate:

> If the fundamental message of attachment research is that children need to be cared for in a consistent and sensitive way, that they love their parents powerfully and need to have that love returned and sustained, then the fundamental message of temperament research is that people are inherently different, that those differences need to be tolerated and respected, and that much of what we once saw as parentally induced is actually part of the nature of human differences (1994, p. 295).

In 1990, Karen interviewed pro-parent researcher Thomas Bouchard, who unabashedly and somewhat illogically explained his motives:

> I think if we recognize that individuals differ from each other in these fundamental ways, we're going to have a lot more respect for one another. We know that we're physically different. We respect and understand that a kid who's only four and one-half feet tall is not going to compete with a kid who's six feet tall. Well, the same may be true for many psychological traits and characteristics (p. 296).

Jerome Kagan agreed with Bouchard in his own interview with Karen, also in 1990:

> There are some people with a very short fuse. They blow up easily; it's hard to get along with them. Many people assume that it's a function of their past and they should be able to control it. So then you get angry at these people. But if you believe that this is partly temperamental, and that their biology prepares them for this, then you become a little more forgiving (p. 296).

Karen paraphrases:

> Kagan also expects temperament research to take the pressure off mothers who, he believes, have got a raw deal as a result of decades of behaviorist and psychoanalytical influence. He quotes with pleasure the words of a famous scientist who suffers from terrible stage fright whenever he makes a speech. After hearing Kagan present his data, he said, "I've been blaming my mother for fifty years, but after hearing this, I'm going to stop" (p. 296).

Karen has found two main points of contention. First, attachment theory blames mothers and ignores "the fact that infants could be difficult or that there could be a poor fit... and [second], attachment theories have not been so eager to let mothers—or caregivers in general—off the hook: They want it understood that sensitive, consistent parenting is vital, and they see proclaiming that as part of their mission" (p. 296). He goes on to say:

The blame issue is similar to the poorness-of-fit concept in that it has been highly charged politically, and the antagonists are often more concerned with the impact certain types of statements will have than whether or not they are true. Many developmentalists recognize that, of course, parents are sometimes blamed for their children's suffering, but they believe that making an issue of it will only tend to generate guilt—and a guilty parent is more likely to do a poor job than one who had been reassured and encouraged... An atmosphere of guilt is so destructive, they lean toward never saying anything, even in professional contexts, that might suggest that mothers never behave badly. Poorness-of-fit and other temperament-based explanations are more reassuring (Karen, 1994, p. 296).

According to practitioner and author Russell Barkley:

The weight of the research points to hereditary and neurological factors as having the lion's share of influence over the expression of this disorder [ADHD], not poor parenting, diet, or excessive television viewing. Genetic effects seem to account for as much as 80% of differences among individuals in these symptoms [a completely unsupported claim]; the common environment accounts for very little, if any, of them. The yoke of moral indignation from others, character indictment, sinfulness, and willful neglect of social responsibilities can therefore finally be lifted from the shoulders of those with ADHD; they need bear it no longer, for it is clear now that to continue to hold such views will bespeak a stunning scientific ignorance about this disorder (Barkley, 1997, p. 349).

To be clear, **there is no evidence genes are responsible for ADHD or any other behavioral issues** (Breggin, 2000; DeGrandpre, 1999; Glasser, 2005; Joseph, 2015; Snyder, 2012), but the main point I want to make is that the common theme of the geneticists or pro-parent theorists is it's just not nice, necessary or productive to "blame" mothers or to actually acknowledge the importance of mothering or parenting in the formation of a personality. Apparently some researchers spend their lives producing theory that protects mothers and parents. The motive makes sense; the logic does not.

Even the notions of temperament or poorness-of-fit are remarkable concepts designed to comfort the guilt of a mother who probably already knows she can't fully tune in, rather than teach her how to respond effectively to her baby. Babies—all of them—are lovely, innocent, dependent and consolable by a consistent and attentive parent who can tune in. They are even trusting until they become fearful that they are not safe, at which point they become cranky. To presume a baby is born difficult is to create blindness and ensure a failure to see the infant's cues to his needs. Any mistrusting baby may recover from crankiness if his life becomes safe enough or the damage is not already too severe to safely remember and cathart.

Others, even the leaders of the pack, have lain down their swords and admitted true research favors environmental explanations for behavior. Unfortunately, it is not clear to pro-parent thinkers this is about education, not blaming parents, as parents were children too.

One reflexive defense I often hear is my parents treated us all the same, and we turned out quite differently. It's important to understand no two children in the same family have the same parents, nor can they possibly be treated the same. The first child may have had parents who idealized parenting or who would learn to parent by making mistakes. Mom might have stayed home for the first child, but not the second, or vice versa. The parent of the first child only has one child demanding attention, while the parent of three has three children demanding attention. Parents can be in different stages of life, or the way their child looks (just like his father) may affect mom's attitude toward the child.

The Patrons of Research

Biological psychiatry is contracted by the pharmaceutical industry to discover or invent, test, authenticate and promote drugs. Biological psychiatry and behavioral researchers have a poor reputation in the sciences for repeating the same research flaws, but it doesn't seem to matter because the marketing budget is so enormous it can readily settle lawsuits. According to Colin Ross and Alvin Pam (1995):

> Biological psychiatry does little to criticize its own premises and thus recapitulates the same errors over time. More, it wields a strong public-relations arm, which manipulates the press into heralding its 'breakthroughs,' although very little of scientific merit is actually occurring. In its march toward scientific 'progress,' biological psychiatry tends to endorse fads—if one may speak of research efforts in this way—that momentarily 'explain' in sophisticated terms the physiological etiology and mechanics of various syndromes and diagnoses. Later, such results are not replicated and specific hypotheses quietly fade away while the general theoretical approach remains... (p. 3).

> As with all rituals, myths and symbols, those of biological psychiatry take on a life of their own, and psychiatrists often forget to look beneath and beyond them... None quite explains how and why a relatively small and not very successful group of researchers transformed themselves into a large, international, influential field of medicine—nor how and why critics within the field...are largely ignored, while the search for genes and enzymes progresses with increasing vigor... (p. 232).

Professions are social organizations that construct, as they form themselves, the means to perpetuate themselves by controlling access and knowledge, and by neutralizing social mechanisms that might control them. This requires political activity, both in relation to potential or actual competitors (p. 233).

In a more recent development, it appears drug companies now install their own representative where the research is being done, as if to ensure the desired outcome. Funding for research often has conditions or agreements not to publish results if genetic causes or other marketing assertions cannot be proven, or if the drugs are not proven to be substantially helpful or safe. Most behavioral research is expected to lead to new, breakthrough wonder drugs. HMOs and insurance companies have come to depend on and expect these medications to produce quicker, cheaper fixes. A related journal article by Henry Mintzberg, "Patent nonsense: Evidence tells of an industry out of social control," reports:

> A great deal has been revealed in recent years about biases in pharmaceutical companies' reports on their medicines. These include 'the preponderance of positive company-sponsored studies,' threats of 'legal action to stop nominally independent researchers from publishing negative material' and research contracts that allow 'the sponsoring company to delete information from the report and to delay publication' (2006, p. 375).

A number of researchers have begun to report that if they fail to produce the results they were paid to produce, they are either penalized financially, or they are required by contract to bury the results, or both (Interlandi, 2006; Mintzberg, 2006). Psychiatrists are being courted, wined and dined (Carlat, 2007; Harris & Carey, 2008, Hensley, 2008). Whistle-blower lawsuits are growing, and the pharmaceutical industry is paying more and more in penalties. However, the penalties are a small percentage of the profit from sales of psychotropic drugs (Brown, 2008; Harris, 2009 and 2010). The penalties are worth it to the drug companies. Peter Conrad, professor of sociology at Brandeis University in Waltham, Massachusetts, points out, "Managed-care organizations are less likely to pay for psychotherapy and family interventions" (Wasowicz, 2007). Finally, study after study has begun to reveal severe side effects for patients, but the push to medicate continues with the public's support. As a matter of fact, research shows patients accept pharmaceutical treatment more readily when they believe their symptoms are genetic (Phelan, Yang & Cruz-Rojas, 2006). The deck is stacked against real therapy, and harmful side medication effects are tolerated as if they're a necessary evil.

According to medical journalist Marcia Angell, Senator Charles Grassley (R-Iowa) launched an investigation in 2008 into the relationship between psychiatrists and drug companies. Grassley uncovered evidence drug companies paid Harvard Medical School psychiatrist Joseph Biederman, who coined the term Pediatric Bipolar Disorder (PBD), $1.6 million in consulting fees between 2000 and 2007, a clear conflict of interest. Two of his colleagues received similar amounts, for which the president of Massachusetts General

Hospital offered sympathy instead of criticism to those being investigated, "We know this is an incredibly painful time for those doctors and their families, and our hearts go out to them" (Angell, 2009, para. 4).

When Senator Grassley called upon Biederman to reveal his income from drug companies, Biederman drastically underreported, as even the drug companies admitted paying him many times more than his reported amount. It is believed Biederman has received millions for promoting the diagnosis of PBD and its pharmaceutical treatment (Harris & Carey, 2008). Biederman may justify the large sums to himself and others, believing the condition is real—and genetic—and somebody must identify and treat it (chemically).

Senator Grassley also uncovered Alan F. Schatzberg, chair of Stanford's Psychiatry Department and president-elect of the American Psychiatric Association, controlled more than $6 million worth of stock with Corcept Therapeutics, a company he owns that is testing an abortion drug, RU-486, also known as mifepristone, as a potential treatment for psychotic depression. Schatzberg was also the principal investigator on a National Institute of Mental Health grant that included research on mifepristone and was an author of three papers on the subject. Schatzberg saw no conflict of interest, but the university replaced him to ensure there was no "misunderstanding" (Angell, 2009, para. 5).

Another of Grassley's discoveries was about psychiatrist Charles B. Nemeroff, chair of Emory University's Department of Psychiatry, co-editor with Schatzberg of the influential manual, *Textbook of Psychopharmacology*. Nemeroff was the principal researcher on a five-year $3.95 million National Institute of Health (NIH) grant, $1.35 million of which went to Emory University for overhead—to study several drugs made by GlaxoSmithKline (GSK). Emory was required to report amounts over $10,000 per year to the NIH, along with assurances of no conflicts of interest. However, Nemeroff failed to disclose to the NIH an income of $500,000 from GSK for giving dozens of talks promoting the company's drugs. Emory conducted its own investigation and found multiple violations by Nemoroff, who responded, "I shall limit my consulting to GSK to under $10,000 and I have informed GSK of this policy" (Angell, 2009, para. 7). Nemeroff received $171,031 from GSK while he reported to Emory just $9,999, one dollar under the reportable threshold. In his defense, Nemeroff wrote the dean:

> Surely you remember that Smith-Kline Beecham Pharmaceuticals donated an endowed chair to the department and there is some reasonable likelihood that Janssen Pharmaceuticals will do as well. In addition, Wyeth-Ayerst Pharmaceuticals has funded a Research Career Development Award program in the department, and I have asked both AstraZeneca Pharmaceuticals and Bristol-Meyers [sic] Squibb to do the same. Part of the rationale for their funding our faculty in such a manner would be my service on these boards (Angell, 2009, para. 9).

WHAT'S THE HARM?

Betrayal of Trust

Critical thinkers have offered differing interpretations of the same problem. Alice Miller saw the blindness of psychiatry as a highly defended blindness to childhood issues that frustrated her until she quit her professional organizations. She wrote about her fellow colleagues:

> I officially broke away from the Swiss as well as the International Psychoanalytical Association. I was forced to take this step when I realized that psychoanalytical theory and practice obscure —*i.e.*, render unrecognizable—the causes and consequences of child abuse, by (among other things) labeling facts as fantasies, and furthermore that such treatments can be dangerous, as in my own case because they cement the confusion deriving from childhood instead of resolving it (1981, p. viii).

Neuroscientist and biologist Steven Rose pointed out the consequence of scientists misleading scientists and the public, implying a misappropriation of priorities, "An immediate social consequence of reductionist ideology is that attention and funding is diverted from the social to the molecular" (1997, p. 297). It appeared the molecular biologists and other geneticists took the same path as the adoption researchers, beginning to hide and fabricate information, if not fully misrepresenting the results of their studies. Then the epigeneticists continued in the same direction.

On the receiving end of adoption studies, twin studies and molecular genetic research are psychiatrists, who are persuaded to believe further in the medical model, the foundation of their profession, and in their own prescription-writing craft. An analysis of the role of biomedical psychiatry was offered in terms of legitimacy and cultural authority by evolutionary biologist Fiona Ingleby. Jay Joseph paraphrases her opinion:

> Science is regarded in our culture as objective and value-free. A pretense of science justifies the clinical approach of biological psychiatry, it's lack of contextual focus, and its lack of attention to issues of power—I say pretense because, in terms of scientific status, biological psychiatry ha s fundamental flaws... (2015, p. 232).

Joseph continues, "In the view of Meyer, Rowan (1977) and Kleinman (1988) positivist ideology provides the rituals, myths and symbols that sustain biological psychiatry" (p. 232) wherein they "take on a life of their own, and psychiatrists often forget to look beneath and beyond them" (p. 232).

According to Joseph, "none of the perspectives of biological psychiatry explains how a relatively small and not very successful group of researchers transformed themselves into a large, international, influential field of medicine—nor how critics within the field, such as Laing, Szasz and

Kleinman, are largely ignored, while the search for genes and enzymes progresses with increasing vigor" (p. 232).

These overcompensating researchers would cause thousands of patients to take drugs that would make them violent or disabled for life with akathisia. They would support mothers in leaving their babies in daycare, thereby dramatically changing the personality of American children as well as the adults they would become, creating "time bombs" and mass shootings.

Psychiatrists are medical doctors who continue their education after receiving their M.D. to specialize in issues of mental health, predominantly according to biological psychiatry. Some of the powerful quotes in this book and in this chapter are by brilliant and heroic psychiatrists who have dared to speak up about the way they were trained, challenging the mythology of their own profession. Unfortunately, most psychiatrists appear to be trained in brain biology, chemistry and medications out of context of causal experiences. These psychiatrists appear to be deprived of a real education in how human beings process relationships and trauma. They don't seem to have learned much about the emotional needs of children and the legacy these needs create in the lifetime of a person, depending on whether or not these needs were met or frustrated. They seem to have little training in the natural ways our bodies are designed to heal emotional trauma. Nevertheless, they assume the position at the top of the pecking order with afforded authority and the power of definition.

Fortunately, some psychiatrists who challenge the medical model of mental illness write critically about how they, and all their fellow students, were trained (Breggin, 1991). We have an opportunity to right a wrong. I write in hopes psychiatrists will study attachment and trauma research, at least as much as described herein. I write in hopes they study how emotional healing works with catharsis and how healing is blocked with repression ethics commonly found in abusive and neglectful families. I also write in hopes they have learned how we grow up to treat our children, our mates and others much the way we were treated as children.

It appears psychiatrists must self-educate or they will not be as well-trained as psychologists in the cause and treatment of mental illness. Psychologists, on the other hand, who are under the influence of the American Psychiatric Association in our curriculum and below psychiatrists in the pecking order of authenticated mental health professionals, are not as well-trained in my experience, as marriage and family therapists (MFTs). MFTs specialize in relationship styles, parenting styles, family systems and prevention, more than the other mental health professions. You might say MFTs are the natural healers. I say this as a psychologist *and* MFT, even though my psychologist license affords me more prestige.

Misdiagnoses

The front page of *Newsweek*, May 26, 2008, held a split photo of 10-year-old Max Blake, showing him both sweet and raging. In an article by Mary Carmichael, we learn Max was diagnosed with Pediatric Bipolar Disorder (PBPD), held to be a genetic disease, at Tufts-New England Medical Center (TNEMC) after his parents searched in vain for someone who could explain and treat his violent and erratic behavior.

The diagnosis at TNEMC was based on Harvard Medical School psychiatrist Joseph Biederman's research on bipolar disorder. Once Max became diagnosed with PBPD, his story became available to *Newsweek* as a means to represent another scientific breakthrough in genetic behaviors, even though the diagnosis is not accepted in the current *Diagnostic and Statistical Manual and no such gene has ever been found.*

Lost in the *Newsweek* article was one sentence revealing that Max's mother, an attorney, returned to work when he was three months old, which could have led to a diagnosis of Reactive Attachment Disorder (RAD). Beiderman has renamed the condition and proclaimed it is genetic, without ruling out RAD. Indeed, the condition of PBPD may be real, however misnamed, if it describes an extreme version of RAD (which is already extreme), as it may be the first time in the history of human evolution that mothers commonly leave their babies with others, often in the care of strangers, even rotating strangers, to return for them in the evenings.

Even though we have known for nearly a century that human attachment is critical, psychiatrists, as well as researchers, forget to consider the probable causes of mental illness, if they ever learned about them in the first place. I would love to see more longitudinal studies on the psychopathology that results in children placed in daycare as newborns or young infants, before one year of age and before two years of age as compared to children who were at least three years old. I predict they will find "pediatric bipolar" results from being placed in daycare in infancy, Reactive Attachment Disorder results in being placed in daycare in the toddler years from one to two, and ADHD and Separation Anxiety result from being placed in daycare between two and three and sometimes later. Additionally, other extreme diagnoses will develop on these fragile foundations identifiable by symptoms of traumatic events to follow. For example, a child with an insecure attachment who is also abused will develop a conduct disorder, while a child who has an insecure attachment and is a victim of incest will likely molest others, and a child who has an insecure attachment and is raised by parents who are incongruent with their beliefs and behaviors, may develop schizophrenia.

The Human Cost of Medication

One of the biggest reasons to question the judgment of medicating psychological symptoms is that once it's begun, the avenue for healing is interrupted. It is much easier and quicker to do therapy when one is not medicated. It is easier to get to the root of the problem and heal it once and for all. When that is done there is no need for medication. Further, prior suffering is often transformed into insight and wisdom. Unfortunately, the profession of psychiatry has long been on the path of medicating symptoms often inconvenient for others, rather than seeking to unearth cause and healing. The driving force in medicine is marketing more than the compassionate healing of injuries.

Some lawsuits have been filed against pharmaceutical corporations for not fully investigating side effects. Some have sold medications that were purely unsafe. Pharmaceutical producer GSK was ordered to pay $750 million in civil and criminal fees for selling 20 different drugs with questionable safety, rife with contamination from a plant in Puerto Rico. Whistleblower Cheryl Eckard warned GSK of the issues and was fired instead of praised for discovering and reporting the problem. Among the affected drugs were Avandia, Bactroban, Coreg, Paxil and Tagamet (Harris & Wilson, 2010, para. 3).

Sometimes medications work. Sometimes they work at first. Sometimes they backfire. The rates of backfiring are very high. The odds of a safe and successful outcome are poor. They are designed to provide Breggin's coined "chemical lobotomy" (1991). Even if that were a reasonable approach, the chemical composition of drugs course through the entire body and brain, creating side effects. They are "shotgun meds" (not expected to hit a specific target). The side effects often make patients very sick. The side effects of psychotropic drugs have been historically very toxic and sometimes deadly. Some side effects create psychosis. When this happens, patients may end up committing homicide or suicide, when they would not have otherwise done so.

Other side effects create physical conditions often worse than the mental condition. One such side effect is tardive dyskinesia, which causes a person to lose physical control over their body. They develop tics that can be both rigid and so exaggerated the patient cannot control their movements all day long, even in their sleep. They are tortured in order to appear sane enough to manage. Unfortunately, once the drug is withdrawn it's often too late to reverse the side effects. I would rather be the victim of murder than of these side effects. It reminds me of politician Joseph Kennedy's decision to give his wife Rosemary a lobotomy because she was too slow and unruly (McNeil, 2014). Psychotropic drugs may create physical conditions in the body that lead to a slow or even quick deterioration, dementia, psychosis or death. Others may create a dramatic weight gain or Type 2 diabetes. Some of these drugs are addictive, such as benzodiazepines (Valium, Xanax). Often prescribing doctors and psychiatrists do not know the statistics on the drugs they prescribe. Drugs of concern to Dr. Breggin from his book *Toxic Psychiatry* (1991):

- Stimulants for Attention Deficit Hyperactivity Disorder (ADHD): Ritalin, Concerta, Adderall, amphetamines and other stimulant medications
- Selective Serotonin Reuptake Inhibitors (SSRIs) for depression: Prozac, Zoloft, Paxil, Luvox, Celexa, Effexor, Wellbutrin and other antidepressants. Evaluated to be no more effective than a placebo.

- Benzodiazapines or tranquilizers and sleeping pills: Xanax, Valium, Ativan, Klonopin and other sedative and highly addictive drugs.
- Neuroleptics or antipsychotic drugs: Thorazine, Trilafon, Zyprexa, Risperdal, Geodon, Seroquel, Abilify and other antipsychotic medications, all presenting major negative side effects.

Schizophrenia is treatable. There are highly competent psychologists who are good at treating psychosis, including Ty Colbert (Orange County) and Bertram Karon (Michigan). One could buy Ty Colbert's book, *Broken Brains or Wounded Hearts* (1996) to see his approach to treating a schizophrenic patient. One can also go online to read Karon's online essay describing his successful treatment of a schizophrenic patient: "The Case of Mr. X: An 'Incurable' Schizophrenic." I have had a few successes myself, but the parents have all refused to cooperate. I have found them to be very defensive, and insist the problem is genetic and has nothing to do with them. I have had parents cruelly re-injure their grown child when they learned the therapy included a review of their childhood issues. Now I only work with such patients when the parents are completely out of the picture or are on board for a review the grown child's earliest experiences, for the sake of their child.

GROUP THINK

Group Denial is a Historical Phenomenon

I wear the hat of a clinician as well as that of a researcher (who compares and studies research). I hypothesize about how educated people who have committed themselves to objectivity could go so far afield at such a high cost to lives and quality of life. I believe it could not happen if they didn't do it together. History is replete with group-think, which seeks agreement and repels disagreement. In my field, we even have a diagnosis *folie à deux*, which means insanity of two (or more), or shared insanity, when either person alone would not have formed the insane beliefs. I realize there are contexts in which a whole community can be completely wrong about something, but that doesn't make them insane. However, one could still argue these scientists together are wrong, rigid, lacking perceptive abilities, prone to bias, shallow, narcissistic, non-self-reflecting, poor at empathy, and probably have some deficits in conscience, the end results of which would be cruel and criminal in another context.

Authorities have done many bad things by surrounding themselves with enforced agreement, and history is replete with group-think, wherein the rest of us agree in order to be accepted:

- Some detectives believe coercion is a valid way to get a confession. Where is the American Psychological Association when we need it?
- Kramer and Sprenger believed witches needed to be tortured to confess, then burned at the stake or drowned. As many as 10 million wildcraft practitioners were executed. These homicidal tactics to force false

confessions were designed to rid the culture of women in leadership and shore up the church. They practiced sadistic ethics and unhealthy relationship skills by abusing power, blaming, controlling, judging, and punishing. They were genocidal terrorists in the name of something allegedly good. They believed they were in the right.
- Southerners before the Civil War were barely conflicted over the right to enslave, torture and exploit the lives of human beings stolen from their homes.
- Adolf Hitler and his loyal Nazis were taught to believe Jews were their enemies within (because Adolf's abusive father was secretly born of a Jewish maid) and extermination was the answer, since they had learned to swallow the truth and their feelings *en masse* for the sake of authority.
- Priests and their superiors have lied about child sexual abuse to protect the church.
- Cult members have been convinced they should follow their cult leader, no matter how badly how s/he behaves.
- The scientists who "proved" genes cause behavior were willing to doctor their results because they *believed* in behavioral genetics so strongly that to report a lack of findings would be a misrepresentation of the truth.

Others have inadvertently been pawns of dishonest authorities:
- Psychiatrists are persuaded that children need pharmaceuticals, not corrective parenting.
- Teachers have been taught that disruptive students need pharmaceuticals.
- Feminists have been persuaded to leave their babies to go work because it is good for them.
- Children's Protective Services have been known to take children from parents who refused to medicate their children.

People Ignore the Truth for Acceptance

It's ironic that a substantial number of the laypopulation has been able to see cause and effect in their daily lives, while geneticists have been blind. It's a perfect case for meditation, isn't it? Meditation brings us face to face with our own self-deception, just as dreams do. There is an overwhelming need for enlightenment experiences by these scientists who cannot see, think or act clearly.

Our psyches are designed to report to us when we are selling others on something that is untrue. That's why polygraphs usually work. Half-healthy people would be having dreams about turning back, driving off a cliff, making a mess, or some sign we are not in accord with reality and we are setting up a long-term disaster. They should be having serious difficulty living with themselves. If not, I suspect they have surrounded themselves with constant affirmations they are on the right track, doing the right thing.

Unfortunately, blinded people have been victims of loyalty ethics, probably to include loyalty to parents and agreement that behaviors are inborn. I would like to see how many of these people who commit these overwhelming offenses against their neighbors and the truth believe they are doing the right thing because they have learned to subsume their own truth for their parents.

Parenting is not just about unconditional love, discipline, family, shelter and education. Many parents think parenting is about sharing a name, roof and food. Parenting is about teaching children how to think about things, what to question and what not to question, and often these lessons are indirectly taught. Parenting teaches us what to see and what not to see, as well as what to feel and what feelings to ignore. The greatest of these instructions—often non-verbal instructions—is how to look at people, events and things.

Children depend on their parents and grown-ups for their worldview. How does a child survive when they experience their parents acting selfishly and hurtfully? Should they swallow any truth or feeling that discredits their parents? Of course. Do they tell the truth, even though it may upset their parents? Of course not. Sometimes swallowing the truth and our feelings is a survival requirement. As clinicians, do we have an eye out for the things children are forbidden to say? Do we know the consequences to the child for expressing thoughts and feelings that upset the parents? What is the most upsetting thing a child could say to a parent? Why?

Sometimes it's not that parents forbid these expressions. Sometimes swallowing feelings and thoughts is a gift children give their parents out of compassion and fear for them, their protectors. They see them struggling or suffering, and so begin taking care of their parents by giving up their authenticity. Sometimes we pretend we are safer than we actually are. Sometime we pretend we are kinder than we are. Sometimes we pretend the way we are being raised is perfection, despite having an underlying drive to outdo others. It's called denial. Whatever denial we learn as children becomes our denial as adults. It becomes our blinders. It determines what we will see or not see and feel or not feel. Most adults become quite contentious, uneasy or avoidant when this very denial is tickled or threatened. We can become emotional about any theory or suggestion that appears to threaten our parents or even parents in general, hence the ongoing and ever unresolved nature/nurture debate.

ORIGINS OF SELF-AWARENESS

A person can't heal without expressing the buried truth and his injured feelings. He also can't heal if he doesn't practice self-awareness, including paying attention to his behaviors and connecting them to original learned assumptions. Self-aware people are more enlightened, more intelligent, more rational, kinder, more understanding, more perceptive and more honest. These are the pro-child thinkers.

When one believes their psychological issues are inborn, they are more inclined to become dull to their own inner workings and less perceptive of others. They also accept pharmaceutical solutions for their psychological issues and if they believe their behavior results from childhood experiences, they are more inclined to do depth therapy or a deeper analysis of their earliest years (Phelan, Yang & Cruz-Rojas, 2006)). When we believe genes determine the way we are, self-inquiry is unnecessary. All great thinkers seem to be self-aware. I am someone who believes everyone could be a great thinker, enjoying the thrill of insight. Those of us who don't self-reflect live lives never knowing the deal—being told the rules, corralled into agreement and loyalty as two primary ethics—which leads to lives of betrayal. Maybe that's why Socrates reportedly said, "The unexamined life is not worth living."

We grow up lots of ways. We may become carpenters or thieves, only responsible to ourselves. Or we can achieve levels of authority and have responsibilities to others. We can grow up to be lovers, parents, teachers, cops, attorneys, judges, clinicians, or behavioral researchers. We may become geniuses or heroes. Some of us defend our own denial, while others seek self-awareness.

Some of us will swallow ourselves to protect our parents. The more important it is to *not* "blame" our parents, the more one is stuck in childhood mandates. **The fear of blaming parents is the point of view of a child**, not a grown-up, yet it's a practice that follows us into adulthood, absent self-awareness (Miller, 1981, 1983, 1984, 1998, 1990, 2001 & 2005). When we don't know or can't know from where our attitudes come, they seem to be inborn.

The adult who has self-reflected doesn't see it as blaming parents. **They give themselves permission to feel their feelings and remember the truth.** As adults, they understand everyone makes wrong choices in life, especially under duress. Most are not interested in blaming their parents, but in acknowledging their own pain, confusion and resulting choices and worldview that perpetuated the problem. They process those feelings and revise their information: Even though my dad said I was a "bad boy," I'm not bad. I never liked playing hockey, but my dad really wanted me to be great at it. I hated my brother because he took time away from my parents. It wasn't his fault; we both needed more attention. I'm not stupid; no one knows things before they learn them. I don't have to put up a false front to be liked; the false front puts people off. Feelings won't kill me; I can handle the pain until it's over. My parents were more afraid of being disrespected than incorrect. I have learned respect is not free; we give respect to get respect. After giving ourselves the appropriate sympathy we need, we can truly forgive our parents even when we acknowledge the way we were treated was wrong. They were children once too and how they were treated was bound to affect us.

Our pro-parent researchers do not ascribe to any principles of self-reflection. As a matter of fact, I suspect they eschew it. Behaviorists assert there is no way to know what causes a behavior because that information is unknowable.

They speak as if it is in a "black box" no one can ever open because you can't trust a person's recollections. You can never truly know what happened between a parent and a child, and even the grown child cannot be considered a valid reporter of what happened. So why bother? Why dredge up old bones? Let the past be the past.

I also say it because if they did believe in self-reflection, this charade would not have gone on so long. How did these two schools of thought—pro-parent and pro-child theories—combine under the heading of psychology? The answer appears to be some of us are driven to protect parents to such an extent we will become professionals to prove our parents were right. Maybe then they would love us and be proud of us.

It appears pro-parent scientists cannot afford to face their own denial. It would be a betrayal of agreements. It would be disloyal to parents and colleagues who believe genes instruct behavior, not parents. Were it not for the monumental impact their conclusions have on children and society, I would have more compassion for their mind-warping plight.

True healing requires the review of life's messages and lessons such that we can make new choices out of self-awareness. The problem of blaming parents is insignificant but is perceived as monumental. Parents were children too, and ultimately when one has faced the truth of what has happened to them, to include their parents' short-comings and long-term impact on their children's development, healing takes place. That's not just healing of the child or grown child. It often includes healing between the parent and child. When grown children review their childhood situation and identify the incidences that negatively impacted their abilities to make healthy choices, they often also review what happened to their parents. Most of my clients end up forgiving their parents and becoming closer. The parents who become the most negatively affected are those who insist on blaming their child rather than self-reflecting. In those moments, the grown child sees clearly who was the most important person in their childhood and why they had to modify their thoughts and feelings to survive.

Clinicians Need to See More Clearly

We need to understand how pathology is born in order to guide. We need to understand cause and effect in order to protect ourselves from the dictates that mislead us and cause us to guide badly. We also need to understand cause and effect in order to qualify for any sort of role as the sage or advocate. There has been enough major replicated research to advise us how to treat children, to predict outcomes of various parenting techniques and childhoods, to recognize what needs to be treated sooner than later, and to understand the behavior of others and ourselves. It's understandable that any one person might not have all that information.

I have written about the groundbreaking and replicated pro-child research from our field in my companion book: *The Predictor Scale: Predicting and Understanding Behavior according to Critical Childhood Experiences*. It presents many examples of people familiar to most of us. I consider *The Predictor Scale* my most important work, as it is designed to be an easy read for clinicians, judges, parents and other professionals, with special hope that behavioral scientists would read it. They could learn these "rule-outs" in the time it takes to read this book. Parents and teachers should read it. Judges and defense attorneys should read it. Criminals in jail should read it. Teachers should read it. Clergy should read it.

There can no longer be any excuse for anyone misinterpreting the significance of childhood experiences and their long-term impacts. We can improve our abilities to prophesy about these long-term effects if we know which ones they are and how to weigh them compared to other experiences. The book also comes with a score sheet for easy yet productive assessment. It's not hard to demystify behavior once we set biases aside.

Psychoanalyzing Scientists

A decision confronts every child born. It is about as genetically determined as procreation, although the decision itself will be determined by environment. It is inherent in our design that we will ultimately learn, predominantly from decisions our parents make *for* us, how to see our parents, others and ourselves. Ultimately our parents will demand loyalty to their point of view, or they will set us free to have our own experiences, on our own terms, to represent ourselves in our own ways. We may be heir to parents for whom good behavior means making them look good, being their mirror, and taking care of their identities by swallowing our own. Or we may be heir to parents who want us to be our own person, given we are respectful, ethical and fair.

If a child wants to be loved and protected, she may have to pay the price of sacrificing her authentic self. It can be decided as early as the first year of life when an infant learns it's not allowed to cry, or when parents withdraw affection when they feel criticized. This decision forms the foundation of temperament and even a personality disorder. It becomes a life-long unconscious commitment if there's no life-altering intervention.

The decision itself will probably be forgotten, but the presumption is deeply held that we put our parents above ourselves, even when they are unethical. From there we determine how to treat our children, often with the same unspecified rules. We will adapt in two possible directions. We may come to judge, blame and scapegoat others for the very things against which we have immunized our parents, or we may learn to interact with others in fear of being discovered as not good enough or not superior after all. We will come to know on some level we can't tell the whole truth, and to have any sort of self-determination we have to live underground where there are no rules. We will advocate others not tell the whole truth either. We will become adults who honor our parents, whatever our parents' issues. We will hold others to the same values. To use the somewhat extreme example of the Menendez Brothers, who killed their parents in 1989, we might believe there are no parents "*that* bad." So if we were on their jury, we would probably have voted guilty, even though their parents mercilessly abused them. One juror said, "I was molested, and I didn't kill my parents." Very few of us know how to assess the most important factors in the creation of personality and behavior. The Menendez Brothers were not a risk to society. They killed their parents in a growing panic of self-defense that may or may not have been a *folie à deux* (shared insanity), since their parents had convinced the boys they were all-seeing, all-knowing and would kill them when they least expected it if they were to report their abuse. They knew of no feasible protection, including authorities. If we meet an adult who had been beaten frequently and intensely as a child, will we want them to "get over it"? Do we have more patience with victims of strangers than victims of parents?

While we hold the grown child responsible, we may excuse their parents for harming a little person, who is clearly less important than a big person. They don't have feelings like grown-ups, right? Wrong. Children are far more fragile and impacted by childhood experiences than adults, including parents. We gravitate to values support the decisions with which we live. When we have experiences that become encapsulated by these long-standing assumptions, we perpetuate long-forgotten values and beliefs with unrelenting fervor.

The greatest evidence I have for this persistent proposition—we are blackmailed into loyalty and inauthenticity—is what happened to Sigmund Freud by fellow psychiatrists. He learned one is not allowed to see some things if one wants to be loved and accepted in the public world and at home. He learned the field of psychiatry—and ultimately psychology—would not tolerate blaming parents for how their children turn out. That's like learning to play golf without a golf club.

The very field dedicated to supporting the mental health of others was born protecting offending parents against their helpless children. This predilection is evident in the fields of law and religion too. It shows up wherever we see the codification of values. It is so pervasive it blinds scientists, judges, clinicians, and parents, even when they have been trained to be objective. So by this point, I trust the reader can accept it is not preposterous to suggest our trusted experts have misled us into believing concepts that harm our best interests.

You have been invited to sit in the front row of an adventure undertaken by the experts of psychology, from the times they committed mass murder against wild-craft practitioners and then against the mentally ill. You have seen researchers build a fraudulent case that heirs of slavery were intellectually inferior rather than educationally deprived. You have seen millions of people murdered for their religion because it was forbidden to recognize the sins of the father (Hitler's father). You have learned of the genocide of the mentally ill and the how the first behavioral researchers attempted to prove mental illness is inborn. You have witnessed the unfolding of the history of psychology, with few heroes and many villains. We have been recognized as an inexact science, not because of how our personalities and behaviors are formed is unknowable to-date, but because we have agreed not to see clearly in another variation on collective denial. Those of us who agree in early childhood not to know the truth about our experiences become adults who cannot perceive clearly or reason well. We become accustomed to hiding our motives and producing "logical" or left-brain explanations in lieu of obvious reasons. We seek solutions essentially designed to cover up and benefit the powers-that-be because it's what we learned as children. We are in the Dark Ages and we don't know it.

The greatest thing I can actually point to now is the issue at hand: the search for the unholy grail. Massive amounts of spending take place in search of genetic explanations or justifications for medicating children and adult patients, rather than understanding them. Today, many if not most of us sign on to a mass injustice in our culture, agreeing it is normal and correct to medicate our children and the mentally ill, in lieu of understanding them. Our experts have been twisting themselves into pretzels to prove the way we are and what we do is inborn. They have gone to exhaustive lengths and recklessly expensive heights to prove something most of us wanted prove,n to justify our own self-denial and our own disregard of our children's perspective. We want to be lied to; it's convenient.

Unfortunately, once we become blind to our own needs, we no longer see clearly. We can't make good political decisions either. When the human race can transcend this conundrum, perhaps we can save the planet from self-destruction. For now, we lack the gift of overview, something we inherited but learned not to use. We can only hope the goal of self-awareness can become important soon enough to save ourselves, declaring we are not blaming parents, but simply ending a legacy by helping them.

To sum up, we have seen the human condition is to sell ourselves short for security, unless our parents are ethical and magnanimous. We agree to sell out our truth and enter together into a collective state of denial. This condition has created a culture that has a taboo against knowing who we are and against seeing our parents and childhoods clearly. It has an ethic of telling half-truths and honoring authorities who hide the truth from us and profit from our ignorance. It is blasphemy to call a spade a spade where explanations for behavior are sought.

Today, the powers-that-be want to sell us drugs for our children more than teach us what our children need, and how they would flourish if we met their needs. In the name of mental health, we are taught that non-existent genes—not needs—determine how and who our children become. We have learned the best behavior is the behavior that doesn't complain about how the body and soul are being treated, and the best treatment extinguishes the symptoms rather than investigating origins of the suffering. We have learned the goal of therapy is to eliminate symptoms, not causes. May it be that in the name of mental health we finally find more compassionate and enlightened ways to care for our progeny.

9: APPENDIX

I: TYPES OF RESEARCH FLAWS

It is not possible to review all the research—even the recent research on genetics—because it just keeps coming. Scientists continue to commit the same errors, despite generous exposure to the criticisms of genetic research. No study contains all errors listed below, but if a study is held to prove genetic influences on behavior, look for any of the following flaws. **To-date, no gene has been isolated and replicated to account for any mental illness.**

Lack of Rule-Outs
- Researchers fail to rule out environmental explanations first, making results invalid (Joseph, 2004).
- Researchers infer genetics when behaviors run in families, disregarding mirror neurons (Siegel, 1999).

Failure to Replicate
- Most of the studies that allegedly detect chemical imbalances cannot be replicated. Often our chemistry changes throughout the day (Colbert, 2000).
- Behavioral scientists have turned upside down their Golden Rule—that a study is not meaningful it if cannot be replicated. Now they declare the lack of ability to replicate is *evidence* there is more than one gene. The number of genes that allegedly create schizophrenia is growing with each new discovery.
- While there are mounds of evidence that have been replicated *ad nauseum* for environmental causes of behavior, there has been no such evidence for genetic causes. Yet the environmental research is essentially ignored.

Revisions of Language
- Chemical "imbalances" such as surges of cortisol or adrenalin and other chemical reactions to stress, loss or trauma, are reported by biogeneticists to be evidence of chemical imbalances presumed to result from genetic inheritance (Whitaker, 2002).
- Many times subjects are reported to have chemical imbalances or show up as having brain abnormalities in brain scans, MRIs and other such tests, but other researchers such as Bruce Perry (2001) and Martin Teicher (2002) have demonstrated these abnormalities result from neglect or trauma. What is proven to be a result is said to be a cause.
- Many times the actual chemical imbalance is caused by long-term or recent use of medication, which is not ruled out in the research design. Again, what is proven to be a result is said to be a cause (Breggin, 1991).

Statistical Problems & Data Tampering
- Two major researchers, Cyril Burt and Franz Kallmann, were exposed for having greatly fabricated/padded their statistics, yet some recent studies still average in all previous research, including the infamous Burt and Kallman studies, in order to inflate results.
- Researchers have been involved in "age correcting," to inflate their results.
- They have to be careful because if they age correct for *every* identical twin not yet (also) schizophrenic, they will exceed the Mendel model of 100%.
- When age correcting, researchers not only tamper with their data, but they reveal their study to not be a true "blind study."
- In order to inflate statistics, scientists have counted half-brothers and half-sisters, not genetically related (Breggin, 1991).

Apparent Research Motives
- The pharmaceutical industry spends more money on misleading marketing than on the research itself (Whitaker, 2002).
- The pharmaceutical industry spends more money than the federal government or any other funding source on medical research, including psychotropic drugs, and most chemists and biogeneticists opt to work for this industry because that is where the money is (Valenstein, 1988).
- It is a known practice for many scientists to be under contract with pharmaceutical research grants that require pro-genetic outcomes and if they do not cause that outcome they don't get paid, don't receive a bonus or are obligated by confidentiality agreements to keep the results quiet (Whitaker, 2010; Colbert, 2000).
- Scientists and publicists are paid to write scientific reports that put a positive spin on negative results. The public relations behind announcing these results and ignoring the failure to replicate are not found in the pro-child research (Whitaker, 2010; Colbert, 2000).
- One researcher's study explored whether people are more likely to seek treatment (with pharmaceuticals) if they believe their mental illness is genetic and found the more people believe in genetics, the more they turn to medication rather than therapy (Phelan, Yang & Cruz-Rojas, 2006).
- Most behavioral-genetic research is used to mislead the public. When their studies are found to be flawed or not replicable, their retractions go unheralded and scientists, whether involved in the studies or not, actually write, speak and continue to represent the studies as if they were sound (Whitaker, 2002).

Specific to Pedigree Studies
- When scientists speak of schizophrenia, it doesn't mean the same schizophrenia mental health professionals would identify and diagnose.
- Schizophrenic spectrum, *not* in the *Diagnostic and Statistical Manual* for mental health professionals, now includes: "borderline states," "inadequate personality," "uncertain schizophrenia" and "uncertain borderline state." The meanings and qualifications for these definitions are unclear and have no clinical significance (Joseph, 2006).
- Even though schizophrenia is supposedly a different gene than bipolar, they often include bipolar in order to boost the statistics. Lately, some scientists say schizophrenics and bipolar personalities are genetically related.
- Contrary to implied results, most schizophrenia studies have few, one or no actual schizophrenics in their purportedly meaningful results (Breggin, 1991).
- Rarely does a real schizophrenic subject come from schizophrenic birth parents or grandparents (Breggin, 1991).
- Scientists have been known in major studies to switch first-degree relatives with second-degree relatives to achieve results. This destroys the validity of the genetic research (because we are no longer talking about genes which were directly inherited), but it pumps up the statistics (Breggin, 1991).

Specific to Adoption Studies
- Adoptions are often represented to have taken place at birth when they often take place up to ten years old.
- Children averaged in at an older age could be more injured and could skew the other results.
- Scientists have replaced Mendel's Model of 100% concordance in genetics for a researcher model of only 8% statistical significance, which does not prove genetics.
- The researcher's model at 8% significance actually proves environment at 92%.

Specific to Identical Twins Separated at Birth
- Twins are often represented as having been "separated at birth," when they were separated at any age up to 15 years old. Separated at four, three, or even two years is too late because the quality of attachment has already been established (secure or insecure). Terminology has sometimes been revised to "reared apart" (Joseph, 2004). "Reared apart" may apply to any twins separated for five years or more, even if they were separated at 15.
- Twins who were not adopted away at birth spent their critical years with the biological parents' environment and with each other before separation (Joseph, 2006).

- In all history, there have only been about ten known pairs of adopted identical twins who both turned out to be schizophrenic. In all known cases they were adopted *after* infancy, usually around three to four years of age. In each case the core damage had been done (Ross & Pam, 1995) and they had similar adult triggers.
- Further, these twins were also all adopted into similar circumstances such as separate orphanages or by grown siblings of the mother, if not the mother's mother, so many of these twins were raised in similar environments (Ross & Pam, 1995).
- Finally, these twins had cause to meet one another again, like looking into a mirror. After meeting and comparing notes, they had the opportunity to wonder what it would have been like to live the other twin's life. These comparisons can lead to profound jealousy and guilt (Joseph, 2004).

Chemistry & DNA
- Researchers infer genetics from chemical imbalance assuming only genes can create a chemical imbalance, when environmental stressors do (Valenstein, 1988).
- Researchers assume if a medication works there is a pre-existing chemical shortage. By that logic, if aspirin works, we could infer there is a shortage of aspirin in the brain (Colbert, 2000*)*.
- Scientists may study large families seeking a gene in common for another family trait and attribute the family psychopathology to the same gene they share for a prominent physical trait.
- The more causes that produce a phenomenon, the more rare it should be.

Obfuscation
- Another explanation for failing research results is "incomplete penetrance" which means while the gene may not be evident, it may be assumed to have been inherited and present, even though its influence has not been realized.
- The Diathesis-Stress Model has suggested if environment affects a person's personality or behavioral development, it is because the person was genetically predisposed (Joseph, 2004).
- The new science of Epigenetics utilizes word play to replace the critical importance of environment to make it appear environment is only effective when genes are predisposed to that environmental influence. In some cases involving physical traits, this is true. In no cases involving psychological traits can this be true, since as always, no such genes have been discovered.

II: DON JACKSON'S 11 CRITICISMS OF TWIN STUDIES

Taken from *The Gene Illusion* by Jay Joseph (2004, p. 55).

- In discussing family (consanguinity) studies, it was noted conditions can run in families for environmental reasons.
- There were no genetic studies of schizophrenia in which researchers made diagnoses blindly. The results of these studies were therefore susceptible to the researchers' bias.
- There were other sources of bias in the diagnostic process, such as the unreliability of schizophrenia diagnoses and the finding people had a better chance of being diagnosed with schizophrenia the longer they stayed in the hospital. A sampling bias as introduced by the methods used to obtain twin subjects, which could lead to inflated concordance rates.
- Contrary to genetic expectations, fraternal twins were more concordant than non-twin siblings, even though both sets have the same genetic relationship to each other.
- Contrary to genetic expectations, female identical pairs were more concordant than male fraternal pairs.
- Contrary to genetic expectations, female fraternal pairs were more concordant than opposite-sex fraternals.
- Contrary to genetic expectations, same-sex fraternal pairs were more concordant than opposite-sex fraternals.
- Individual case histories of reared-apart identical twins concordant for schizophrenia do not provide important evidence for genetic factors because they were few in number (two), and because the pairs grew up in similar environments and had an interactive relationship with each other.
- Identical twins grow up in a more similar environment and are treated more similarly than fraternal pairs. Therefore, similar environments can explain greater resemblance of identical pairs for schizophrenia.
- The unique psychological bond or "ego fusion" of identical twins contributes to their higher concordance rate for schizophrenia on the basis of association and identification. Furthermore, the nature of the identical twinship itself might create conditions leading to the identity problems often experienced by people diagnosed with schizophrenia.
- There is a striking similarity between reports of *folie à deux* (shared psychotic disorder) and the case histories of identical twins concordant for schizophrenia.

III: KEY QUESTIONS TO CONSIDER WHEN STUDYING GENETIC RESEARCH

- Who is funding the study?
- Why are they funding the study?
- What is the desired outcome of the study?
- Did the project end with a recommendation or prophesy that the best solution is a chemical solution?
- Has the study been replicated? How many times?
- Does the *actual* data match the author's *interpretation* of the data?
- Have all environmental causes been ruled out?
- Were attachment issues from the first three years of life ruled out?
- Was the study actually blind?
- Is the results language clear?
- For studies of schizophrenia, do the results show patients actually diagnosed with schizophrenia, or were they merely on the "schizophrenic spectrum"?
- Have definitions changed after the study concluded?
- Were there changes in the terms to alter the outcome?
- Has the design of the study changed?
- Were findings based on phenotypes (family intergenerational behaviors) rather than (isolated) genes?

IV: REFERENCES

Ainsworth, M. (1978). *Patterns of Attachment*. Hillsdale: Lawrence Erlbaum Associates, Inc.
Allen, M. G., Cohen, S., & Pollin, W. (1972). Schizophrenia in veteran twins: A diagnositic review. *American Psychiatry, 128*, 939-945.
American Psychiatric Association (2013). *Desk Reference to the Diagnostic Criteria from DSM-5*. Arlington: American Psychiatric Association.
Angell, M. (2009, Jan). Drug Companies & Doctors: A Story of Corruption. *The New York Review of Books,* Retrieved from http://www.nybooks.com/articles/2009/01/15/drug-companies-doctorsa-story-of-corruption/
Anonymous (2000, June). Human genome projects: work in progress. *Nature, 405*, 981. doi:10.1038/35016692
Asbury, K. & Plomin, R. (2013). *G is for genes: what genetics can teach us about how we teach our children*. Oxford: Wiley.
Baillargeon, R., Needham, A., & DeVos, J. (1992). The development of young infants' intuitions about support. *Early Development and Parenting, 1*, 69-78.
Baillargeon, R., & Wang, S. (2002). Event categorization in infancy. *Trends in Cognitive Sciences, 6*, 85-93.
Bandura, A. (1963, April). The Role of Imitation in Personality Development. *The Journal of Nursery Education, 18*, 3.
Barkley, R. (1997). *ADHD and the Nature of Self Control*. New York: The Guilford Press.
Belsky, J. (1986). Infant day care: a cause for concern? *Zero to Three: Bulletin of the National Center for Clinical Infant Programs, VII*(5).
Bentall, R. P. (2009). *Doctoring the Mind: Is Our Current Treatment of Mental Illness Really Any Good?* New York: New York University Press.
Bouchard, T. J. & McGue, M. (2003, January). Genetic and environmental influences on human psychological differences. *Journal of Neurobiology, 54*(1),4-45.
Bowlby, J. (1969). *Attachment, Volume I*. New York: Basic Books.
Bowlby, J. (1973). *Separation, Volume II.* New York: Basic Books.
Bowlby, J. (1980). *Attachment and Loss, Volume III: LOSS, Sadness, and Depression.* New York: Basic Books.
Bowlby, J. (1988). *A Secure Base*. London: Basic Books.
Boyd, D. & Bee, H. (2006). *Lifespan Development*. New York: Pearson Education, Inc.
Breggin, P. (1991). *Toxic Psychiatry.* New York: St. Martin's Press.
Breggin, P. (1998). *Talking Back to Ritalin.* Maine Common Courage Press.
Breggin, P. (2000). *Reclaiming Our Children: A Healing Plan for a Nation in Crisis.* New York: Perseus Publishing.
Breggin, P. (2001). *The Anti-Depressant Fact Book: What Your Doctor Won't Tell You about Prozac, Zoloft, Paxil, Celexa and Luvox.* New York: Perseus Books Group.
Breggin, P. (2008). *Medication Madness: The Role of Psychiatric Drugs in Cases of Violence, Suicide and Crime.* New York: St. Martin's Griffin.
Breggin, P. & Cohen, D. (1999) *Your Drug May Be Your Problem: How and Why to Stop Taking Psychiatric Medications.* Cambridge: Perseus Publishing.
Brown, D. (2008, Sept. 6). FDA to List Drugs Being Investigated. *The Washington Post*.
Buchen, L. (2010, Sept. 8). Neuroscience: In Their Nurture. *Nature 467*, 146-148. doi:10.1038/467146a
Bullock, M., Gelman, R., & Baillargeon, R. (1982). The development of causal reasoning. In W. J. Friedman (Ed.), *The Developmental Psychology of Time*. New York: Academic Press.
Bynum, W. F. (1964, October). Rationales for therapy in British psychiatry: 1780-1835. *Medical History, 18*(4): 317–334.
Calhoun, J. F. (1977). *Abnormal Psychology Current Perspectives*. 2nd ed. New York: Random House.
Carlat, D. (2007, November 25). Dr. Drug Rep. *The New York Times Magazine*, 64.

Caspi, A.; McClay, J.; Moffitt, T. E.; Mill, J.; Martin, J.; Craig, I. W.; ... Poulton, R. (2002, August 2). The Role of Genotype in the Cycle of Violence in Maltreated Children: Fears of the Future in Children and Young People. *Science,* 297(5582), 851-4.
Colbert, T. (1996). *Broken Brains or Wounded Hearts: What Causes Mental Illness.* Santa Ana: Kevco Publishing.
Colbert, T. (2000). *The Four False Pillars of Biopsychiatry: One Hundred Years of Medical Nonsense.* Santa Ana: Kevco Publishing.
Colbert, T. (2001). *Rape of the Soul: How the Chemical Imbalance Model of Modern Psychiatry Has Ailed Its Patients.* Santa Ana: Kevco Publishing.
Collins, F. & Galas, D. (1993, Oct 1). A New Five-Year Plan for the US Human Genome Project. *Science 262,* 43-46.
Craighero, L.; Metta, G., Santini, G.; Fadiga, L. (2007) The mirror-neurons system: data and models. *Progress in Brain Research 164,* 39-59.
DeGrandpre, R. J. & Hinshaw, S. P. (2000). ADHD: Serious Psychiatric Problem or All-American Cop-out? *Cerebrum: The Dana Forum on Brain Science,* 12-38.
DeGrandpre, R. J. (1999). *Ritalin Nation: Rapid-fire Culture and the Transformation of Human Consciousness.* New York: W. W. Norton & Co.
Dorfman, D. D. (1978, Sep 29). The Cyril Burt Question: New Findings. *Science, 201*(4362), 1177-1186, doi: 10.1126/science.201.4362.1177
Dulbecco, R. (1986, Mar 7). A Turning Point in Cancer Research: Sequencing the Human Genome. *Science 231,* 1055-1056.
Dumont, M. P. (1984). The nonspecificity of mental illness. *American Journal of Orthopsychiatry, 54,* 326-334.
Dupre, J., (2004). Understanding Contemporary Genomics. *Perspectives on Science 12,* 320-338.
Ellenberger, H. (1970). *The Discovery of the Unconscious: The History and Evolution of Dynamic Psychiatry.* New York: Basic Books.
Ewald, P. W. (1994). *Evolution of Infectious Disease.* New York: Oxford University Press.
Fancher, R. T. (2009). *Cultures of Healing.* New York: Freeman.
Felitti, V. J., MD; Anda, R. F., MD; Nordenberg, D., MD; Williamson, D. F. PhD; Spitz, M. S., MPH; Edwards, A. M., BA; ... Marks, J. S., MD. (1998) The Adverse Childhood Experiences (ACE) Study: The Relationship of Adult Health Status to Childhood Abuse and Household Dysfunction. *American Journal of Preventive Medicine, 14,* 245–258.
Fuentes, A. (2012). *Race, Monogamy, and Other Lies They Told You: Busting Myths about Human Nature.* Los Angeles: University of California Press.
Galves, A. & Walker, D. (2002). *Debunking the Science Behind ADHD as a Brain Disorder.* Retrieved from http://www.academyanalyticarts.org/galves-debunking-science-behind-adhd
Gannett, L. (2008). "The Human Genome Project" *The Stanford Encyclopedia of Philosophy* (Winter 2008 Ed.), Retrieved from http://plato.stanford.edu/archives/sum2016/entries/human-genome/
Geetz, C. (1973). *Interpretation of Cultures.* New York: Basic Books.
Gilbert, S. F. (2005). Mechanisms for the environmental regulation of gene expression: Ecological aspects of animal development. *Journal of Biosciences, 30,* 65-74.
Glasser, H. (2005). *101 Reasons to Avoid Ritalin Like the Plague.* Tucson: Nurtured Heart Publications.
Gosselin, P. G. (2000, June 27). Public Project's Chief: Quiet, But No Pushover. *Los Angeles Times.*
Gottesman, I. I. (2007). Gold Medal Award for Life Achievement in the Science of Psychology. *American Psychologist,* 62(5), 394-396. doi:10.1037/0003-066X.62.5.394
Gottesman, I. I., & Shields, J. (1966). Schizophrenia in twins: 16 years' consecutive admissions to a psychiatric clinic. *British Journal of Psychiatry, 112,* 809-818.
Gottesman, I. I., & Shields, J. (1972). *Schizophrenia and Genetics: A Twin Study Vantage Point.* New York: Academic Press.

Gottesman, I. I., & Shields, J. (1984). *Schizophrenia: The Epigenetic Puzzle*. Cambridge: Cambridge University Press.

Gottesman, I. I., & Shields, J. (1991). *Schizophrenia Genesis*. New York: W. H. Freeman.

Greally, J. (2015, Aug. 23). "Over-Interpreted Epigenetics Study of the Week." Retrieved from http://epgntxeinstein.tumblr.com/post/127416455028/over-interpreted-epigenetics-study-of-the-week

Griffiths, P. E. & Stotz, K. (2006, Dec). Genes in the Post-Genomic Era. *Theoretical Medicine and Bioethics, 27*, 499. doi:10.1007/s11017-006-9020-y

Hall, N. (1992, June/July). The Painful Truth. *Parenting Magazine*.

Harlow, H.; Dodsworth, R. O.; Harlow, M. K. (1965, July). Total social isolation in monkeys. *Proceedings of the National Academy of Science of the United States of America, 54*(1), 90–97.

Harlow, H. F. (1964). Early social deprivation and later behavior in the monkey. In A. Abrams, H. H. Gurner & J. E. P. Tomal (Eds.), *Unfinished tasks in the behavioral sciences* (154-173). Baltimore: Williams & Wilkins.

Harlow, H. F. & Suomi, S. J. (1971, July). Social Recovery by Isolation-Reared Monkeys. *Proceedings of the National Academy of Science of the United States of America, 68*(7), 1534-1538.

Harris, G. & Berenson, A. (2009, Jan 15). Lilly Said to Be Near $1.4 Billion U.S. Settlement. *New York Times*. Retrieved from http://www.nytimes.com/2009/01/15/business/15drug.html

Harris, G. & Carey, B. (2008, June 8). Researchers Fail to Reveal Full Drug Pay. *New York Times*. Retrieved from http://www.nytimes.com/2008/06/08/us/08conflict.html

Harris, G. & Wilson, D. (2010, Oct 26). Glaxo to Pay $750 Million for Sale of Bad Products. New York Times. Retrieved from http://www.nytimes.com/2010/10/27/business/27drug.html

Haworth, C. M. A., & Plomin, R. (2010). Quantitative genetics in the era of molecular genetics: Learning abilities and disabilities as an example. *Journal of the American Academy of Child and Adolescent Psychiatry, 49*, 783-793.

Hensley, S. (2008, June 9). Harvard Psychiatrists Under Fire for Drug-Company Funding. *Wall Street Journal*. Retrieved from http://blogs.wsj.com/health/2008/06/09/harvard-psychiatrists-under-fire-for-drug-company-funding/

Herman, J. P. (2013, Aug 8). Neural control of chronic stress adaptation. *Frontiers in Behavioral Neuroscience, 7*, 61. doi: 10.3389/fnbeh.2013.00061

Heston, L. L. (1966). Psychiatric disorders in foster home reared children of schizophrenic mothers. *British Journal of Psychiatry, 112*(489), 819–825.

Hickok, G. (2014). *The Myth of Mirror Neurons: The Real Neuroscience of Communication and Cognition.* New York: W. W. Norton & Co.

Hoffer, A. & Pollin, W. (1970). Schizophrenia in the NAS0NRC panel of 15,909 veteran twin pairs. *Archives of General Psychiatry, 23*, 469-477.

Hubbard, R. & Wald, E. (1999). *Exploding the Gene Myth: How Genetic Information is Produced and Manipulated by Scientists, Physicians, Employers, Insurance Companies, Educators and Law Enforcers.* Boston: Beacon Press.

Hudziak, J. J. & Faraone, S.V. (2010, Aug) The new genetics in child psychiatry. *American Academy of Child and Adolescent Psychiatry, 49*(8), 729-35. doi: 10.1016/j.jaac.2010.06.010

Interlandi, J. (2006, Oct. 22). An Unwelcome Discovery. *New York Times Magazine*.

Issa, J. (2008, Feb.). Burgeoning epigenetics field holds huge promise: Montrealers pioneer new science of environment's impact on genes. *National Review of Medicine, 5*, 2.

Jackson, D. (1960). A critique of the literature on the genetics of schizophrenia. In D. D. Jackson (Ed.), *The Etiology of Schizophrenia* (37-87). New York: Basic Books.

Jacobson, S. W. (1979, June). Matching behavior in the young infant. *Child Development, 50*(2), 425-30.

Jones, S. S. (1967, October) Imitation or Exploration? Young infants' matching of adults' oral gestures. *Child Development, 67*(5), 1952-1969.

Jones, S. S. (2009, August 27) The Development of Imitation in Infancy. *Philosophical Transactions of the Royal Society Biological Sciences, 364*(1528), 2325-2335. doi: 10.1098/rstb.2009.0045

Joseph, J. (2004). *The Gene Illusion: Genetic Research in Psychiatry and Psychology Under the Microscope.* New York: Algora Publishing.

Joseph, J. (2006). *The Missing Gene: Psychiatry, Heredity and the Fruitless Search for Genes.* New York: Algora Publishing.

Joseph, J. (2015). *The Trouble with Twin Studies: A Reassessment of Twin Research in the Social and Behavioral Sciences.* New York and London: Routledge, Taylor & Frances Group.

Karen, R. (1994). *Becoming Attached: First Relationships and How They Shape Our Capacity to Love.* New York: Oxford University Press.

Karon, B. P. (2008). An "Incurable" Schizophrenic: The Case of Mr. X. *Pragmatic Case Studies in Psychotherapy, 4*(1), 1-24. doi: 10.14713/pcsp.v4i1.923

Keller, E. F. (2000). *The Century of the Gene.* Cambridge: Harvard University Press.

Kendler, K. (1983). Overview: A current perspective on twin studies of schizophrenia. *American Journal of Psychiatry, 140,* 1413-1425.

Kety, S. S. (1978). Heredity and environment. In J. Shershow (Ed.), *Schizophrenia: Science and Practice* (p. 47-68). Cambridge: Harvard University Press.

Kety, S. S., Rosenthal, D., Wender, P. H., & Schulsinger, F. (1968). The types and prevalence of mental illness in the biological and adoptive families of adopted schizophrenics. In Rosenthal, D., and Kety, S. S. (eds.),*The Transmission of Schizophrenia (p. 345-362).* Oxford: Pergamon Press.

Kluckhohn, C. (1959). *Mirror for Man: The Relation of Anthropology to Life.* New York: McGraw Hill.

Kramer, H. & Sprenger, J. (1971, 1948, 1928, 1486). *The Malleus Maleficarum (The Witch Hammer).* New York: Dover Publications.

Kresser, C. (2008, June 30) The "chemical imbalance" myth. Retrieved from http://chriskresser.com/the-chemical-imbalance-myth/

Kuchment, A. (2009, Apr 13). Study of Rodents Sheds Light on Nature-Nurture Debate. *Columbia University Record, 34*(9), 5.

LeDoux, J. E.; Romanski, L. & Xagoraris, A. (1991). Indelibility of subcortical emotional memories. *Journal of Cognitive Neuroscience, 1,* 238-243.

Lee, Thomas F. (1991). *The Human Genome Project: Cracking the Genetic Code of Life.* New York: Plenum Press.

Leo, J. (2000). Attention Deficit Disorder: Good Science or Good Marketing? *Skeptic, 8*(1), 63-9.

Leo, J. (2003). The Fallacy of the 50% Concordance Rate for Schizophrenia in Identical Twins. *Human Nature Review, 3,* 406-415. Retrieved from http://human-nature.com/nibbs/03/joseph.html

Lewontin, R. C., Rose, S. & Kamin, L. J. (1984). *Not in Our Genes: Biology, Ideology & Human Nature.* New York: Pantheon Books.

Lipton, B. (2001a). Evolution by BITs and Pieces: An Introduction to Fractal Evolution. Retrieved from https://www.brucelipton.com/resource/article/fractal-evolution

Lipton, B. (2001b). Insight into Cellular Consciousness. Retrieved from https://www.brucelipton.com/resource/article/insight-cellular-consciousness

Lipton, B. (2001c). Nature, Nurture and Human Development. Retrieved from https://www.brucelipton.com/resource/article/nature-nurture-and-human-development

Lipton, B. H.; Bensch, K. G. & Karasek M. A. (1991, Mar). Microvessel endothelial cell transdifferentiation: phenotypic characterization. *Differentiation 46,* 117-133. doi: 10.1111/j.1432-0436.1991.tb00872.x

Lissek, S. & Grillon, C. (2012). Learning Models of PTSD. In J. G. Beck & D. Sloan (Eds.), *The Oxford Handbook of PTSD Disorders.* Oxford: Oxford University Press. doi: 10.1093/oxfordhb/9780195399066.013.0013

Main, M. (1995). *Attachment Theory: Social, Developmental & Clinical Perspectives.* Hillsdale: Analytic Press.

Main, M. & Solomon, J. (1990). Procedures for identifying infants as disorganized/disoriented during the Ainsworth Strange Situation. In M. Greenberg, D. Cicchetti & E. M. Cummings (Eds.), *Attachment during the Preschool Years: Theory, Research & Intervention.* Chicago: University of Chicago Press.

Main, M. & Weston, D. R. (1981*). The Place of Attachment in Human Behavior.* C. P. Parkes & J. Stevenson-Hinde (Eds.). New York: Basic Books.

Markman, A. (2011, Sep 22). Infants and Imitation: How much do infants understand when they imitate? *Psychology Today: Ulterior Motives.* Retrieved from https://www.psychologytoday.com/blog/ulterior-motives/201109/infants-and-imitation

Masson, J. M. (1984). *The Assault on Truth: Freud's Suppression of the Seduction Theory.* New York: Simon & Schuster.

Masson, J. M. (1985). *The Complete Letters of Sigmund Freud to Wilhelm Fliess, 1887-1904.* Cambridge: Harvard University Press.

Maté, G., MD. (2003). *When the Body Says No: Exploring the Stress-Disease Connection.* Hoboken: John Wiley & Sons.

Maté, G., MD. (2010): *In the Realm of Hungry Ghosts: Close Encounters with Addiction.* Berkeley: North Atlantic Books.

Maté, G., MD [compassion4addiction]. (2015, Jan 6). *Gabor Mate: Attachment, Disease and Addiction.* Retrieved from https://www.youtube.com/watch?v=x9cvEa5qFQc

McInerney, J. & Rothstein, M. (2008). Behavioral Genetics. Human Genome Program. *Human Genome Project Information.* U.S. Department of Energy Office of Science, Office of Biological & Environmental Research. Retrieved from http://www.ornl.gov/sci/techresources/Human_Genome/elsi/behavior.shtml

McNeil, L. (2014, Nov 6). The Truth about Rosemary Kennedy's Lobotomy. *People Magazine.* Retrieved from http://www.people.com/article/rosemary-kennedy-timothy-shriver-fully-alive

McPherson, C. B. (1975). *The Political Theory of Possessive Individualism: Hobbes to Locke.* Toronto: Oxford University Press.

Meltzoff, A. N. (1999). *Born to Learn: What Infants Learn from Watching Us.* Department of Psychology, University of Washington. In N. Fox & J. G. Warhol (Eds.), *The Role of Early Experience in Infant Development* (145-164). Skillman: Pediatric Institute Publications.

Milgram, S. (1965). Some Conditions of Obedience and Disobedience to Authority. *Human Relations, 18*(1), 57-76. doi:10.1177/001872676501800105

Milgram, S. (1974). *Obedience to Authority, an Experimental View.* New York: Harper & Row.

Miller, A. (1981). *The Drama of the Gifted Child: The Search for the True Self.* New York: Basic Books.

Miller, A. (1983). *For Your Own Good.* New York: Noonday Press.

Miller, A. (1984). *Thou Shalt Not Be Aware: Society's Betrayal of the Child.* New York: Basic Books.

Miller, A. (1990a). *Banished Knowledge: Facing Childhood Injuries.* New York: Bantam Doubleday Dell Publishing Group, Inc.

Miller, A. (1990b). *Breaking Down the Wall of Silence: The Liberating Experience of Facing Painful Truth.* New York: A Meridian Book.

Miller, A. (1998, Fall). The Political Consequences of Child Abuse. *Journal of Psychohistory, 26*(2). Retrieved from http://psychohistory.com/articles/the-political-consequences-of-child-abuse/

Miller, A. (2001). *The Truth Will Set You Free: Overcoming Emotional Blindness and Finding Your True Adult Self.* New York: Basic Books.

Miller, A. (2005). *The Body Never Lies: The Lingering Effects of Cruel Parenting.* New York: W.W. Norton & Co.

Miller, G. (2010, July 2). The Seductive Allure of Behavioral Epigenetics. *Science, 329,* 24-7.

Mintzberg, H. (2006, Aug 15). Patent Nonsense: Evidence tells of an industry out of social control. *Canadian Medical Association Journal, 175*(4), 374-6.

Moss, L. (2004). *What Genes Can't Do.* Cambridge: MIT Press.

Nance, R. D. (1970). G. Stanley Hall and John B. Watson as child psychologists. *Journal of the History of the Behavioral Sciences, 6*(4), 303-316.

Nijhout, H. F. (1990). Metaphors & the role of genes in development. *BioEssays, 12*(9), 441-6.

Perry, B. D. (2001) The neuroarcheology of childhood maltreatment: the neurodevelopmental costs of adverse childhood events. In: *The Cost of Maltreatment: Who Pays? We All Do.* (Eds., K. Franey, R. Geffner & R. Falconer). San Diego: Family Violence and Sexual Assault Institute.

Petersen, M. (2008). *Our Daily Meds: How the Pharmaceutical Companies Transformed Themselves into Slick Marketing Machines and Hooked the Nation on Prescription Drugs.* New York: Sarah Crichton Books.

Phelan, J. C., Yang, L. & Cruz-Rojas, R. (2006). Effects of Attributing Serious Mental Illnesses to Genetic Causes on Orientations to Treatment. *Psychiatric Services, 57*(3).

Plomin, R. (1990, Apr 13). The Role of Inheritance in Behavior, *Science, 248*(4952), 183-8.

Plomin, R. (2000). Behavioral genetics in the 21st century. *International Journal of Behavioral Development, 24,* 30-34.

Plomin, R. (2005). Finding genes in child psychology and psychiatry: When are we going to be there? *Journal of Child Psychology and Psychiatry, 46,* 1030-1038.

Plomin, R. (2011). Commentary: Why are children in the same family so different? Non-shared environment three decades later. *International Journal of Epidemiology, 40,* 582-92.

Plomin, R. & Rende, R. (1991). Human behavioral genetics. *Annual Review of Psychology, 42,* 161-190.

Plomin, R., DeFries, J. C., Craig, I. W., & McGuffin, P. (2003). *Behavioral genetics in the postgenomic era.* Washington, DC: American Psychological Association.

Plomin, R.; DeFries, J. C.; Knopik, V. S.; Neiderhiser, J. M. (2013). *Behavioral Genetics (6th ed.).* New York: Worth Publishers.

Plomin, R.; DeFries, J. C.; Knopik, V. S.; Neiderhiser, J. M. (2016). Top 10 Replicated Findings from Behavioral Genetics. *Perspectives on Psychological Science, 11*(1), 3-23.

Plomin, R.; DeFries, J. C.; McClearn, G. E., & Rutter, M. (1997). *Behavioral Genetics (3rd ed.).* New York: W. H. Freeman and Company.

Plomin, R.; DeFries, J. C.; McClearn, G. E., & Rutter, M. (2008). *Behavioral Genetics (5th ed.).* New York: Worth Publishers.

Plomin, R., & McGuffin, P. (2003). Psychopathology in the postgenomic era. *Annual Review of Psychology, 54,* 205-228.

Plomin, R. and Davis, O. S. P. (2009). The future of genetics in psychology and psychiatry: microarrays, genome-wide association, and non-coding RNA. *Journal of Child Psychology and Psychiatry, 50*: 63–71. doi:10.1111/j.1469-7610.2008.01978.x

Plomin, R., & Asbury, K. (2005). Nature and nurture: Genetic and environmental influences on behavior. *The Annals of the American Academy of Political & Social Science, 600,* 86-98. 10.1177/0002716205277184

Ramachandran, V. (2000, May). Mirror Neurons and imitation learning as the driving force behind the great leap forward in human evolution. *Edge.* Retrieved from https://www.edge.org/conversation/mirror-neurons-and-imitation-learning-as-the-driving-force-behind-the-great-leap-forward-in-human-evolution

Rizzolatti, G. (2005, Dec). The mirror neuron system and its function in humans. *Anatomy Embryol (Berl), 210*(5-6), 419-21.

Rizzolatti, G & Craighero, L. (2004). The mirror-neuron system. *Annual Review of Neuroscience, 27,* 169-92.

Rizzolatti, G.; Fadiga, L.; Gallese, V. & Fogassi, L. (1996, Mar). Premotor cortex and the recognition of motor actions. *Cognitive Brain Research, 3*(2), 131-41.

Rose, S. (1997). *Lifelines: Biology Beyond Determinism.* New York: Oxford University Press.

Rosenthal, D. (1970). *Genetic Theory and Abnormal Behavior.* New York: McGraw Hill.
Ross, C. (2004). *Schizophrenia: Innovations in Diagnosis and Treatment.* New York: The Hayworth Press.
Ross, C. & Pam, A. (1995). *Pseudoscience in Biological Psychiatry: Blaming the Body.* New York: Wiley & Sons, Inc.
Schore, A. N. (1994). *Affect Regulation & the Origin of the Self.* Hillsdale: Lawrence Erlbaum Associates.
Schore, A. N. (2001). The Effects of Early Relational Trauma on Right Brain Development, Affect Regulation & Infant Mental Health. *Infant Mental Health Journal, 22*, 201-269.
Schore, A. N. (2002a). Dysregulation of the Right Brain: A Fundamental Mechanism of Traumatic Attachment & the Psychopathogenesis of Posttraumatic Stress Disorder. *Australian & New Zealand Journal of Psychiatry, 36*, 9-30.
Schore, A. N. (2002b). Advances in Neuropsychoanalysis, Attachment Theory & Trauma Research: Implications for Self Psychology. *Psychoanalytic Inquiry, 22*, 433-484.
Schore, A. N. (2003a). *Affect Regulation & the Repair of the Self.* New York: W.W. Norton & Co.
Schore, A. N. (2003b). *Affect Dysregulation & Disorders of the Self.* New York: W.W. Norton & Co.
Shields, J. (1962). *Monozygotic twins brought up apart & brought up together.* London: Oxford University Press.
Siegel, D. J. (1999) *The Developing Mind: Toward a Neurobiology of Interpersonal Experience.* New York, London: Guilford Press.
Snyder, F. (2010). *The Politics of Memory: When One Is Instructed to Shut the Eyes.* Los Angeles: Clifton Legacy Publishing.
Snyder, F. (2012). *The Manual: The Definitive Book on Parenting and The Causal Theory.* Los Angeles: Clifton Legacy Publishing.
Snyder, F. (2012). *ADHD: A Diagnosis in Denial.* Los Angeles: Clifton Legacy Publishing.
Snyder, F. (2014). *The Predictor Scale: Predicting and Understanding Behavior by Critical Childhood Experiences.* Los Angeles: Clifton Legacy Publishing.
Spitz, R. A. & Wolf, K. M. (1946) Anaclitic depression: an inquiry into the genesis of psychiatric conditions in early childhood, II. *Psychoanalytic Study of the Child, 2*, 313-342.
Stern, D. (2000, orig. pub. 1985). *The Interpersonal World of the Infant.* London: Basic Books.
Stern, D. (2003). Attachment & Intersubjectivity. Conference on New Developments in Attachment Theory: Applications to Clinical Practice. UCLA Extension & Lifespan Learning Institute.
Teicher, M. (2002). Scars That Won't Heal: The Neurobiology of Child Abuse: Maltreatment at an early age can have enduring negative effects on a child's brain development & function. *Scientific American, 286*(3), 68-75.
Tienari, P. & Wynne, L., Moring, J., Lahti, I., Naarala, M., Sorri, A., Wahlberg, K. E.,... Kaleva, M. (1994). The Finnish adoptive family study of schizophrenia. *British Journal of Psychiatry Supplement, 23*, 20-26.
Tienari, P. & Wynne, L., Sorri, A., Lahti, I., Läksy, K., Moring, J.,...Wahlberg, K. E. (2004). Genotype-environment interaction in schizophrenia-spectrum disorder: Long-term follow-up study of Finnish adoptees. *British Journal of Psychiatry, 184*, 216-222.
Torrey, E.F., Bowler, A.E., Taylor, E.H. & Gottesman, I.I. (1994). *Schizophrenia & Manic-Depressive Disorder.* New York: Perseus Books.
Trzaskowski, M., Dale, P. S. & Plomin, R. (2013). No Genetic Influence for Childhood Behavior Problems from DNA Analysis. *Journal of the American Academy of Child and Adolescent Psychiatry, 52*, 1048-1056.
Turner, E. H.; Matthews, A. M.; Linardatos, E.; Tell, R. A. & Rosenthal, R. (2008, Jan 17). Selective Publication of Antidepressant Trials and Its Influence on Apparent Efficacy. *New England Journal of Medicine, 358*, 252-260. doi: 10.1056/NEJMsa065779

Turkheimer, E. (2011a). Still Missing. *Research in Human Development, 8*(3-4), 227-241. doi: 10.1080/15427609.2011.625321

Turkheimer, E. (2011b). Commentary: Variation and Causation in the Environment and Genome. *International Journal of Epidemiology, 40*(3), 598-601. doi: 10.1093/ije/dyq147

Turkheimer, E., Pettersson, E. & Horn, E. E. (2014). A Phenotypic Null Hypothesis for the Genetics of Personality. *Annual Review of Psychology, 65*, 515-540. doi: 10.1146/annurev-psych-113011-143752

Umilta, M. A.; Kohler, E.; Gallese, V.; Fogassi, L.; Fadiga L.; Keysers, C. & Rizzolatti, G. (2001, July 19). I know what you are doing: a neurophysiological study. *Neuron, 31*(1), 155-65.

Valenstein, E. S. (1988). *Blaming the Brain: The Truth about Drugs and Mental Health.* New York: The Free Press.

van der Kolk, B. (1989). The Compulsion to Repeat the Trauma: Re-enactment, Revictimization, and Massochism. *Psychiatric Clinics of North America, 12*(2), 389-411.

van der Kolk, B. (1994a). Childhood Abuse and the Loss of Self-Regulation. *Bulletin of Menninger Clinic, 58*(2), 145-68.

van der Kolk, B. (1994b). *The Body Keeps The Score: Memory & the Evolving Psychobiology of Post Traumatic Stress.* Retrieved from Trauma Information Pages: http:\\www.trauma-pages.com

van der Kolk, B. (1995). The Body, Memory, and the Psychobiology of Trauma. In Judith L. Alpert (Ed.), *Sexual Abuse Recalled: Treating Trauma in the Era of the Recovered Memory Debate* (29-60). Northvale: Jason Aronson Inc.

van der Kolk, B. (2014). *The Body Keeps the Score: Brain, Mind and Body in the Healing of Trauma.* New York: Penguin Group.

van der Kolk, B.; McFarlane, A. & Weisaeth, L. (Eds.). (1996). *Traumatic Stress: the Effects of Overwhelming Experience for Mind, Body & Society.* New York: Guilford Press.

Wahlsten, D. (2012). The hunt for gene effects pertinent to behavioral traits and psychiatric disorders: from mouse to human. *Developmental Psychobiology, 54*, 475-492.

Wasowicz, L. (2007, July 17). Ped Med: Non-drug options slighted? *United Press International.* Retrieved from http://www.upi.com/Health_News/2007/07/16/Ped-Med-Non-drug-options-slighted/67251184591581/

Watson, J. B. (1928). *Psychological Care of infant and Child.* New York: Norton and Company, Inc.

Watson, J. D. & Berry, A. (2003). *DNA: The Secret of Life.* New York: Alfred A. Kopf.

Watters, E. (2006, Nov 22). DNA Is Not Destiny: The new science of epigenetics. *Discover Magazine.* Retrieved from http://discovermagazine.com/2006/nov/cover

WebMD. (2008). *Webster's New World Medical Dictionary, Third Ed.* Hoboken; Wiley Publishing, Inc.

Whitaker, R. (2002). *Mad in America: Bad Science, Bad Medicine, and the Enduring Mistreatment of the Mentally Ill.* New York: Basic Books.

Whitaker, R. (2010). *Anatomy of an Epidemic: Magic Bullets, Psychiatric Drugs and the Astonishing Rise of Mental Illness in America.* New York: Crown Publishers.

World Health Organization. (2015, Oct 26). IARC Monographs evaluate consumption of red meat and processed meat. Press Release No. 240. Retrieved from https://www.iarc.fr/en/media-centre/pr/2015/pdfs/pr240_E.pdf

Winerman, L. (2005). The mind's mirror. *Monitor on Psychology, 36*(9), 48.

Winnicott, D. W. (1992). *The Child, The Family, and The Outside World. 2nd Ed.* Cambridge: Perseus Publishing.

Yehuda, R.; Daskalakis, N. P.; Bierer, L. M.; Bader, H. N.; Klengel, T.; Holsboer, F. & Binder, E. B. (2015). Holocaust Exposure Induced Intergenerational Effects on FKBP5 Methylation. doi: 10.1016/j.biopsych.2015.08.005

Zombardo, P. (2007). *The Lucifer Effect: How Good People Turn Evil.* New York: Random House.

IV: EPIGENETICS LANGUAGING CODES (TEAR-OUT)

(1) fails to rule out alternative explanations
(2) confuses cause and effect with vague languaging (ex. "associated with")
(3) tends to be over-technical, failing to explain invented terminology for other laypeople or scientists to follow
(4) tends to be sloppy with language, like substituting "genotype" for "phenotype"
(5) key sentences over-state the value of the study
(6) key sentences over-state the results of the study
(7) key sentences reveal bias, with the assumption in the hypothesis
(8) key sentences reveal the hypothetical and unfounded nature of the study, buried amidst other text
(9) terminology implies existence of something that is speculative (ex. "epigenetic mechanisms")
(10) assumes facts not in evidence
(11) uses terms that imply proof, but actually represent a circular logic (ex. "demonstrated")
(12) language designed to distance from or mitigate failed results
(13) overgeneralized language
(14) key sentences promote the use of pharmacological interventions
(15) proves the opposite (pro-child) research and theory
(16) erroneous
(17) relevance not clear

www.ingramcontent.com/pod-product-compliance
Lightning Source LLC
Chambersburg PA
CBHW032048150426
43194CB00006B/450